ENGLISH EMBLEM BOOKS

Tempus erit.

Will: Marshall sculpsit.

From Francis Quarles
Hieroglyphikes of the Life of Man 1638

English Emblem Books

by

Rosemary Freeman

1970

OCTAGON BOOKS

New York

Originally published 1948 by Chatto & Windus (London)

Reprinted *1966*
by special arrangement with Chatto & Windus Ltd.

Second Reprinting 1970

OCTAGON BOOKS

A DIVISION OF FARRAR, STRAUS & GIROUX, INC.

19 Union Square West

New York, N. Y. 10003

LIBRARY OF CONGRESS CATALOG CARD NUMBER: 66-18037

Printed in U.S.A. by
NOBLE OFFSET PRINTERS, INC.
NEW YORK 3, N. Y.

To my Mother

Foreword

IN reading past literature it is humanly natural to select the easiest portions, those most in accord with our own habits of thought. People rejoice to see an English squire reappearing in Chaucer's knight, a refined English old maid reappearing in his Prioress. Or, in more serious mood, we dwell on the permanence of the passions displayed in the *Iliad*, delighted that by this means we may bridge the years and see in the past not the strange and the alien but the known and the reassuring. There is no harm in such pleasures, if we remember that they concern but a fraction of the truth.

Other portions of the truth are less easy to grasp, though when grasped they may bring their reward. And if we are to gain the reward that comes from knowing something of the way men thought in this or that age we must regard not the familiar and permanent things but the typical, which are usually just the reverse. Chaucer's translation of the *Romaunt of the Rose* and his *Book of the Duchesse* are less attractive than his Prologue to the *Canterbury Tales*, but the very things in them which (initially) fail to attract—the rigid conventions they embody—are the most valuable in making us familiar with mediaeval habits of thought. And such familiarity not only teaches us history, it protects us from imagining the literature of the past which we enjoy to be more 'modern' than it actually is. To refer to Chaucer once more, we may, by knowing a little of contemporary conventions, refrain from applying to his *Troilus and Criseyde* the standards of a modern realistic novel.

The English habit of mind between 1560 and 1660 is more remote from our own than we are usually prepared to admit. We anthologise the literature of the time to suit our tastes rather than guide our reading by what were then thought the master-pieces. It is unusual, for instance, for moderns to assimilate the whole of *Arcadia* or *The Faerie Queene*.

FOREWORD

Now one of the then habits of mind most prevalent yet most remote from ourselves was the emblematical, an adjective whose meaning I need not explain, since such explanation is found in the body of Miss Freeman's book. The chief general interest of the English Emblem Books is that they present in a very simple and striking form one of the ruling mental principles of a whole century. Their very ingenuousness and their popularity prove how deeply the emblematical way of thinking had penetrated the consciousness of England.

Miss Freeman has mastered her subject, and, as well as presenting a scholarly survey of the whole field, has given us an insight into the general psychology of the time which is of great interest to students of history and of literature alike.

But the English Emblem Books are more than a minor manifestation of an important general mode of thought: they touch and illumine great literature at several points. Miss Freeman has shown excellent judgment in not pressing the intrinsic importance of the Emblem Books too far. She can therefore speak with all the more authority when she sees their relation to Spenser and Herbert and Bunyan. A. C. Bradley wrote of Wordsworth that the way to get to the heart of him was through not round his strangenesses. The same is true of these three great writers; and the Emblem is one of those strangenesses through which their intimacies can be reached. Miss Freeman's sensitive literary perception makes her an admirable guide. Her book, as well as expounding an important phase of thought, has high merit as a work of literary criticism.

E. M. W. TILLYARD

Author's Preface

IN the pages which follow I have tried to explore a literary form which had much vitality in the sixteenth and seventeenth centuries although little is heard of it, except as a curiosity, to-day. The study has seemed worth making both for the merits of the now almost forgotten emblem books themselves and for their bearings on other, more important, writing. Although the form was not one which attained to great eminence as literature, it was serious enough to attract men of considerable minor ability, and there are emblem books, notably those of Quarles and Henry Hawkins, which deserve to be valued for their own sake. In its connections with Elizabethan and seventeenth-century poetry the convention offers much that is interesting and often illuminating: good poets used it as a means to an end rather than as an end in itself, and its transformations and applications in contemporary literature are as diverse as they are frequent.

The chief difficulty in treating a subject the marginal interests of which are so many and the literary merits so relatively few, has been to preserve a proper balance between information and criticism. Since the material is so little known, space has been given to exposition and illustration, and a bibliography of English emblem books to 1700 has been added. For the same reason at least one reproduction from each book has been included, even where the book in question is discussed only briefly; for the pictures formed an essential element in the make-up of emblem books and the plates were intended to be read as part of the text. It is to be hoped that so close an attention to detail in what is, for all its ramifications, a comparatively small subject will not exaggerate its literary importance, and that the sections on George Herbert and on Bunyan will amend any critical distortions which may have resulted from the use of the magnifying-glass elsewhere.

I began this work as a thesis for a research degree, and my debt

AUTHOR'S PREFACE

to all who helped me with it in its various stages is one of long standing. Too many thanks are tedious, too few would be ungracious. Pleading, therefore, that the brevity of its expression is no measure of the extent of my gratitude, I should like to record my thanks to Girton College and to Smith College, Massachusetts, for scholarships without which it would have been impossible to begin; to my three research supervisors, Miss M. G. Lloyd Thomas, Dr. M. C. Bradbrook, and Dr. E. M. W. Tillyard, for many criticisms and suggestions and for a patience and an endurance which often outran my own; and to Miss Rosemary Beresford whose imaginative understanding of literature enabled me to turn a thesis into a book. I am also greatly indebted to Canon F. E. Hutchinson for his criticism of part of the chapter on Herbert, and to the late Mr. Bernard Newdigate, who lent me his notes on Sir Henry Godyere and his photostat of a manuscript in the Huntington Library. Birkbeck College generously assisted me in the provision of plates for the illustrations, and the authorities of the following libraries and institutions have kindly allowed me to reproduce emblems from books and embroidery in their possession: the British Museum, the Bodleian Library, the Cambridge University Library, the Victoria and Albert Museum, and the Henry E. Huntington Library.

ROSEMARY FREEMAN

BIRKBECK COLLEGE,
UNIVERSITY OF LONDON
February 1946

Contents

List of Illustrations

LIST OF ILLUSTRATIONS

INTRODUCTION

EMBLEM books were first introduced into England from the Continent during the reign of Queen Elizabeth. They quickly became popular, and translations of foreign collections together with some original works were published in the vernacular. They continued to flourish in the seventeenth century and were finally extinguished in the general change in taste that took place at the end of that period. It is the purpose of this book to study the development of the form from its first appearance in England in 1586 to the time when it ceased to be regarded as a serious branch of literature.

The work of the English emblem writers is not in itself of any great bulk or merit. Compared with that of Continental authors their output was small and, if judged by absolute standards, rarely of any permanent value. It is impossible to claim for even the best of them anything more than minor distinction as poets. Yet the convention in which they worked was of considerable literary importance. It has an intrinsic value in that it is peculiar to the age which produced it; and it also deserves notice as a mode of expression that was adapted by contemporary poets and dramatists to serve ends more complex than its own.

As a contemporary document it reflects the mind of the age. It shows how persistent and how deep-rooted was the Elizabethan and Jacobean taste for allegory; and it shows, too, something of the form which that taste for allegory took. In the reign of Elizabeth allegory was still an essential part of life, as it had been, only more profoundly, in the Middle Ages. Its basis was social: it entered into the occupations of every day. The accounts of the progresses of the Queen represent an England in which nothing had a single meaning and nothing lacked significance. The towns, the villages, the manors into which she came greeted her with pageants and with poetry. She was entertained in allegorical performances; her very clothes and jewelry were symbolic. Nor had

I

allegory its province only at Court: a firework display, visible to many, included 'the seven Deadly Sins in their lively colours, shape, and characters', and on top of a pinnacle 'a fierce lion couchant signifying sudden vengeance'; Perdita in the shepherd's cottage distributes flowers, explaining their significance as she does so. Colour and decoration, gesture and action had a double meaning which was everywhere emphasised.

As the seventeenth century progressed allegory found a less public and more psychological sphere. The material of *The Faerie Queene* is derived in part from the social life of the Court, from its tournaments, its ceremonial, its setting. The personified figures which Spenser uses so frequently might be found painted on a ceiling, embroidered on a cloak, or woven in a tapestry; but the material of Herbert's *Temple* is to be found in the human heart. The same individual sense of the dual meaning of things continues, but the interest has turned inward:

> Who can sit in his studie and looke on his houreglasse, and say not to himselfe, *Ut hora, sic fugit vita*? . . . Canst thou feele the wind beat on thy face, and canst thou forget that thou holdest thy tenement by a puffe of winde? canst thou sit by the river side, and not remember that as the river runneth, and doth not returne, so is the life of man? Canst thou shoot in the fields, and not call to mind that as the arrow flieth in the aire, so swiftly doe thy dayes passe? [1]

Bunyan's *Pilgrim's Progress* is the last coherent formulation of this way of thinking. It became possible, and then customary, to observe the river independently of its significance, and individual experience broke free of the haunting presence of a perpetual *memento mori*. The old mentality ceased to exist, and the new generation was categorical in its condemnation of the past. Rymer, writing on Spenser in 1674, could complain that 'it was the vice of those Times to affect superstitiously the *Allegory*; and nothing would then be current without a mystical meaning'.[2] *The Pilgrim's Progress* was an anachronism before it was born.

[1] Elizabeth Grymeston, *Miscelanea*. 1604.
[2] Thomas Rymer, 'Preface to the Translation of Rapin's *Reflections on Aristotle's Treatise of Poesie*.' 1674.

The reasons for this change are many, and they are probably connected largely with the development of scientific knowledge during the second half of the seventeenth century. Science, which interests itself in the universe as it is, independently of human values and human endeavour, needed a rejection of allegorical habits of thought before it could act fully and freely. In a world in which the importance of things was estimated by their significance rather than by their nature, no scale of strictly scientific values could be evolved. The study of cause and effect is merely hampered by the perception of symbolical relations everywhere; and the purpose of the new scientific movement was, as its founder Francis Bacon proclaimed, 'to search out the causes of things'.

After three centuries of scientific 'progress', however, it is not so much towards the origins of modern ways of thinking that enquiry turns as towards the question of how thought could ever have been different. The Elizabethan love for emblems and for allegory in all its forms can, no doubt, be attributed in part to an unreflecting acceptance of mere fashion: emblem writing was a gentlemanly accomplishment of the same type as the ability to play the lute or to dance the lavolta. It can also be attributed in part to the recurrent and restless desire in human nature to exercise the power of reason with which it is endowed. What was primarily emphasised in the emblem fashion by those who defended it was its 'wit'; and, although the intelligence required to perceive that wit may not have been of a particularly high order, the man who had successfully followed an emblem writer through his exposition of the connection between a symbol and its significance was left with the same pleasant assurance that his reason had not been allowed to fust in him unused as is the man who to-day follows the oblique approach of an advertiser to his subject or guesses a clue in a crossword puzzle. For both, it is the wit, the apparent lack of any relation between two ideas and the subsequent establishment of an intellectually convincing link between them, that pleases; it does not matter how forced and arbitrary the link may seem to common-sense or to feeling. Puns, in Elizabethan drama and modern music-hall alike, afford the same sort of satisfaction. But explanations such as these account only for the popularity of allegory once it is established. It is much less easy to see why the need for intellectual stimulus should have found its outlet in that form rather than in any other. Any reasons that could be given are necessarily larger than the scope of this book, for they would have to be based upon an analysis of the strange mixture of mediaeval and modern ideas which constituted sixteenth and seventeenth century thought. The presence of allegory in mediaeval literature and life is undisputed; the absence of serious allegory after the end of the seventeenth century is also undisputed. In between lies a period in which allegories like *The Faerie Queene* (1590 and 1596) and *The Purple Island* (1633) were published side by side with Bacon's *Essays* (1597) and Donne's *Songs and Sonets* (1633). It is a period which cannot be summed up or explained in a simple formula; it did, after all, produce Shakespeare. All that can be said here is that the taste for emblems was part of a wider taste for allegory, and that wider taste for allegory formed one side, though by no means the whole, of the sixteenth and seventeenth century man's view of the world in which he found himself. It was certainly a legacy from the Middle Ages, but it was inherited as a living not a dead tradition. Bacon himself, who wrote essays essentially sceptical and rational in outlook, who was revered by the scientists of the Restoration as the father of the movement which turned the emblematic habits of thought into ridicule, could nevertheless find allegory in the myths and legends of the ancients [1] and could share with Spenser and Fletcher their love of a 'dark conceit'. His approach to classical literature, allowing for his own scientific bias, was that of many of his contemporaries; in it he resembles Chapman who read the *Iliad* as an allegory of 'the body's fervour and fashion of an outward fortitude', and the *Odyssey* as that of 'the mind's inward, constant, and unconquered empire'.

Emblem books depended for their existence upon the validity of these allegorical ways of thinking; they depended also upon a

[1] In *De Sapientia Veterum.* 1609.

4

close interrelation between the arts of poetry and painting. While poetry was regarded as 'a speaking picture' and painting as 'dumb poetry', the emblem convention, in which poem and picture were complementary to each other, could flourish; when they were, on the contrary, thought to have totally different spheres of activity any attempt to link them became merely artificial. The emblem book developed finally into an illustrated book in which the picture was no longer to be 'read' in the same way as the poem but became merely an extraneous ornament, of antiquarian interest if the original seventeenth century plates were copied and of practical value if the emblems were intended for educational purposes. It was no longer an essential factor, and with this divorce the most distinctive feature of the convention was lost.

Outside the emblem books themselves the convention had a positive influence. If it was one of the normal accomplishments of a courtier, it was also one of the normal devices of a poet. In the reign of Elizabeth emblems were so well established as a part of social life that they slid everywhere into literature. At a time when it was natural and intelligible for a man to scratch an emblematic poem on his friend's window pane, taking the brittleness of the glass for his 'picture' and his theme, it was impossible to ignore them. They occur frequently in the drama: in *Cynthia's Revels* they are parodied in the burlesque courtship scene where prizes are given for the best court compliment:

For the *bare Accost*, two *Wall-eyes*, in a *face forced*: For the *better Reguard*, a *Face favorably simpring*, with a *Fanne waving*: For the *solemne Addresse*, two *Lips wagging*, and never a wise word: For the *perfect Close*, a *Wring by the hand*, with a *Banquet* in a corner.[1]

Nashe, too, was acutely enough aware of the convention to mock at it. It fulfilled, indeed, the necessary requirements of a subject of parody: it was a matter of common knowledge and it had a clearly defined set of rules. The fashion also lent itself to serious treatment, and it could make a positive contribution to dramatic

[1] Ben Jonson, *Cynthia's Revels*. V. iii. 106–110. *Works*. ed. C. H. Herford and P. Simpson. Vol. IV. 1932. p. 138.

effect. Chapman's tragedies contain long and elaborate emblems which, to an Elizabethan, would have taken the place of incident and which, therefore, though readily detachable, formed an essential part of the play's structure. Byron upon his horse, for instance, is described by Savoy in these terms:

> Your Majesty hath miss'd a royal sight:
> The Duke Byron on his brave beast Pastrana,
> Who sits him like a full-sailed Argosy
> Danced with a lofty billow, and as snug
> Plies to his bearer, both their motions mix'd;
> And being consider'd in their site together,
> They do the best present the state of man
> In his first royalty ruling, and of beasts
> In their first loyalty serving (one commanding,
> And no way being mov'd; the other serving,
> And no way being compell'd) of all the sights
> That ever my eyes witness'd; and they make
> A doctrinal and witty hieroglyphic
> Of a blest kingdom: to express and teach
> Kings to command as they could serve, and subjects
> To serve as if they had power to command.[1]

Here a speaking picture, its interpretation, and its moral lesson, are all present; an emblematist would have had a woodcut in place of the description of Byron, but the passage otherwise conforms with the pattern of the poems which made up the content of the emblem books.

In this book I have attempted to trace the history of the emblem fashion for a century—the period during which it was vital and important—and to bring out its connections with the literature of the time. The first English emblem book was published in 1586; the first emblem book intended specifically for children in 1686, a date which can be taken as marking the end of the life of the convention. The early chapters are concerned with emblem books in the first phase of their development, when they were still closely connected with decoration and rhetoric, and with some

---

[1] *Byron's Conspiracy*. II. 2. 66–81. *The Tragedies of George Chapman*. ed. T. Parrott. 1910.

comparisons which may be drawn between them and Elizabethan poetry, particularly the poetry of Spenser. In the seventeenth century they became more literary and their potentialities as a poetic form are developed; in Chapter 5 the work of Francis Quarles and his imitators is discussed, and in Chapter 7 some prose adaptations of the form considered. In Chapter 6 I have tried to work out the relation of the poetry of George Herbert to the fashion, since, apart from some poems in which even the material of the emblem books is used, there is much in his writing that is generally emblematic, and the convention seems to provide an approach by which his real merits can be estimated and in which his peculiarities appear natural. To apply the same method to the work of the other metaphysical poets would be lacking in a sense of perspective: for, although the emblem books were at hand for any writer to draw upon, Herbert's poetry is primarily and consistently emblematic where theirs was only spasmodically so. Since the fashion was as much a symptom as a production of the period, it is impossible to define the boundaries between the emblematic and the metaphysical except in terms of technique; one critic has, indeed, maintained that an emblem is a metaphysical conceit in little.[1] It is Herbert's technique which resembles that of the emblematists, and the convention is therefore particularly illuminating in relation to his poetry.

In the development of English emblem books through the century there emerges a distinct change in the scope of allegory: interest turned from what was public, external, and impersonal to a field more private, individual, and literary. It is a change which has its counterpart in the difference between the allegorical methods of *The Faerie Queene* and *The Pilgrim's Progress*; and these appear to represent the two poles upon which the subject turns. Chapter 8 is therefore mainly concerned with the work of Bunyan, in which the convention found its final expression.

[1] T. O. Beachcroft, 'Quarles and the Emblem Habit.' *Dublin Review*. Vol. 188. Jan. 1931. pp. 80–96.

I

From George Wither: *A Collection of Emblemes 1635*
[slightly reduced]

From Lord Shaftesbury: *Characteristicks 1714*

Chapter 1

THE METHODS OF THE EMBLEM
WRITERS

I

EMBLEM books are picture books made up of emblematic pictures and explanatory words. Some of the words will probably be familiar enough to readers of seventeenth century literature, for they are the constantly repeated tags of Elizabethan morality such as *Festina Lente*, and *Vincit qui patitur*; others will be strange only because they were not so constantly repeated. The pictures, however, present more serious difficulties: they appear curious, if not uncouth, to an unaccustomed eye, and they demand an inspection perhaps too prolonged for so meagre a reward. They rarely, in fact, achieve any great merit as art. Since, therefore, a part of this study presupposes serious consideration of a number of them, some explanation of their purpose and character is needed, both as an apology and as an apparatus of approach.

The two engravings on the opposite page are intended to define to the eye the scope of this book. They are contrasted as different methods of solving the same problem; together they establish the province and limits of the term 'emblematic'. The first, drawn from George Wither's *A Collection of Emblemes* has affinities sometimes quite obvious, sometimes more remote, with all the reproductions which are to follow in this study. It is, in fact, a representative emblem. The second, drawn from Lord Shaftesbury's unfinished *Second Characters or the Language of Forms* (1713) shows what an emblem was *not*.[1] It was designed with the conscious

---

[1] The term *Character* is here used by Shaftesbury in a sense in which it obtained throughout the seventeenth century. He means signs or symbols of any kind. A chart is appended to the book, in which Characters are divided into three groups, FIRST CHARACTERS or linguistic symbols, SECOND CHARACTERS

9

aim of proving that certain subjects could be represented in painting 'without necessary recourse to what is absolutely of the emblem kind', and in the very acute discussion which accompanies it, Shaftesbury fastens immediately on the points at issue and clearly distinguishes between the principles underlying the two methods. That he is led finally to dismiss all that is represented by Wither's picture as 'magical, mystical, monkish and Gothic', does not diminish the penetration of his analysis and, since he stood outside the emblem tradition, he was able to look back to it and could be more articulate about it than those who were within. It is, therefore, useful to be able to compare the two pictures and to set beside a plate engraved when the emblem literature was at its height, criticism written when it was meaningless.

The two pictures are divided by exactly a century. Wither's *A Collection of Emblemes* was printed in 1635 but its plates were all drawn from Gabriel Rollenhagen's *Nucleus Emblematum Selectissimorum* which had appeared in 1611–13. Emblem books were then already popular both in England and on the Continent; a hundred years later the interests of both reader and writer had changed, as Shaftesbury's categorical condemnation of their previous tastes must show. The original picture for his *Second Characters* was painted by an Italian working in France, Paolo de Matteis. Shaftesbury accompanied the commission with a little treatise in French for the painter's better understanding of the principles of his art. This theoretical discussion, entitled 'A Notion of the Historical Draught of Hercules', was published first in the *Journal des Sçavans* in 1712, and translated into English in the following year. Its author had intended that the essay, together with an engraving of the finished picture, should form one section of the projected work, *Second Characters*, but this he never lived to complete.[1] Enough, however, of the book exists in notes

[1] It has been edited from the MSS. by Benjamin Rand: *Second Characters or the Language of Forms*, by the third Earl of Shaftesbury. Harvard 1914. All references are to this edition.

or statuary and painting, and THIRD CHARACTERS or emblematical designs which group he also terms MIDDLE as falling somewhere between the first and second. See Appendix 2. p. 241.

and brief treatises to indicate its direction, and the 'Notion' itself is complete.

The theme of the two pictures is the same. It was one familiar in various guises to contemporary readers, and Rollenhagen found no occasion to go to the original source but clings to a current conception of Virtue as an old man. The exact story, however, is recorded by Xenophon, and Shaftesbury's picture is based on that. The fable describes the meeting of Hercules and two goddesses, Virtue and Pleasure, their conflicting invitations to him, the long debate which follows, and the final decision of the hero.

The story offers an opportunity for what Shaftesbury calls 'history painting', that is, painting where 'not only men, but manners, and human passions are represented', and not only human passions but human actions. The artist is asked to set before the eye struggles which are agitating only within the mind and to transfix in one instant events which take place in time. Shaftesbury and Wither have different methods of solving this problem. In the engraving of Hercules Shaftesbury has appointed his time carefully: he rejects three possible alternatives and finally chooses the moment when Pleasure has ceased to plead and Virtue is still speaking. Hercules is leaning towards her with the memory of Pleasure's inducements still in his mind, and the ensuing conflict is conveyed by his attitude and expression. In Wither's picture none of the three characters has any particular interest in the others: it is a tableau in which each is posed in an attitude appropriate to his own nature. There is no sense of dramatic moment.

These two opinions as to the importance of the element of time in pictures of this kind are part of a wider issue which resolved itself finally into the eighteenth century critical battle over the exact interpretation of the Horatian formula, *Ut pictura pœsis*. Both pictures are expressly based on this formula, but it bears a wholly different interpretation in each. Shaftesbury often anticipates Lessing in his determination of the proper spheres of poetry and painting, and his conclusions are always abruptly at variance with the practice of the emblem artists.[1] Aiming at 'a just conformity with historical truth, and with the unity of time and action', he can only represent the fable 'by setting in view such passages or events as have actually subsisted, or according to nature might well subsist, or happen together in one and the same instant. And this is what we may properly call the rule of consistency.'[2] The emblem writers had no such rule of consistency; often several events which could not by any chance have subsisted together in one time are found side by side within the single frame of an emblem from Wither or Whitney. The encroachments of the painter upon the domain of the poet occur everywhere in the emblem books.[3] Whitney's Arion, for example, is cast into the waves and is seen simultaneously riding away upon the dolphin in another corner of the picture.

Divergence upon the question of time is, however, only one side of the difference. Shaftesbury next transfers his attention to the posture and form of the three figures. In Wither these are represented with small regard for those 'living appearances' which constituted for Shaftesbury the chief province and the true criterion of painting. The characters of Vice and Virtue are indicated in their outward form, but they are made even more distinct by the collection of objects which surround them. Vice holds a whip in her hand, at her feet is a lute, and beside her a vase of flowers;[4] the mask which she holds in front of her face barely conceals her real nature. Virtue, a sober old man, bears a book in his hand, and the rod of Mercury, the symbol of wisdom, lies at his feet. Behind is a sunflower, the emblem of constancy in the pursuit of an ideal, which is balanced on Vice's side by crossed

[1] The treatise was translated into German and did have considerable influence on German thinkers. See Benjamin Rand's introduction to his edition, p. xxii.

[2] Shaftesbury, op. cit. p. 36.

[3] This encroachment was exemplified for Lessing by Titian's Prodigal Son. 'His dissolute life, his misery and repentance are all represented on one canvas.' *Laokoon*. Ch. 18.

[4] The flowers are lilies. Cp. John Webster, *The White Devil*. V. 4. 118, where Brachiano's ghost appears to Flamineo bearing 'a pot of lilly-flowers with a skull in it'.. For the association of lilies with corruption cp. Shakespeare's 'lilies that fester smell far worse than weeds'.

bones and a skull. Shaftesbury will have none of this; he insists on the visual, not the symbolical:

By the word moral are understood, in this place, all sorts of judicious representations of the human passions. . . . As the moral part is differently treated in a poem from what it is in history, or in a philosophical work; so must it, of right, in painting be far differently treated from what it naturally is, either in the history, or poem. . . . For the completely imitative and illusive art of painting, whose character it is to employ in her works the united force of different colours; and who, surpassing by so many degrees, and so many privileges, all other human fiction, or imitative art, aspires in a directer manner towards deceit, and a command over our very sense; she must of necessity abandon whatever is over-learned, humourous, or witty; to maintain herself in what is natural, credible, and winning of our assent: that she may thus acquit herself of what is her chief province, the specious appearance of the object she represents. [1]

Even where it seems to him advisable to add what he calls 'some exterior marks more declaratory and determinative of these two personages, Virtue and Pleasure', the claims of the probable must be respected. The two attributes of Virtue, forbearance and endurance, may be indicated by a bit or bridle placed somewhere by her side, and a helmet, 'especially since they are each of them appurtenances essential to heroes (who in the quality of warriors, were also subduers and managers of horses), and that at the same time these are really portable instruments such as the martial dame who represents virtue, may be well supposed to have brought along with her'. [2]

From such a contrast as this some of the principles of the emblem writer begin to emerge more plainly. For him, all objects have an allegorical significance. Both in their patterned arrangement and in the fact of their being present at all, the claims of verisimilitude are ignored. The vase of lilies and the death's head cannot be numbered among 'portable instruments', nor has Vice any plausible reason for having brought them along with her; the reader is not even required to suppose that she did. Shaftesbury's criterion of the natural and credible is irrelevant

[1] Shaftesbury, op. cit. pp. 53-5.   [2] Ibid. p. 58.

here since in such pictures objects are introduced not for their 'specious appearance' but for their significance. Dryden raised the same issue when he criticised the symbolic representation of the theatrical army: 'What is more ridiculous than to represent an army with a drum and five men behind it?' [1] The emblem writer dispenses even with the five men; he entrusts his meaning to the drum alone, and relies upon the reader's ability to accept a symbolical connection between things. His pictures are, in fact, allegorical, and allegorical in certain specific ways. Shaftesbury's strictures are of a piece with the kind of criticism implied in Dryden's rewriting of Shakespeare's plays; they mark the first appearance of the standards by which Quarles's and Whitney's Victorian editors were to judge their emblems, and in distinguishing Wither's methods from those of Shaftesbury it is possible to disentangle the conceptions of the seventeenth century emblem writers from those which have been since current almost to the present time.

The apologists of the emblem books, both the writers in their prefaces and the critics, unite in one common critical formula. It is the phrase quoted by Plutarch from Simonides that poetry is a speaking picture and painting dumb poetry; Henry Hawkins, for instance, prefaces his translation of a French emblem book with the injunction: 'If you eye wel and marke these silent Poesies, give eare to these speaking pictures.' [2] The chief end of an emblem, according to a French handbook on the subject, is 'to instruct us, by subjecting the figure to our view, and the sense to our understanding'.[3] Wither describes the process in greater detail:

> When you have heeded, by your *Eyes* of *sense*,
> This *Helmet*, hiving of a Swarme of *Bees*,
> Consider, what may gather'd be from thence,
> And, what your *Eye* of *Understanding* sees.[4]

[1] Dryden, Essay of Dramatic Poesy. *Works*. Ed. Scott. 1892. Vol. XV. p. 323.
[2] *The Devout Hart or Royal Throne of the Pacifical Salomon*. 1634. pp. 4–5.
[3] *L'Art de faire les Devises*, by Henri Estienne. Paris. 1645. Translated from the French by Thomas Blount, *The Art of Making Devises*. London. 1646. All quotations are from the edition of 1650.
[4] George Wither, *A Collection of Emblemes*. 1635. p. 90.

14

He calls the pictures without their mottoes 'dumb figures' or, 'dumb showes'; indeed the dumb show of the stage is in both form and function only a much more elaborate version of the pictures in an emblem book. Harington makes the same point when he explains the purpose of the engravings which he had made for his translation of *Orlando Furioso*, the merits of which he, 'though partial', does not hesitate to describe:

The use of the picture is evident, which is, that (having read over the booke) you may reade it (as it were againe) in the very picture.[1]

This conception of the double medium was one which was assumed rather than explored by the seventeenth century critics; it was frequently invoked as a ready-made critical tag to be introduced whenever necessity arose, and it was rarely elaborated. Further comment was added merely to prove the inferiority of painting since that can speak only to the sense. 'The conceits of the mind are pictures of Things and the tongue is the interpreter of those pictures.' Henri Estienne, speaking of a related mode, the device, says:

Moreover, the invention is pleasing and efficacious, since to the contentment of the sight, it adds a ravishing of the mind, and that to the satisfaction both of the one and the other; it brings also some profit and utility, which is the perfection of a work; wherefore it surpasseth not onely all other Arts, but also Painting, since this onely representeth the body and exquisite features of the face, when as a Device exposeth the rare conceipts, and gallant resolutions of its Author, far more perspicuously, and with more certainty, then Physiognomy can, by the proportions and lineaments of the face.[2]

This is a questionable contention, but it holds good if painting is conceived as no more than dumb poetry. It is relevant here, too, to recall that contemporary pictures sometimes closely resembled devices. Drummond of Hawthornden in a letter to Sir George Keith describes the pictures at the Fair at St. Germains in terms not unlike those of Estienne:

[1] Ariosto, *Orlando Furioso*, in English Heroical verse by John Harington. 1591
[2] Estienne, op cit. p. 14.

I was much taken with the daintiness of the many Portraicts there to be seen. The devices, Posies, Ideas, Shapes, Draughts, of the Artificers were various, nice, and pleasant. Scarce could the wandering thought light upon the Storie, Fable, Gayetie which was not here represented to the view. If *Cebes* the *Theban* Philosopher made a Table hung in the Temple of *Saturn*, the Argument of his rare *Moralities*, and *Jovius* and *Marini*, the Portraicts in their *Galleries* and *Libraries* the subject of some books; I was brought to think I should not commit a great fault, if I sent you for a token, from this Mart a Scantling of this Ware which affordeth a like contentment to the Beholder and possessor.

He then lists the pictures, which consisted mainly of classical subjects—'on this Table *Flora* her bewitching Twins, on that not far from these *Mars* is surprized by the *Lemnian*, and the Senate of the Gods are all laughing; near by *Jupiter* is comming down in a Golden Showre in his *Danaes'* lap'. In another the painter had drawn Venus 'lying on a Bed with stretched out arms, in the hand she presented to a young man (who was adoring her, and at whom little Love was directing a Dart) a fair face, which with much ceremony he was receiving, but on the other side, which should have been the hinder part of that head, was the Image of death; by which *mortality* he surpassed the others more than they did him by *Art*'. Emblems were, of course, a special interest for Drummond, but even if it was his choice to isolate those particular pictures they were none the less there. Finally, there were the double pictures or perspectives which were so fascinating to his contemporaries. He describes several:

> Here were many double Pictures, the first view shew old men and young Misers gathering carefully, the second view shew young men and prodigals spending riotously with *stultitiam patiuntur opes*. Churchmen and grave Senatours consulting and seriously deliberating, the one face of the Picture represented, the other Fools dancing, Souldiers dicing and fighting.[1]

In these one image was super-imposed upon the other, so that as Cleopatra said of Antony, the figure was painted 'one way like

[1] William Drummond of Hawthornden, 'Letter to S.G.K.' in *The History of Scotland*. 1655. pp. 249–52.

16

a Gorgon, the other way a Mars' and a moral lesson could be drawn from the contrast between the two. All these pictures stand somewhere between the painted sign and the written word. They verge on the emblematic, and it remained for Shaftesbury in the detachment of the succeeding century to establish a schematic account of them. He distinguishes precisely between what he terms the true, or 'emblematic', in pictures, and the false or 'enigmatic'; and this distinction corresponds to the difference between his Hercules and that of Wither. Everything that characterises the seventeenth-century emblem book belongs, for him, to the region of the enigmatic: the true emblematic is constituted by 'the relief works and inwrought of the polite ancients' (presumably coins stamped with Athena's owl, etc.). He, therefore, divides those representations which cannot be classified with painting proper into two types:

1. *True, natural and simple*: Emblematical designs: whether graphical or plastical. The Greek and Roman anaglyphs of this narrative, historical and didactic, with what answers to the same in drawings, prints, etc. Paintings or full colours have hardly place here: because of wrong situation, loss of distances, and confusion of perspective.
2. *False, barbarous and mixed*: Enigmatical, preposterous, disproportionable, gouty and lame forms. False imitation, lie, impotence, pretending. Egyptian hieroglyphics. Magical, mystical, monkish and Gothic emblems.[1]

Wherever Shaftesbury grants his Hercules any share of the emblematic it is always of the first order.[2] Virtue and Pleasure are themselves of this category: if the strength of Virtue is to be conveyed the painter may do so by designing her to stand firmly on one foot, the other raised upon a piece of rocky ground; there is no need for her to be poised triumphant upon a globe. Literal translation of the conceits of the mind into pictures is no longer the basis of historical painting:

[1] Shaftesbury, op. cit. p. 91.
[2] In a letter to Sir John Cropley (Feb. 16, 1712) he says that his own designs 'run all on moral emblems', and the minute instructions which he sent to Micklethwayte for the emblematic engravings in *Characteristicks* show his principles in practice.

The moral part in painting lies but little in the forms . . . but is expressed in the air, attitude, feature, action, motion; and is therefore wholly lodged in that part of painting called the movements, where action, passion, the affections are shown.[1]

In the 'enigmatical' emblems which are to be the concern of this book it is an axiom that the moral part does lie in the forms. The illustrations to this and the succeeding chapters will show how frequently and easily the meaning was externalised. Occasion, for instance, in Plate 2, conveys little by her 'air, attitude, feature, action, motion', spirited though these are: the razor, the winged feet and the long forelock were what made her recognisable to contemporaries. In the same way, in the 'Hercules', all the factors which are involved in the decision the hero has to make are projected into pictorial form; and the sense of the picture lies in the total effect of these pictorial details.

II

This assumption that the meaning of the picture was to be conveyed in allegorical rather than naturalistic terms remained a constant factor in the constitution of emblems although the range of subject matter and the manner of its presentation in the books themselves changed as the century progressed. The picture and the word or poem were to be very closely interrelated: in the words of Bargagli, one of the Italian exponents of the science of emblem writing, they were to be 'so strictly united together, that being considered apart, they cannot explicate themselves distinctly the one without the other',[2] and one of the means by which this close interrelation was achieved was to be found in the use in the picture itself of detail which had a literary rather than a visual significance. It was taken for granted that the allegory in the picture as well as in the poem should assume a literary form. It is, of course, not necessarily of the nature of things that this should be so: Shaftesbury was at pains to point out that an allegorical meaning could be bestowed on pictures through other means, and Blake's paintings prove how successfully it could be conveyed in

[1] Shaftesbury, op. cit. p. 98.   [2] Quoted in H. Estienne, op. cit. p. 10.

To my Kinſman M. GEFFREY WHITNEY.

W HAT creature thou? *Occaſion I doe ſhowe.*
On whirling wheele declare why doſte thou ſtande?
Bicauſe, I ſtill am toſſed too, and froe.
Why doeſt thou houlde a raſor in thy hande?
That men maie knowe I cut on euerie ſide,
And when I come, I armies can deuide.

But wherefore haſt thou winges vppon thy feete?
To ſhowe, how lighte I flie with little winde.
What meanes longe lockes before? *that ſuche as meete,*
Maye houlde at firſte, when they occaſion finde.
Thy head behinde all balde, what telles it more?
That none ſhoulde houlde, that let me ſlippe before.

Why doeſt thou ſtande within an open place?
That I maye warne all people not to ſtaye,
But at the firſte, occaſion to imbrace,
And when ſhee comes, to meete her by the waye.
Lyſippus ſo did thinke it beſt to bee,
Who did deuiſe mine image, as you ſee.

From Geoffrey Whitney: *A Choice of Emblemes 1586*
[slightly reduced]

the visual forms, in the shape and placing of the figures, and in the pattern of the picture as a whole. But for the emblem writers it was a first principle. The essence of the term 'emblematic' lies in such a detailed pictorial and allegorical presentation of ideas, and the pleasure of the reader lay in identifying the significant details and correlating them with the moral doctrines taught in the accompanying poem.

Emblematic ways of perception in this sense were widely current in all forms of art in the sixteenth and seventeenth centuries. Shaftesbury in his rejection of the whole method as enigmatical, monkish and Gothic is voicing the prejudice of a classical age against anything which appears to be mediaeval. In reality, however, the emblems are not so much mediaeval in their interests as renaissance: they draw upon stock mediaeval symbols for some of their material, but some of it is also classical, and is derived from Greek and Roman legends, from classical history, and from Ovid. In Italy, where they first appeared, their classical affinities were at least as important as their mediaeval, and through the epigram and pithy moral saying which accompany the picture they are related to the Greek anthology. It is, indeed, this epigrammatic element and their use of classical themes that make them peculiarly characteristic of Renaissance literature. Furthermore, although the fashion is linked through its allegorical material with the surviving interests of the Middle Ages, the way in which the themes are treated is not mediaeval at all. The mediaeval conception of the world was disappearing and with it the mediaeval genius for allegorical presentation of people and ideas. Sidney makes an illuminating comment on the intellectual state of his own age when in writing to Languet in 1574 he says:

. . . in your letters I fancy I see a picture of the age in which we live: an age that resembles a bow too long bent; it must be unstrung or it will break. . . . [1]

[1] Translated from the Latin by Steuart A. Pears, *The Correspondence of Philip Sidney and Hubert Languet.* London. 1845. The original letter is printed by Feuillerat, *Works of Sidney*, C.U.P. 1923. Vol. III. p. 86: . . . ex tuis enim litteris quasi imaginem nostrum temporum videor mihi videre, quae iam sane ut arcum nimis diu intensum, aut relaxari aut frangi oportet . . .

His image of the bow symbolises the nature of much Elizabethan
literature. Ideas are held together by tension and no longer by the
interlocking of a system. For the mediaeval man the whole world
had been symbolic, and all the details of experience had formed
part of one unified allegorical conception of the meaning of life:

> Omnis mundi creatura
> quasi liber et pictura
>   nobis est in speculum,
> nostrae vitae, nostrae sortis,
> nostri status, nostrae mortis
> fidele signaculum.[1]

For the Elizabethans this great framework no longer existed as a
single unity: it had not completely vanished but it had broken up,
leaving fragments of the old allegorical ways of thinking still
present in men's minds, but present only as fragments and not
co-ordinated.

Inevitably the disappearance of a unified framework into which
each small detail was known to fit had distinct effects upon the
way in which allegorical ideas were presented. The change is not
reflected only in emblem books: it is clearly marked in all forms
of allegorical expression in the sixteenth century, and it constitutes the great difference in method between Spenser's presentation of an allegorical theme and that of his predecessors. The new
technique is perhaps best seen in the treatment of personification
where the distance from a naturalistic conception is always most
clearly apparent. In the first place a much greater freedom of
presentation was possible when a unified allegorical picture of
the world existed. The personified figures of the later Middle Ages
were often accorded a treatment far more realistic than that which
the Elizabethans were able to provide. They could move and act
naturally because their place in the symbolised world was assured.
They derived their meaning from, and were always referred back
to, an established and integrated scheme. The Elizabethan symbol
is isolated, and partly perhaps for that reason, is treated statically

[1] Alan of Lille. Quoted by F. J. E. Raby, as an example of the mediaeval
symbolical outlook in *A History of Christian-Latin Poetry*. 1927. p. 355.

and quite unrealistically. Dunbar's Seven Deadly Sins dance by
their own vitality:

> Me thocht, amangis the feyndis fell,
> Mahoun gart cry ane dance
> Off schrewis that wer nevir schrevin . . .
> 'Lat se', quod he, 'Now quha begynnis;'
> With that the fowll Sevin Deidly Synnis
> Begowth to leip at anis.
> And first of all in dance wes Pryd,
> With hair wyld bak and bonet on syd,
> Lyk to mak waistie wanis.[1]

The figures in the emblem books, however, are turned about by
their authors to show off their symbolical properties; and in
Spenser, too, the personifications which constitute most of the
minor figures in *The Faerie Queene*, such as those of the Seven
Deadly Sins in the House of Pride, or the figures in the Masque of
Cupid, do not move freely and naturally with their own life but
are made to move by the author, and to move more for the sake
of display than of action. Secondly, this stiffness and lack of freedom in presentation is accompanied by a passion for allegorical
detail for its own sake. The emblem writers, however familiar
their material might be, never wearied of explaining its significance: over and over again the points of likeness between the
picture and what it stands for are elaborated. They are not taken
for granted and made a part of the living human being as they are
by Dunbar or by Skelton in the *Bouge of Court* or by Chaucer in
his list of personifications in the *Knight's Tale*. Instead, the details
are laboriously enumerated and attached to a figure that is, and
remains, lifeless.

These two characteristics are perhaps rather unexpected as
results of the disintegration of a unified allegorical conception of
the world: it might have been supposed that the effects would be
a greater, and not a diminished, freedom in the presentation of
the isolated parts. But in practice when the validity of any relation-

[1] Dunbar, 'The Dance of the Sevin Deadly Synnis.' *The Poems of William
Dunbar*, ed. W. Mackay Mackenzie. 1932. p. 120. The poem was written some
time between 1496 and 1507.

ship ceases to be taken for granted, the free and unselfconscious movement which is based upon it is no longer possible: and this is what happened to allegory in the sixteenth century. Whereas the mediaeval personification could spring spontaneously into being and carry its meaning lightly with it, the Elizabethan personification had to be established, and made intelligible by careful analogy; hence the stiffness of the figures and the long lists of parallels between the image and the idea it expresses. Because the relationship between symbol and thing symbolised had changed, the method had to be one of manipulation rather than exploration. Spenser cannot penetrate into the nature of his symbolical figures as Chaucer or Dunbar can, absorbing the allegorical into the human: he has to impose their significance upon them by external means. The emblem books themselves, indeed, provided a peculiarly suitable form for this kind of symbolisation, and this may account in part for their popularity in the late sixteenth century. In them the personifications, and the other forms of symbolic representation too, were required only to exist, not to function; they had not to live and move credibly, and consequently those elements in the mediaeval scheme which still had meaning locally could be preserved in them without reference to, or need for, a coherent framework. In *The Faerie Queene* the lack of vitality in such figures as Occasion, Ignaro, or the ladies and the servants in the House of Alma, weakens the force of the allegory and remains one of the great defects of the poem.

Personification is, of course, only one of the forms through which allegorical thinking is expressed but what holds true for it, holds true for the others also. All differ from the mediaeval type of allegory in this way. The forms which occur most frequently in the emblem books apart from the personified figures are the short anecdote and the abstract symbol. The first, the anecdote, was drawn from classical myth and legend, from historical incidents, from jest books, collections of fables and other sources of that kind. 'The Choice of Hercules' is a representative example of this sort of emblem, and it is characterised by the same stiffness of presentation and love of allegorical detail as is found in the personifications. The abstract symbol was more widely used still. It formed the staple of the emblem writer's stock-in-trade and was employed both as part of a composite picture, where it contributed one more significant detail to the personification or the anecdote, and also by itself as the single subject of an emblem: the sunflower, for instance, which adds something to the allegorical conception of the 'Choice of Hercules', was elsewhere treated independently. These symbols are emblematic in just the same way as are the personifications and the moral anecdotes, but because their make-up is considerably simpler, they reflect more plainly the virtues and the limitations of the whole method. For that reason it is useful to consider them more fully than the other two.

Symbols have been used so variously and with such complex effect in poetry at different periods that it is necessary to elucidate the sense in which the term is here applied. They were included, as one of the descendants of the Hieroglyphic, among devices and other related forms by critics who discussed the nature of the emblem and its kin in the sixteenth and seventeenth centuries, and the word 'symbol' is therefore used in a special and limited sense in that connection.[1] It has, however, acquired a much wider significance for the modern critic, and to cling to this limited sense would be to ignore the difficulties that must be encountered in using the word at all. A poetic symbol in the modern sense is a concrete image, complete in itself, which stands for some abstract idea or series of ideas in the poetic mind. By this definition all emblems are symbols: they present an ethical concept in the form of a picture, real or imagined, and the picture is not to be interpreted literally but figuratively. The picture itself may be of various different types: Shaftesbury's ideal emblematic picture is very different from Wither's: but both have some kind of symbolic purpose. Since, however, the symbols used by poets often bear a very rich and complex meaning, the term is sometimes used in a qualitative as well as in a merely explanatory sense.

---

[1] e.g. by Henri Estienne, op. cit. p. 4; Abraham Fraunce, *Insignium, Armorum, Emblematum, Hieroglyphicarum, et Symbolorum* . . . *explicatio.* London, 1588. Book III. passim; and Claude Mignault in the preface to his edition of Alciati.

Thus, although Blake and Herbert both wrote poetry in which concrete images stand for abstract ideas those images are described without hesitation as 'symbols' in Blake's poems, whereas in Herbert's there may be some doubt as to the propriety of the term and something a little less laudatory such as 'conceits' may be used instead. In this narrower sense no emblem could be called a symbol since no emblem ever achieved the fulness and richness of the emotional content of one of Blake's symbols. When, therefore, the term is used in connection with the images in the emblem books it is used in a purely factual way, and no standard of value is implied. It remains to be considered, however, whether the failure of the emblem writers to create in their poetry symbols of the richest kind is inherent in the method they chose, and follows inevitably from the kind of symbol they adopted and from the way they related it to the ideas they wished it to convey.

The critics who discussed the theory of emblem writing did, of course, realise to some extent how highly involved the question was. They saw that the relationship between the symbol and the thing symbolised could vary greatly in kind and complexity. Henri Estienne, the French critic, who had read widely in the theories of the Italians and usefully summarises their views in his book, tried to get to the root of the matter through the actual nature of the symbol itself. He distinguishes between two kinds of resemblances between things—the 'intrinsicall, occult, naturall and essentiall' on the one side, and on the other the 'extrinsicall, manifest, artificall, knowne and accidentall'. The example he takes to illustrate the distinction is somewhat absurd, but it makes his point. The Egyptian hieroglyphic of an enfranchised slave is a hat:

As if you consider a hat, as it is an instrument invented to keep off the sunne and raine, you consider it purely according to its nature; but if you take it for a figure of liberty, you suppose then that either God or man have already imposed this signification upon it.[1]

It is, in that case, a symbol of the accidental kind, and the relation

[1] Op. cit. p. 41.

24

between the image and its significance is purely arbitrary. Estienne then goes on to insist, quite rightly, that the best symbols are intrinsic, and he maintains that these are to be found in those similitudes and relations which we discover 'walking in the spacious fields of the wonderful secrets of nature and qualities of things'. In this, too, he is probably right, for only in nature and human nature are to be found symbols of permanent validity: the penny-farthing was soon superseded as a symbol of speed whereas a winged foot is unlikely ever to lose its significance. But his distinction breaks down in the end because it ascribes everything to the kind of symbol chosen and nothing to the method by which this is related to the ideas for which it stands: his theory will hold good for the very simple type of pictorial symbol, which is most effective when its relation to what it represents is both self-evident and fundamental—the hammer and sickle is a better symbol than the stars and stripes—but in literature, where it must be used in a context, other factors come into play and something more than an intrinsic image is needed before a successful symbol can be produced. Indeed, it may even be true that a good symbol can be made out of an apparently external and accidental image provided that it is adequately related to the ideas within the poem.

The limitation of Estienne's classification is seen if it is applied to the emblem books themselves. There the symbols are largely of the kind which he deprecates and the correspondence between idea and image is mainly arbitrary. But there are some which he would have called intrinsic. The skull and crossed bones, for instance, which was frequently used by emblem writers, has a connection with death which is by no means arbitrary, and it is a self-evident and intrinsic symbol of mortality; the sunflower or the marigold, which was commonly supposed to turn about on its stalk in accordance with the movement of the sun, is a perfectly just image of faithfulness. There is no question in either emblem of forcing a significance upon an unsuitable image. Yet in the hands of the emblem writers these images appear not to have any greater degree of plausibility than Estienne's hat. It is the method which matters, and it must be admitted that even when they are based on images which do bear a fundamental resemblance to the idea which is to be expressed, the emblems are unsatisfactory as poetic symbols. In spite of the accumulation of parallels which he can produce, the emblem writer fails in the end to provide any convincing reason for his choice of that particular image. It remains arbitrary. Wither, for instance, takes the symbol of the Marigold and gives it a religious significance:

> When, with a serious musing, I behold
> The gratefull, and obsequious *Marigold*,
> How duely, ev'ry morning, she displayes
> Her open brest, when *Titan* spreads his Rayes;
> How she observes him in his daily walke,
> Still bending towards him, her tender stalke;
> How, when he downe declines, she droopes and mournes,
> Bedew'd (as 'twere) with teares, till he returnes;
> And, how she vailes her *Flow'rs*, when he is gone,
> As if she scorned to be looked on
> By an inferiour *Eye*; or, did contemne
> To wayt upon a meaner *Light*, then Him.
> When this I meditate, methinkes, the *Flowers*
> Have *spirits*, farre more generous, then ours;
> And, give us faire Examples, to despise
> The servile Fawnings, and Idolatries,
> Wherewith, we court these earthly things below,
> Which merit not the service we bestow.
>   But, oh my God! though groveling I appeare
> Vpon the Ground, (and have a rooting here,
> Which hales me downward) yet in my desire,
> To that, which is above mee, I aspire:
> And, all my best *Affections* I professe
> To *Him*, that is the *Sunne of Righteousnesse*.
> Oh! keepe the *Morning* of his *Incarnation*,
> The burning *Noone* tide of his bitter *Passion*,
> The *Night* of his *Descending* and the *Height*
> Of his *Ascension*, ever in my sight:
>   That imitating him, in what I may
>   I never follow an inferiour *Way*.[1]

[1] George Wither, op. cit. p. 109. The Marigold, Sunflower, Heliotrope and Girasole were regarded as interchangeable terms in the seventeenth century.

There are plenty of likenesses yet the Marigold carries no conviction as a symbol of religious life in the poem, and Wither
might multiply his points of resemblance indefinitely without
ever being able to persuade the reader that they are anything
more than accidental. The fault does not lie in the Marigold but
in what Wither does with it. Blake will take the same image,
draw no explicit comparisons and yet invest the flower with the
whole meaning of his poem:

> Ah, Sun-flower! weary of time,
> Who countest the steps of the Sun,
> Seeking after that sweet golden clime
> Where the traveller's journey is done:
>
> Where the Youth pined away with desire,
> And the pale Virgin shrouded in snow
> Arise from their graves, and aspire
> Where my Sun-flower wishes to go.[1]

It is perhaps unfair to contrast so good a poem with one so poor,
but the difference in method cannot otherwise be defined.
Wither's Marigold behaves towards the sun as a man should be-
have towards God, fixes its eye upon him, laments his absence
when he is gone, and follows no lesser light: the actions of the
flower and of man are equated at each point. But Blake does not
equate, he identifies. His poem is about time and about aspiration:
the Sunflower which follows, and grows weary of following, the
sun, and which, in following, seeks for some unattained golden
world associated with it, combines in itself those two themes.
Everything in the poem enriches the meaning of the symbol; the
movement of the sun marks the passage of time, 'weary', 'count-
est', 'steps' build up the impression of the gradualness and tedium
of the process, and at the same time contribute to the idea of
aspiration, linking up with the traveller in the fourth line. The
'sweet golden clime' is the world to which the sun retreats or it
may be the world which the sun represents; in its general associ-

[1] Blake, *Songs of Experience*. 1794. *The Poetry and Prose of William Blake*, ed.
Geoffrey Keynes. 1941.

ations with Paradise it has an application for all humanity which is carried on in the next line by the 'traveller's journey' with its suggestion of pilgrimage and the journey of human life. In the second stanza these ideas are developed further: the conception of the 'sweet golden clime' is further defined by the extremes of heat and cold, of passion and frigidity which have destroyed the Youth and the pale Virgin; and when they rise from their graves, the 'time' of the opening lines is shown to be not only time as it is in itself, wearisome, slow and yet a condition of human life, but also as it is in contrast to eternity. The more the vocabulary is explored the fuller and richer the meaning of the whole poem becomes; and this meaning is strengthened by the actual structure of the poem with its curious circular movement. Both the incomplete syntax and the way in which the ideas are developed lead back again to the beginning: the movement of the Sunflower is embodied in the movement of the poem. The symbol is an entirely valid one because it is made so within the poem.

Such an achievement would have been impossible for an emblem writer because his method really precludes it. He chooses his image and imposes some significance upon it: in practice the image was generally ready to hand in the emblematic plate, but even poets who made their own plates, like Peacham, always begin with the picture and then make an interpretation for it. Blake, on the other hand, begins with his ideas and concentrates them into the single image of the Sunflower, which then becomes their symbol invested with all the richness of a complex meaning. The existence or non-existence of an essential connection between the symbol and what it stands for has little to do with its success: what matters is whether it is established as essential, and so made wholly convincing within the poem. In Blake the connection is recognised to be intrinsic, in Wither it remains arbitrary.

In this imposition of meaning upon a predetermined image lies the essential weakness of the emblem writer's method. The point by point comparison which they adopted to explain the likeness could not, in the nature of things, be fruitful because the symbol always remained detached from what it stood for. The fact that the images of the emblem writers were almost wholly visual may also have contributed something to their lack of success as symbols: each detail in them is a pictured detail, to be seen by the eye, and this inevitably limits the scope of the comparison. The weakness of the technique is that although the symbol is plausibly and persistently equated with the idea or ideas it represents, it is never actually identified with them: it does not become the idea itself, wholly inseparable from it, as Blake's Sunflower is inseparable from the ideas of time and aspiration. There may be nothing wrong with the emblem writer's symbol as such, yet it fails to convince the reader. For his method, with its detailed equation of picture and meaning, is the method of fancy rather than of imagination, as Wordsworth and Coleridge were later to define the distinction. He deals in fixities and definites, establishing parallel after parallel in a purely objective way. His symbol is a matter of choice not of necessity, and because he deduces his ideas from it instead of concentrating them in it, it remains the arbitrary product of a fanciful rather than an imaginative experience.

This limitation within the emblem technique itself must be admitted at the outset, although since the emblem writers were never poets of much merit the ultimate value of their symbols was rarely tested. Their methods were, however, used to better purpose by better men, and the issue becomes important when the work of those contemporary poets who made use of their technique is considered. The one among these who owes most to it is George Herbert, and the connections between his poetry and the emblem books will be indicated in a later chapter. As has already been suggested, Herbert's images can only doubtfully be called symbols. They almost always belong to the second group of connections indicated by Estienne—those which are artificial and accidental by nature—and they are largely visual. In both these ways they resemble the images of the emblem writers. They are to some degree like emblems also in the manner of their presentation. Herbert does not labour his parallels point by point as Wither and Quarles do, but his method is nevertheless that of equation rather than of identification. The image remains independent of the ideas it conveys, and does not wholly embody them as Blake's does. Yet within the poem the parallel is convincing: the pulley and the church floor can be accepted as credible symbols even though they are arbitrary. Herbert succeeds in making them the focus for complex ideas and emotions, and so combines in his poems something of the richness of meaning which Blake's symbols have with the detachment which characterises the emblem writer's treatment of them. His images are symbols in precisely the same sense as the images of the emblem writers, and yet they are the means by which he achieves his success as a poet. The degree of success varies from poem to poem according to the quality of the meaning concentrated in them, but it is always achieved through, and not in spite of, the emblem method. The emblematic image remains the basis upon which the poem is built, and if it appears fanciful in itself it is nevertheless made valid by the use to which Herbert puts it.

The poems of Herbert show that there were potentialities of success within the emblematists' use of symbol. Some modifications of method were necessary even then, but these were not fundamental, and the connections between his poems and those of the emblem writers are close enough to prove that their arbitrary and largely visual symbols had a value for poetry. They were, indeed, employed widely by seventeenth century poets as a form of imagery and as an incidental element in their poems, but it is only rarely that they constitute the basic principle of construction as they do for Herbert. Although its introduction in a poem is no guarantee of success, the intrinsic symbol undoubtedly has certain advantages over the arbitrary type: inasmuch as it has a significance outside its context and is part of general human experience, it is more accessible and more immediately productive of emotional response and therefore helps the poet in his task. Similarly the symbol that is not purely pictorial has also more in its favour at the outset than one which appeals only to the eye, for it is less clearly defined and so more elastic and capable of wider application. The emblem writer's type of symbol was probably, therefore, by nature less open to imaginative treatment, and, poor poets as they were, they were never able to make much of it. But in more competent hands it could be used successfully and although, with the single exception of Herbert, no poet of distinction was willing to entrust the responsibility for the whole of his poem to it, many were content to make it a part. The extent to which the imagery of seventeenth century poetry is visual and clearly outlined yet at the same time rich with meaning is proof of the fruitful way in which it penetrated contemporary habits of thought.

The emblematic image, then, had potentialities as a medium for poetry. In all its forms it remains unlike the earlier type of allegory: in the emblem books the treatment of the abstract symbol, the stiffness of the personified figures, the imposition of moral significance upon straightforward unallegorical stories, the introduction of purely figurative detail in the plates and the interpretation of realistic detail there in a figurative way, all bear witness to the forced and arbitrary nature of Elizabethan and Jacobean symbolism. And yet the allegorical way of thinking was pervasive and habitual; if it had not been, the emblem books would not have existed at all. It had, however, ceased to be pervasive and habitual in the mediaeval fashion: allegory had become an interest for its own sake instead of a means of interpreting the universe. For the emblem writers, the establishment of likenesses is an end in itself rather than a means to an end, and even for poets like Spenser and Herbert, who are still using allegory and symbol for a purpose, there is a new selfconsciousness in the handling of the medium. Spenser shows it in his elaboration of allegorical detail and his lack of freedom in the treatment of his characters, Herbert in his search for unusual and unexpected analogies. Yet, although this selfconsciousness is a sign of the decline of allegory as a mode of thought and reflects the disintegration of the old mediaeval framework, the emblematic image nevertheless had great vitality. Not until the Restoration was it dismissed altogether as a needless obscurity. In eighteenth century poetry symbolism apart from personification has small place:

with Blake it returns to English poetry as a mode of thought, but this is individual and personal thought, not the collective experience of everyone that it had been in the Middle Ages.

III

The emblematic image, as reflected in the emblem books, underwent some changes during the hundred years of its popularity in English literature. It did not change in its fundamentals; but the material with which the emblem writers deal and, in some degree, their manner of dealing with it, altered in accordance with changes in contemporary taste. The first emblem book introduced into England, Whitney's *A Choice of Emblemes* which appeared in 1586, was introduced in response to a demand already well established, and others which were published in imitation of it continued to satisfy the same taste in much the same way for about forty years. In 1635, however, Quarles brought a wholly new type of emblem book to England and this replaced the by now outworn formulas of the older variety.[1] Finally the fashion began to decay, and when in 1683 Philip Ayres published a third version of the form, the interests of English poets had gone elsewhere and his emblem book had none of the seriousness and the vitality which mark the two previous types.[2] These three authors all found their models abroad: their books are translations or adaptations of foreign emblem books. But in importing them, they and their successors made them a part of English literature, and although the impulse came originally from abroad, it remains none the less true that each type is closely related to a particular phase of English literary taste.

Of the three groups it is only the first two which can be said to have a serious bearing on English literature: the third merely marks the departure of poetic energy into other channels. The first group, that introduced by Whitney in 1586, is characterised by a wide range of content but complete unity of method and

[1] Francis Quarles, *Emblemes*. 1635.
[2] Philip Ayres, *Cupids Addresse to the Ladies. Emblemata Amatoria*. 1683.

3

From Sir Henry Godyere: *The Mirrour of Maiestie 1618*

From Francis Quarles: *Emblemes 1635*

intention; whereas the second, whose most representative figure is Quarles, is more limited in its field but far more elastic in its applications. As might be expected, the first is accompanied by a compact and consistent body of criticism, whereas the second, although it may provoke some interesting speculation from contemporary poets, has no commonly accepted rules or definition. The differences of method and intention are reflected in various ways. The same emblematic characteristics—the persistently literary nature of the symbolisation and the arbitrary way in which the significance is imposed—lie behind both, but they find different forms of expression in each. There is, in the first place, a change in theme, a shift in the later emblems from what is impersonal, to more individual and subjective types of material. If, for instance, the two plates opposite are contrasted the difference can easily be seen: both treat the theme of shipwreck: but for H.G. this symbolises the errors of the Catholic Church, for Quarles, the state of the soul alienated from God: his interest is psychological where H.G.'s is wholly objective. As a consequence of this new interest, the later emblem writers preferred to invent their own images or to adapt familiar ones and apply them in their own way, whereas the earlier writers were content very often with the conventional symbols and personifications or with traditional episodes from history, legend, or fable. Secondly, and corresponding to the difference of theme, there is a difference in the handling of the material. The earlier type of emblem is much less complicated in its nature and its treatment. The words and the picture in it each formed self-contained statements of the author's conception and they were equally appropriate carved in jewels, blazoned on shields, embroidered on hangings or engraved in books. The author indeed needed a certain kind of wit rather than any poetic ability. The presentation of a single image or episode, with its appropriate moral significance indicated briefly in the motto and the poem, was enough. The emblem was then considered complete.

In the second type of emblem, however, literature claims what had been regarded as no more than a 'sweet moral symbol', and it becomes no longer sufficient in itself, but something that must be made use of, and turned to all kinds of literary purposes. It was made into verse by Quarles, and transformed in poetry by George Herbert; it was made an element of refreshment in a manual of devotion by the Jesuit, Henry Hawkins, and the basis of a series of meditations by another religious writer. Consequently emblems of this later kind are differently conceived; original in design, they are considerably more complicated, and often include a far wider range of ideas than did the earlier ones. They could not be used outside literature as the earlier ones so often are: and, whereas in such books as those of Peacham and Whitney the personifications, abstract symbols and episodes are all indiscriminately classed as emblems, these later authors adopt the principle of one type to one volume, and it is the narrative type which is commonly assumed to constitute the true emblem. Hawkins, in fact, makes a clear division between a 'device' and an 'emblem' in his book, the one being the representation of a single object with an interpretative motto, the other a highly complicated allegorical picture accompanied by an explanatory poem. Such a distinction cannot in practice be made in the earlier emblems, though both the critics and the authors of the emblem books make attempts to draw one. In one sense their narrative emblems are much less emblematic than the later type: they are not full of symbolical detail and do not include abstract symbols and personifications in the elaborate way the later books do. That is because they are still close to the device, still seen as single moral symbols, where Quarles's emblems are complex and the picture needs to be explored in detail.

The second group of emblem books has then a different province and requires a different mode of approach. Briefly, the first group is the production of the men whom R. L. Stevenson in a frivolous little rhyme about the *ars emblematica* characterised as the 'ambidextrous Kings of Art', men who were equally at home with the engraving tool and the pen, and whose interests lay as much in the decorative and pictorial aspects of their work as in its verse. The second group is primarily literary. The emblem books in it need to be considered individually and for their literary merit rather than collectively and in relation to the other arts as the first type must be.

Towards the end of the century the form was banished from serious literature as a childish toy. At best it could survive in the nursery through a conscious didacticism; at worst in the drawing room archly 'dedicated to the Ladyes'. Philip Ayres's emblem book *Emblemata Amatoria* is an elegant volume containing verses written in copper-plate in four languages and pictures representing the amorous adventures of Cupid. It had considerable popularity, for it appeared in two editions in 1683, and was reprinted at least twice; but its province is made clear in the sub-title *Cupids Addresse to the Ladies*. The days of serious emblem writing were over; and this volume bears much the same relation to Whitney's and Quarles's conception of the emblem book as do Lady Mary Wortley Montagu's shooting activities to the tournaments in *Arcadia*:

> The next day I was to wait on the empress Amelia, who is now at her palace of retirement half a mile from the town. I had there the pleasure of seeing a diversion wholly new to me, but which is the common amusement of this Court. The empress herself was seated on a little throne at the end of a fine alley in the garden, and on each side of her were ranged two parties of her ladies of honour with other young ladies of quality, headed by two young archduchesses, all dressed in their hair full of jewels, with fine light guns in their hands; and at proper distances were placed three oval pictures, which were the marks to be shot at. The first was that of a CUPID, filling a bumper of Burgundy, and the motto, *'Tis easy to be valiant here.* The second a FORTUNE, holding a garland in her hand, the motto, *For her whom Fortune favours.* The third was a SWORD with a laurel wreath on the point, the motto, *Here is no shame to be vanquished.*[1]

Heraldry and chivalry have become a civil game and such an account burlesques the solemn ritual that a Tournament once was:

> But by and by, even when the Sunne (like a noble harte) began to shew his greatest countenaunce in his lowest estate, there came in a

[1] Lady Mary Wortley Montagu, 'Letter to the Countess of Mar.' 14 Sept. 1716. *Letters and Works*, ed. Lord Wharncliffe. London. 1893. Vol. I. p. 243.

Knight called *Phebilius*, a Gentleman of that country, for whom hate-full fortune had borrowed the dart of Love, to make him miserable by the sight of *Philoclea*. For he had even from her infancie loved her, and was striken by her, before she was able to knowe what quiver of arrowes her eyes caried; but he loved and despaired; and the more he despaired, the more he loved. He sawe his own unworthines, and thereby made her excellencie have more terrible aspect upon him: he was so secrete therein, as not daring to be open, that to no creature he ever spake of it, but his harte made such silent complaints within it selfe, that while his senses were attentive thereto, cunning judges might perceave his minde: so that he was knowne to love though he denied, or rather was the better knowne, because he denied it. His armour and his attire was of a Sea couler, his *Impresa*, the fishe called *Sepia*, which being in the nette castes a blacke inke about it selfe, that in the dark-nesse thereof it may escape: his worde was, *Not so*. *Philocleas* picture with almost an idolatrous magnificence was borne in by him.[1]

Symbols had become frivolous, and emblem books became frivolous too: the only alternative to frivolity was childishness, and so the fashion ends, charmingly in the nursery with Bunyan's *Country Rhymes for Children*, or lightly in the drawing-room with graceful picture books like Ayres's. Indeed it must have been hard for the reader of the 1680's to understand how it had ever been an adult taste at all.

[1] Sidney, *Arcadia*. 1590. Bk. I. Ch. 17. ed. A. Feuillerat. C.U.P. 1912. p. 107.

NON TIBI SED RELIGIONI.

Isidis effigiem tardus gestabat asellus,
Pando uerenda dorso habens mysteria.
Obuius ergo deam quisquis reuerenter adorat,
Piasq; genibus concipit flexis preces.
Ast asinus tantum praestari credit honorem,
Sibi, & intumescit admodum superbiens.
Donec eum flagris compescens dixit agaso,
Non es deus tu aselle, sed cum uehis.

IN I. LAVDATA LAVs
dante.

SPES PROXIMA.

Bdelychca auis praesto tibi motacilla paretur,
Quam quadriradiam circuli in orbe locos.
Ore crucem & cauda, & geminis ut complicet alis,
Tale amuletum carminis omnis erit.
Dicitur hoc Veneris signo Pegaseus Iason,
Phasiacis laedi non potuisse dolis.

Innumeris agitur respub. nostra procellis,
Et spes uenturae sola salutis adest.
Non secus ac nauis medio circum aequore uenti,
Quam rapiunt, salsis iamq; fatiscit aquis.
Quodsi Helenae aduentum lucentia sidera fratres,
Amissos animos spes bona restituit.

From Andrea Alciati: *Emblematum Liber 1531*
[slightly reduced]

Chapter 2

THE BEGINNINGS OF EMBLEM WRITING IN ENGLAND

I

EMBLEM writers in England did not create the taste which they satisfied; they imported the fashion from abroad when a marked interest in it had already shown itself in various ways. The word 'emblem' according to Geoffrey Whitney, the first serious exponent of the fashion in England, had indeed existed in the language well before the beginning of the sixteenth century:

> ... thoughe it be borrowed of others, & not proper in the Englishe tonge, yet that which it signifieth: Is, and hathe bin alwaies in use amongst us, which worde being in Greeke επεμβάλλεσθαι, vel εμβλῆσθαι is as muche to saye in Englishe as *To set in, or to put in*: properlie ment by suche figures, or workes, as are wroughte in plate, or in stones in the pavements, or on the waules, or suche like, for the adorning of the place.[1]

In this sense it continued to be used through the seventeenth century, and Milton so uses it.[2] But however familiar it may have been before the Renaissance, it was newly established in the vocabulary in the mid-sixteenth century to mark a distinct literary form—strictly the contents of a book of emblems. This consisted of a collection of pictures, of the kind already illustrated from Wither, each accompanied by a motto and a moral exposition usually in verse. In seventeenth century terminology it was generally the picture alone that was the 'Emblem', the motto was

---

[1] Geoffrey Whitney, *A Choice of Emblemes*. Leyden. 1586.
[2] *Paradise Lost*. IV. 700–3:

> Underfoot the Violet,
> Crocus, and Hyacinth with rich inlay
> Broider'd the ground, more colour'd then with stone
> Of costliest Emblem:

called the 'Word', and the poet added verses or 'moralised the emblem'. Thus Georgette de Montenay's *A Booke of Armes* is represented on the title page as containing 'one Hundered Godly Emblemata, in peeces of brasse very fine graven, and adorned pleasant to be seen'; and *The Mirrour of Maiestie* has 'emblemes annexed, poetically unfolded'. This same distinction between the different parts occurs also in single emblems outside the collections; the poem called 'Wither's Motto', for example, had an engraved emblematic frontispiece matched by a set of verses called 'The Explanation of the Emblem', which begins:

> This little Emblem here doth represent
> The blest condition of a man Content.

The parts of the picture are then listed and are each regarded as 'expressing' the author's meaning. These explanatory poems were often designated *The Meaning of the Emblem*, or *The Mind of the Frontispiece*. Another example of a complex emblematic frontispiece was that published in *Eikon Basilike* in which Charles I is represented surrounded by the symbols of his fate. Single emblems of this kind were a later extension of the method of the emblem book proper and became enormously popular in the mid-seventeenth century; often a number of small pictures would be engraved within the main frame of the frontispiece to indicate the general drift of the text. In Burton's *Anatomy of Melancholy*, for instance, there are emblematic pictures representing the different forms of melancholy.

The word 'emblem' had then in the sixteenth century acquired an entirely new sense; and even though it was already familiar in the language there is no question of any actual continuity from mediaeval usage. It was imported into England along with the literary form it described.[1]

The first emblem book made its appearance in Italy in 1531. It

---

[1] The term 'emblem' was current in three senses in the late sixteenth and the seventeenth centuries. It was used in connection with decoration to describe certain kinds of inlaid work, in connection with rhetoric to describe a particular rhetorical figure (see below, Chapter 4. pp. 86 ff.) and thirdly as a name

was the work of a distinguished Italian lawyer, Andrea Alciati, who was responsible for both the form and its name. The name he derived from G. Budé's *Annotationes in Pandectas* where the word 'emblem' is used in the old sense of mosaic.[1] The form is less easily traceable, being an amalgamation of several different influences. The question of origins is not of any historical importance for English literature since the emblems reached this country in the shape in which Alciati had formed them and were not re-created out of their sources, but it has a certain critical interest as it helps to emphasise the distinctive features of the convention.

Henri Estienne in *L'Art de faire les Devises* gives his subject its due importance by placing the first emblem in the Garden of Eden:

Those (whose scrutiny into the Origin of Devises soares highest) doe derive them from God himselfe, and affirme that he is the first Author of them, since he planted the Tree of Life, or rather the Tree

---

[1] Mario Praz, *Studies in Seventeenth Century Imagery.* 1939. p. 18. The history of the form is discussed in detail by Professor Praz in his first chapter.

---

for a particular literary form. The best contemporary set of definitions is that of Maximilian Sandaeus in *Theologia Symbolica.* 1626. pp. 169–70. who expands the number of senses to five:

'(1) Ipsum illud opus ex tessellis insititiis aptatum, atque consertum, dictum est *Emblema.*

(2) Oratio culta, rerum verborumque luminibus, ut totidem flosculis, aut gemmulis nitens, *Emblema* vocari potest.

(3) Florente Republica, vocabantur *Emblemata* in vasis aureis, argenteis, Corinthiis ornamenta quaedam exemptilia.

(4) *Emblema*, pro ornatu quolibet temporario & exemptili ponitur.

(5) Poetis, *Emblemata*, sunt *Carmina*, seu *Epigrammata*, quibus imagines, ἀγάλματα, *Symbola*, simulachra, pegmata, atque alia id genus scite adinventa, varie, atque erudite explicantur, ut post Claudium Mynoen in Syntagmate de *Symbolis*, docet Iacob. Pontan. . . . . Itaque *Emblema* ab illis vocatur *Epigramma*, quod *Emblema complectitur* μετωνυμικῶς, ut fatentur.

Requirunt autem Poeticae Magistri ad *Emblema* tria quaedam : *Epigraphen*, id est, sententiolam aliquam scitam & concinnam, tanquam rei totius animam: *Picturam* seu *Imaginem*, & *Poesin*, quae se ita explicent, ut altera alteri sit interpres. Et *Pictura*, tanquam corpus, *Poesis* habetur ut animus (*sic*).'

of Knowledg of Good and Evil in the terrestrial Paradise, explaining himself by these words, NE COMEDAS.[1]

He then suggests more helpfully that 'if the sense of devises have not so noble and ancient an origin it must at least be derived from the hieroglyphics of the Egyptians'. This was a derivation much favoured by Italian theorists and was generally accepted in England whenever origins were considered; Quarles, in fact, called his second emblem book *Hieroglyphikes of the Life of Man* and offered it as an 'Ægyptian dish'. The connection between the two is obviously close, and the affinity grows more marked when direct reference is made by contemporary critics to a book of Egyptian Hieroglyphics which was circulating in the sixteenth century. This was the collection made by Horapollo, a Greek Grammarian of Phonebethis in Egypt, who was teaching in Constantinople in A.D. 408–50. It was supposedly written in Coptic and was translated into Greek by a certain Philipus, the only form in which it is extant.[2] In 1505 Aldus issued an edition of it at Venice under the title of *Hieroglyphica*, and other editions and translations of it into Latin, French, Italian and German were published during the sixteenth century. There was no contemporary English version, but it was certainly known in the foreign texts, for references to 'Orus Apollo' are frequent among English authors and critics. The other main source of the convention was the Greek epigram. The emblems were pictures, but they were also 'pithy moral sayings'. Professor Praz has stressed the importance of the *Planudean Anthology* as an influence upon Alciati. Forty-four out of the whole two hundred and twelve emblems he finds to be directly derived from the Greek Anthology, and the remainder are, in his view, conceived in the same spirit, so that,

---

[1] Op. cit. p. 16.
[2] See Samuel Sharpe, 'Notes on the Hieroglyphics of Horapollo Nilous'. *Original Papers read before the Syro-Egyptian Society of London.* 1845. Vol. 1. Part I. pp. 45–62. Mr. Sharpe argues on the grounds that the author always spoke of the Egyptians as 'they', attempted to explain Egyptian words by the Greek language, and clearly had a very imperfect knowledge of the hieroglyphics he was interpreting, that it was a Greek work written by Philipus from Horapollo's explanations which he did not fully understand.

granting the Hieroglyphics their share of influence, Alciati's real model was the Greek epigram.[1] This account gives greater weight to the verbal, the 'witty' side of the emblem form than to the pictorial and consequently minimises its significance as a branch of symbolism. But the apologists fastened upon the hieroglyphics as the prototype of the emblems and of all other symbolical writing, and appealed directly to Horapollo because his collection best exemplified that mode of expression in which word and picture are completely united. In Estienne's opinion, every branch of symbolical writing, the 'Enigma, Emblem, Fable and Parable', depended upon and had an affinity with the science of Hieroglyphics; they are all, as Shaftesbury later observed, forms half way between pictures and words.[2] Furthermore, interest in hieroglyphics was bound up with a wider issue, with the view of nature held by such writers as Sir Thomas Browne in the early part of the seventeenth century. Nature was for him a 'Universal and publick Manuscript' written in hieroglyphics:

> The Finger of God hath left an Inscription upon all his works, not graphical or composed of Letters, but of their several forms, constitutions, parts and operations, which, aptly joyned together, do make one word that doth express their natures. By these Letters God calls the Stars by their names; and by this Alphabet Adam assigned to every creature a name peculiar to its Nature.[3]

Quarles prefaces his *Emblemes* with a statement which explicitly links this doctrine with the emblem method:

> Before the knowledge of letters GOD was knowne by *Hierogliphicks*. And, indeed, what are the Heavens, the Earth, nay every Creature, but Hierogliphicks and *Emblemes* of his Glory?

Besides acknowledgements to the Egyptians, the critics produced several pictorial parallels from the Classics. Abraham Fraunce, in a critical work on emblems and devices, refers to the description

---

[1] 'Between an emblem of Alciati and an epigram of the Anthology there is a difference only in name.' Op. cit. p. 21. See also p. 26.

[2] See Shaftesbury's classification of Characters in Appendix 2. p. 241.

[3] Sir Thomas Browne, *Religio Medici*. 1635. *Works*, ed. G. Keynes. 1928. Vol. I. p. 75.

of Achilles' shield in the *Iliad*, and Estienne to the devices on the shields carried in the *Seven Against Thebes*.[1] The seals and coins of the Roman Emperors are also included among the early forms of the device, and two pages of examples were engraved for *The Art of Making Devises*. All these references tend to emphasise the pictorial aspects of the emblem books, and it is evident that this is what constituted their chief interest in contemporary eyes. The emblems do clearly have affinities with the epigram, 'that fag end of poetry', as Edward Phillips called it; Alciati's emblems come within the category of 'flourishes of wit' in Hoole's list of useful models for children in schools, and they were also discussed by English critics among the figures of rhetoric;[2] but it was for their pictures that they were read and remembered in their own time and afterwards.

Alciati's particular contribution consisted in taking over a familiar method, and often familiar themes, and translating them into literary terms. The result was a book the popularity of which was so great as to be almost inconceivable to the modern reader. It went into ninety editions in the sixteenth century alone, was wedged between solemn and cumbrous annotations, translated into French, Italian, English and Spanish, and finally modified and imitated all over Europe. Its popularity had in no measure decreased in the seventeenth century; it was commented upon at even greater length than before by John Thuilius, a professor of Latin in Germany, and even in the eighteenth century when the impulse behind the allegorical method had altogether vanished, five editions of his work are known, and the fashion which he had set on foot reached even to Russia.[3]

Some account of Alciati's book as the begetter of offspring so numerous and so various may be given here. It originally appeared in manuscript and had been in circulation for ten years before

---

[1] Estienne, op. cit. p. 18.

[2] Charles Hoole, *A New Discovery of the Old Art of Teaching Schoole.* 1660. p. 159.

[3] H. Thomas, *The Emblemata Amatoria of Philip Ayres.* 1910. p. 22. A bibliography of Alciati's emblem book was made by Henry Green, *Andrea Alciati and his Book of Emblems.* 1872.

From Andrea Alciati: *Emblemata 1584*

Steyner printed the first edition in 1531. This contained a hundred and four emblems with ninety-eight cuts. Three years later Wechel issued another edition from Paris with eleven new emblems, and in subsequent editions the numbers were gradually increased to a total of two hundred and twelve—a hundred and ninety-eight emblems and fourteen trees. New sets of cuts were made by the various presses and they were often surrounded by elaborate borders. In 1549 Aneau rearranged the emblems according to subjects; in 1571 Claude Mignault embedded them in copious notes; and from the presses of Roville and Bonhomme at Lyons came a whole series of translations in French, Italian and Spanish. This ceaseless labour of expansion and editing offers a surprising contrast to conditions in England where there is no evidence of any emblem books having been enlarged. They rarely attained even a second edition. The salient exception is Quarles, for whose work there was a continual demand, and several other writers of his type such as Edmund Arwaker and Christopher Harvey reprinted their books at least once. The early emblem writers emulated the continental model but they did not oust it, and therefore it is not to Whitney but to Alciati that reference is always made by English writers. Whitney, Combe and P.S. and those who wrote like them, wrote to prove that 'as the Latins have these emblematists . . . so we have these . . .' but they wrote for a literate and articulate class to whom the language of the originals presented no difficulty. The emblem book was a developing mode in Italy, still tentative and exploratory; by the time it reached England its scope had been defined and its exponents could proceed along familiar lines.

Alciati's emblems are drawn chiefly from natural history, fable and mythology; the verses are in Latin, sometimes only of two lines and rarely of any great length. Plate 4 (p. 37) shows two examples from the *Emblematum Liber*. The emblem of the ass which thought that the homage of the crowd was directed towards itself and not to the shrine on its back, was used again by Whitney. A few of Alciati's emblems were dedicated to friends or patrons—a gesture which became popular later in England. The 'arbores', which appear all together at the end of the book, are interesting as a collection of those trees which had fixed and formalised associations arising from mythology or from their natural properties, but they were not adopted by Whitney and have small bearing upon the one English emblem book which does contain trees alone—a little devotional work called *Ashrea; or, The Grove of Beatitudes* (1665), in which eight trees are made pivots for a scheme of meditation.[1] The reproduction from Alciati in Plate 5 shows 'Alcides' speckled poplar tree', which, along with the vine and the oak, is one of those specially connected with a god; among others are the lemon tree bearing the golden apples of Venus—golden, but γλυκυπίκρος—the box, the tree of lovers, for 'Pallor inest illi, pallet et omnis amans', the victorious laurel which was also memorable for its remarkable property that 'Subdita pulvillo somnia vera facit'. They probably owe their inclusion to the classical tradition of the tree lists which came down from Vergil and Ovid and made their way to England in the fourteenth century. There is one in the *Parliament of Foules* as well as that at the burial of Arcite: they appear again in *The Faerie Queene*, in Drayton's *Endymion and Phoebe*, in Matthew Royden's *Elegy on Sidney*, and there is a last remnant of the same tradition in Dyer's *Grongar Hill*.

The *Emblematum Liber* was rapidly imitated by Alciati's contemporaries and by the time it reached England it was accompanied by a train of imitations and apologies. For Francis Meres, Reusner and Sambucus had already begun to share the platform with Alciati; and the French writers too were acquiring authority.[2] Alciati was translated into French by J. Le Fèvre as early as 1536, and again by Aneau in 1549, who then set out to produce a similar book of his own; de la Perrière's *Le Theatre des bons Engins* appeared in 1539, Corrozet's *Hécatomgraphie* a year later, and Paradin's *Devises Heroiques* in 1557. Although the output was

[1] See below, Chapter 7.
[2] Francis Meres, *Palladis Tamia*. 1598. p. 285v. 'As the Latines have these *Emblematists*, Andreas Alciatus, *Reusnerus*, and *Sambucus*: so we have these, *Geffrey Whitney, Andrew Willet*, and *Thomas Combe*.'

not comparable with that in Italy, it is evident that the fashion was widespread in France as at least eight independent books of emblems apart from translations of Alciati, Hadrian Junius, and Sambucus had appeared there before 1586.

France was not the only country in which the fashion took root. In Spain it was given fresh impetus by the way in which the Jesuits took the emblem books over for educational and missionary purposes; one Spanish emblem book of this kind, a treatise on the education and conduct of princes, written, however, by a layman, was translated into English by Sir James Astry in 1700.[1] In Holland it was adapted to suit the tastes of a democratic middle class. The tournament devices, which had filled the pages of the Italian and French books and which became popular in England too, were replaced for Dutch readers partly by emblems of love representing the adventures of the young Cupid, and partly by emblems of a more realistic kind upon domestic subjects. The emblems of love drew their material chiefly from Ovid; they had already appeared among others in the work of Alciati and his imitators, but it remained for the Dutch to develop them into an elaborate convention. An example of this type of work can be seen in the plate from Philip Ayres (Plate 6). Ayres was an English writer but most of his plates are copied from those of Cornelius Boel in Otho Vaenius's *Amorum Emblemata* and are characteristic both of the matter and the manner of the Dutch emblems.[2] The success of the emblem fashion in the Low Countries was to a considerable extent an engraver's success. While in England the art was still only slowly being developed, goldsmiths on the Continent had from the middle of the fifteenth century been working at copper plates, and by the end of the sixteenth a flourishing trade of engraving and printselling had sprung up, in which whole families were often engaged. From Antwerp especially the output was enormous: engravings of paintings and of maps, portraits, illustrations and decorative borders for books

---

[1] *Idea de un Principe politico cristiano*. By Diego Fajardo. 1640. Translated by Sir James Astry, *The Royal Politician*. 1700.
[2] See below, Chapter 5, p. 116.

were turned out in huge quantities; Flemish books of patterns were used by English craftsmen and Flemish plates by English printers. Some engravers such as Simon van de Passe, and later his brother Willem, and Marten Droeshout to whom we owe the portrait of Shakespeare in the first folio, migrated to London where they had no difficulty in finding employment. Others were invited over by patrons who were interested in their work: the Earl of Arundel, for instance, brought Lucas Vorsterman to England after his quarrel with Rubens and found him employment.[1] The emblem books offered yet another field in which the Dutch and Flemish engravers could excel and the standard of their plates is high. The pictures of Jacob Cats's emblems formed one of the early models of Sir Joshua Reynolds, who owned a copy of Vaenius's emblems from Horace as well—presumably also for the sake of their engravings.[2] Cats's emblems gave much more scope to the artist than did those of other Dutch writers like Heinsius and Vaenius because they were not concerned with the Ovidian theme of Cupid but with aspects of social and domestic life. 'Father Cats' as he was called, shared the interests of the Dutch interior painters: his emblems show scenes of family life, a housewife in the kitchen with her maid, illustrating the English proverb: 'A little pot is soon hot', a man and a woman playing battledore and shuttlecock, with the motto, *Amor, ut pila, vices exigit*, incidents in the streets or in the country. The central figure is often highly emblematic but the pictures still have carefully detailed naturalistic backgrounds. Cats's work was known in England and there was an attempt to translate some of it by Thomas Heywood in *Pleasant Dialogues and Drammas*, a hotchpotch of verse dialogues, elegies, emblems and epitaphs drawn from various sources and translated.[3]

[1] Sidney Colvin, *Early Engravings and Engravers in England*. 1905. p. 73.
[2] C. R. Leslie and T. Taylor, *Sir Joshua Reynolds*. 1865. Vol. I. p. 13. See also F. W. Hilles, *The Literary Career of Sir Joshua Reynolds*. 1936. p. 119.
[3] 'Monita Amoris Virginei . . . 1622', translated by Thomas Heywood in *Pleasant Dialogues and Drammas*. 1637. pp. 203-30.

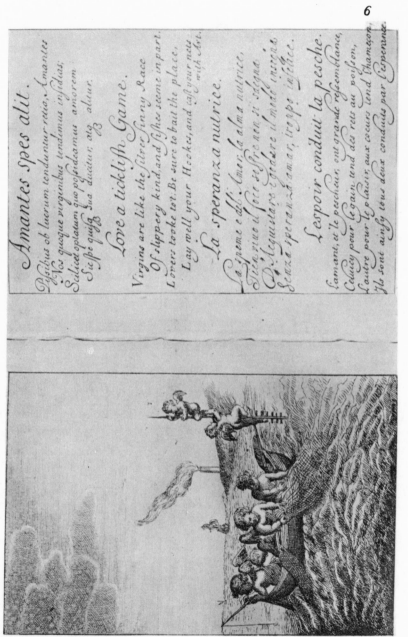

Amantes spes alit.

Piscibus ut lucrum tenduntur retia, Amantes
Nos quoque virginibus tendimus insidias;
Scilicet optatam quo possideamus amorem
Sicse quisq; sua ducitur, atq; alitur.

Love a ticklish Game.

Virgins are like the silver finny Race
Of slippery kind, and Fishes seeme in part.
Lovers tooke tot. Be sure to bait the place,
Lay well your Hookes, and cast your nets
with Art.

La speranza nutrice.

La speme e dell' Amor la alma nutrice,
Vien vuo d'l' ore e' ... non si sdegna
D'acquistar è godere il modo insegna,
Senza speranza amar, troppo infelice.

L'espoir conduit la pesche.

L'amant, et le pescheur, ont grande resemblance,
Celuicy pour le gain, tend des rets au poisson,
L'autre pour le plaisir, aux cœurs tend l'hameçon,
Ils sont ainsy tous deux conduits par l'esperance.

From Philip Ayres: *Emblemata Amatoria* 1683
[slightly reduced]

II

It is clear from any consideration of the development of emblem books on the Continent that their counterparts in England must be regarded as dependent on, rather than contributory to, the general European movement. Not only were they not a native invention, but nothing very new was added to them by their English adaptors in the course of the hundred years during which they were a vital interest, nor was their popularity, though considerable, in any degree comparable with the emblem-mania which overtook Italy, and to a lesser extent France. The works of Alciati and Ruscelli and some of the French emblematists had long been familiar to English readers before Whitney's collection made its appearance. Travellers on the Grand Tour had certainly read and had probably brought back with them some of the books and works of criticism from abroad. Sidney, for instance, writing to Languet in 1573 from Venice offered to send him a copy of Ruscelli's *Imprese*, which he recommended among various other 'elegantes libri'.[1] Edward VI owned Giovanni Marquale's Italian version of Alciati printed in 1549,[2] and Whitney had a copy of the 1562 edition of Paradin.[3] The introduction of emblems into the vernacular did not diminish the popularity of Alciati: a painstaking reader would even annotate an edition of Whitney with page references to his source,[4] and the frequent quotations from the *Emblematum Liber* rather than from Whitney show that the *Collection* in no way superseded it. Before any emblem book was published in England Samuel Daniel had translated the *Dialogo dell'Imprese Militari et Amorose* of Paolo Giovio, adding certain devices of his own choice which he had collected in Italy and, as a preface, a long letter written by a certain N.W. which bears

[1] Sidney, op. cit. p. 81.
[2] Now in the British Museum. See 'A Collection of the Emblem Books of Andrea Alciati in the Library of G. E. Sears'. Pr. printed, New York. 1888.
[3] See Sotheby's *Catalogue of Emblems sold in 1884*. Item 108: Paradin's *Devises Heroiques*. 1562. 'With motto and autograph of G. Whitney . . . *Constanter et syncere* Galfridus Whytney. Cestreshire.'
[4] The Folger Library copy has notes in a contemporary hand.

witness to wide reading in French and Italian emblems. N.W.'s account is interesting as a statement of the current notion of what constituted a device. He sets out with customary bashfulness:

But concerning the arte of Imprese I neede not draw the petigree of it, sith it is knowne that it descended from the auncient *Aegiptians* and *Chaldeans*, in the Schoole of *Memphis*: who devised meanes before Charecters were founde out, to utter their conceiptes by formes of Beastes, Starres, Hearbes, (as you have declared) and these notes were called ιἑρογλήφικα i.e. sacrae notae . . .

But to what end served this? to shadow suerly their intents and purposes by figures. So counsayled *Plato*: so practised the first parents of Philosophie. As by the picture of a Stork they signified Αντιπελαργια. By a Serpent pollicie. By an Olive peace. By a Gote lust: drawing these Charecters from the world, as from a volume wherein was written the wonders of nature. Thus was the first foundations layd of *Imprese*: From hence were derived by succession of pregnant wittes *Stemmata* Coates of Armes, *Insignia* Ensignes, and the olde Images which the *Romanes* used as witnesses of their Auncestors, *Emblemes* and *Devises*. Then what was the intent of these Ensigns and *Devises*? What cause can bee pretended for them? What did they import? *Iamblicus* saieth that they were conceiptes by an externall forme representing an inward purpose: so *Fergusus* the first Scottishe King did beare in his Standard a *Lion geules*, to bewray his courage, testifie his stomache, and dismaie his adversarie, which being well marshalled, is borne for the achievement of the Kings ever since. So did the *Athenians* beare their Owle; the *Thebans* their *Sphinx*; the *Switzers* their Beare. But among all inventions surpasse for witt and art your *Imprese*: neither less renowned, than the *Insegnes*, nor less heroicall than the Armes called by *Paradin*, *Symbola Heroica*, by *Symeon*, *devises illustres*.[1]

Only two years after the appearance of Whitney's collection of emblems, Abraham Fraunce issued a treatise on Insignia in which he drew freely upon the criticism of continental theorists. There is no doubt that interest in emblems was widespread in the 1580's, and even though the direct literary expressions of it were still few the taste was well established in other fields. A sense of

---

[1] *The Worthy Tract of Paulus Iovius . . . of Rare Inventions . . . called Imprese*, by Samuel Daniel. London. 1585.

the emblematic was so much a part of the disposition of the age
that it asserted itself on every side. The devices for tournaments
which occupied a prominent place in Elizabethan court life gave
it full scope: 'things worthy of observation' in Whitehall were for
a visitor, Paul Hentzner, 'a variety of emblems on paper cut in the
shape of shields, with mottoes, used by the nobility in tilts and
tournaments, hung up here for a memorial'. The Progresses of
Elizabeth provided another opportunity: the usual mode of
greeting in Oxford, for example, was a 'banket' and 'thousands
of verses and emblematical poetries' hung upon the outer walls
of the colleges. The Queen herself delighted in them and in one
of her visitations she 'casting her eyes on the walls of St. Mary's
Church, All Souls, University and Magdalen Colleges . . . was
often seen to give gracious nods to the Scholars'.[1] In her first
public procession through London she found emblematical
tableaux and verses set up at various points in the City representing the qualities of good government. At Cheapside there
were two hills, each with a tree on it, one withered to represent
a 'decayed commonweale', the other green to represent a
'flourishing commonweale', and between the two came forth
Truth and Time. The point of this was not lost on Elizabeth who
is said to have cried, 'And Time hath brought me hither!'[2] A
smaller and more personal form of the same interest is seen in
jewelry. Among the New Year gifts presented to Elizabeth are
many, the designs of which were to become familiar themes in the
emblem books later. Some needed only verses to turn them into
emblems proper: there was for instance among the presents 'a
juell of golde, being a woman ennamuled called VIRTUTE, a pair
of compasses in one hand and a green garlande in the other, standing upon a rainbow';[3] and her suitor, Anjou, gave her 'a shakyll

[1] J. Nichols, *Progresses of Queen Elizabeth*. 1823. Vol. III. p. 148.
[2] For an interesting account of this emblem see F. Saxl, 'Veritas Filia Tem-
poris' in *Philosophy and History*, ed. R. Klibansky and H. J. Paton. 1936. pp.
197–222. Dr. Saxl traces its development and use as a political symbol during
the Tudor period and after. Another example of its use which is not, however,
mentioned by Saxl is the Darnley Jewel.
[3] The compasses represented Constancy, the garland and rainbow Victory
and Peace. See below, p. 146.

of golde with these words graven, SERVIET ETERNUM DULCIS QUEM TORQUET ELIZA, and a padlocke of golde hanging by a little chayne of golde'. The Darnley Jewel which Lady Margaret Douglas had made in memory of her husband, the Earl of Lennox, comes perhaps most close to the literary form. It has figures of Faith, Hope, Victory and Truth, each with their emblems, enamelled on the front, and the crowned salamander in flames and the pelican in her piety on the back. Inside are emblematic pictures including Truth, the daughter of Time, with the motto TYM GARES AL LEIR.[1] This was made at least fifteen years before the publication of Whitney's book.

The same tendencies can be seen also in sixteenth-century domestic architecture and household decoration. The Tudor rose, for instance, that decorated the bedchamber of Wolsey, the heraldic beasts on the ceiling of Plas Mawr in Wales built in 1577, the Wheel of Fortune in Little Morton Hall all have their counterparts in the engravings of Whitney. Personified figures peopled the tapestries and embroidered hangings on Elizabethan walls, though these again are clearly a legacy from the Middle Ages and cannot be confined to any single period. One specifically emblematic piece of decoration which was made prior to 1586 was the bedspread embroidered by Mary Queen of Scots which William Drummond saw and described in detail to Ben Jonson.[2] Drummond's interest in emblems and devices led him to make a list of those he had seen and he tells Jonson that it 'will embellish greatly some pages of your book and is worthy your remembrance'. The emblems are all accompanied by mottoes and many were derived from Paradin and other French emblematists whose work Mary would have known at the French Court. There are imprese of the outstanding French, English, and Italian noblemen and churchmen in the late sixteenth century—the crowned Salamander in flames, the Phoenix, the Palm-tree, the Portcullis

[1] See Joan Evans, *English Jewellery*. 1921. pp. 88–91. for an account and picture of the Darnley Jewel.

[2] Letter to Ben Jonson dated July 1, 1619. The book referred to is Jonson's projected verse account of his journey to Scotland. For a full text of the letter see Herford and Simpson, *Ben Jonson*. Oxford. 1925. Vol. I. pp. 208–10.

of Henry VIII, the bird in the cage with the hawk above, all of which became the commonplaces of emblematic decoration and of the emblem books themselves. Some reappeared in Whitney, coming direct from Paradin,—'the Impressa of the Cardinal of Lorrain her Uncle, a Pyramide overgrown with Ivy, the vulgar word, Te Stante Virebo', for example. There was also on the bedspread an emblem of two women upon the Wheel of Fortune, one holding a lance, the other a cornucopia, 'which Impressa seemeth to glaunce at Queen Elizabeth and her self', as Drummond said. Mary referred again to her own fortunes in another emblem which she wore on her signet ring and which she also embroidered on a cushion; it had this sentence: VIRESCIT VULNERE VIRTUS, 'and a hand with a knife cutting down the vines as they use in the spring time'.

Emblems had, too, appeared tentatively in literary form before Whitney made his collection. One work, A Theatre for Worldlings, has more than once been described as the first emblem book printed in England.[1] It is known now chiefly because Spenser is reputed to have been the translator of some of its verses. Originally written in Flemish, it was translated into French the same year, and in 1569 Henry Bynneman brought out an English version with woodcuts copied from the engravings of the original.[2] Its full description is 'A Theatre wherein be represented as wel the miseries & calamities that follow the voluptuous Worldlings, as also the great ioyes and plesures which the faithful do enioy', and its main object is an attack on the Pope, who is represented as the Beast of Revelation and the 'begetter of the Mysterie of iniquitie'. The text consists of six poems translated from Petrarch, eleven from Du Bellay, and four sonnets, based on the Apocalypse, composed by van der Noot himself; these are interpreted at length in prose. Spenser's hand in the book is not acknowledged, and the translation of the prose is

[1] C. H. Herford, Literary Relations between England and Germany in the Sixteenth Century. 1886. p. 369. Harold Stein, Studies in Spenser's Complaints. 1934. p. 111.
[2] A Theatre wherein be represented as wel the miseries & calamities that follow the voluptuous Wordlings, as also the great ioyes and plesures which the faithful do enioy . . . Devised by S. Iohn vander Noods. London. Henry Bynneman. 1569.

ascribed at the beginning to Theodore Roest. But when the Complaints were published in 1591 Spenser included in them the 'Visions of Petrarch and the Visions of Bellay', which are revised versions of the translations in the Theatre. It is more than probable, therefore, that they were the early work of Spenser. Something even closer to the work of Alciati was produced by Gascoigne, who included three unmistakable emblems in his Hermit's Tale, a story told three times over in three languages and presented in manuscript with many professions of the author's worthiness, to the Queen.[1] The pictures are drawn in pen and ink and set in scroll-work frames. The first represents a foot, trampling upon a snake, the motto being Spretaque sic vivunt, sic concultata resurgunt. Alciati would, of course, have added a poem enlarging upon the theme, but, though lacking this, the design has both the matter and the manner of the emblem proper. Ownerless legs or arms stretching from the sky are as common in the emblem books as they are in the Castle of Otranto. The motto explains the picture, the picture particularises the motto, each depends on the other. A poem to bring home a point which was without doubt perfectly clear to the Queen is all that is needed to complete it. In the other two emblems, one of which was copied from Alciati, poems are supplied in place of the motto.[2] All three treat of the same subject —Gascoigne's plea for royal favour. They bear no immediate relation to the story and were obviously intended to be an additional attraction to catch the eye of the Queen. A book full of them would have constituted an emblem book. Doubtless there were other appearances of single emblems such as those of Gascoigne; but it was not till 1586 that a complete emblem book in the English language was published.

[1] B.M. Royal MSS. 18.A. XLVIII. Printed in Gascoigne, Complete Works, ed. J. W. Cunliffe. 1910. Vol. II. pp. 473–509. where the pictures are also reproduced.
[2] Alciati. Emblem 192. This is one of the emblems woven in the borders of the Hatfield Tapestries. See below. p. 95.

III

There were various reasons why, despite this background of knowledge and interest, emblem books themselves were so late in appearing in the vernacular in England and so relatively few when they did come. In the first place these early emblem books are inseparably related to devices and heraldry—the prerogative of a limited class—and their readers would have been those for whom French and Italian presented no difficulties and to whom English was still an insular rather than a European language. But this is not an altogether sufficient explanation; for in France the first, at least, of these conditions existed and yet French emblematists sprang up as soon as the fashion reached the country. But England was still conscious of inferiority to the Continent in respect of the polite arts, and the ever increasing number of these publications while offering a wide selection to a man like Whitney and awakening the desire for emulation in a man like Henry Peacham, had also an inhibiting effect. One English emblem writer, Andrew Willet, for instance, is articulate over his hesitation where others may have remained quite mute. Willet was famous for his immense learning and huge literary output; he produced two theological works a year, provoking an astonished contemporary to describe him as one that 'must write as he sleeps it being impossible he should do so much waking'. He had apparently read widely in the emblem books of France and Italy, and he criticises a previous emblematist, unnamed but from all appearances Whitney, for thinking it enough to have translated old material drawn from abroad or to have added new merely of the same kind. He then continues:

Ego, ne actum (quod aiunt) agerem, vel in alienam messem falcem immitterem, ad sacrum tantum fontem digitum intendens et intingens pedem, tentare volui, an in eodem genere, sed alia incedens via nostris placere possem.[1]

The size of the foreign harvest may have been the least of reasons, but it did seem to set up a standard which the English found hard

---

[1] Andrew Willet, *Sacrorum Emblematum Centuria Una.* Cambridge. n.d. sig. A.2ʳ.

to attain. Whitney's emblems appeared in 1586 at a time when there clearly was room for them; this was followed by Willet's little volume,—remarkable historically perhaps for its attempt to do something new, but otherwise only for the feebleness of its verse,—and two translations from the French. After this no more was published in England until Peacham's *Minerva Britanna* in 1612; Peacham does, it is true, comment on the slender collection of emblemata in the vernacular:

I have heere (kind Reader), sent abroad unto thy view, this volume of *Emblemes*, whether for greatnes of the chardge, or that the Invention is not ordinarie: a Subiect very rare. For, except the collections of Master *Whitney*, and the translations of some one or two else beside, I know not an *Englishman* in our age, that hath published any work of this kind: they being (I doubt not) as ingenious, and happy in their inventions, as the best French or Italian of them all. Hence perhaps they term us *Tramontani Sempii*, Simple and of dull conceipt, when the fault is neither in the Climate, nor as they would have it, in the constitution of our bodies, but truely in the cold and frozen respect of Learning, and artes, generally amongst us: comeing far shorte of them in the iust valewing of well deserving qualities.

Compared with Italy, there was doubtless a cold and frozen respect of learning and the arts generally in England, but it can hardly be said that the invention was not by this time ordinary. The explanation is more nearly to be found in the practical difficulties of producing picture books in England. The cost of printing was a continual cause of complaint among the emblematists; and not only were the plates expensive to print, they had also to be acquired. The backward state of engraving in England compared with that on the Continent effectively checked the publication of illustrated books. John Harington, advertising the engravings in his translation of *Orlando Furioso* in 1591, for instance, emphasises both their singularity and their costliness:

I will not praise them too much, because I gave direction for their making, and in regard thereof, I may be thought partiall, but this I may truely say, that (for mine owne part) I have not seen anie made in England better, nor (in deede) anie of his kinde, in any booke, except it were in a treatise, set foorth by that profound man, maister Broughton the last yeare, upon the Revelation, in which there are some 3 or 4 pretie figures (in octavo) cut in brasse verie workemanly. As for other books that I have seene in this realme, either in Latin or English, with picturs, as Livy, Gesner, Alciats emblemes, a booke de Spectris, in Latin, & (in our tong) the Chronicles, the booke of Martyrs, the book of hawking and hunting, and M. Whitneys excellent Emblems, yet all their figures are cut in wood, and none in metall, and in that respect inferior to these, at least (by the old proverbe) the more cost, the more worship.

Harington's account is not strictly accurate in detail but the general truth of his statement is unquestioned; the first appearance of copper-plates for illustration of an English book was in 1540,[1] but there was no real demand for them until the beginning of the seventeenth century. Nor was woodcutting in a much better state. The emblem writers met the difficulty in various ways. Willet solved the problem by publishing 'naked emblems', or emblems without pictures. Whitney's *Choice* was published by Plantin and illustrated with woodcuts already in the printer's stock. Peacham made his own. Wither imported Rollenhagen's plates from Holland, which he admired though they were prefixed with verses 'so meane' that he cut them off.[2] In general, however, it seems that the production of emblem books in England was much retarded by the practical difficulties which their make-up presented.

[1] *The Byrth of Mankynde*, a book on midwifery.   [2] See below, p. 142.

Chapter 3

ELIZABETHAN AND JACOBEAN
EMBLEM BOOKS

I

THE published emblem books of the early type which are still extant are six in number, and besides these there are several works in manuscript. There may too have been others of which all trace is now lost; certainly some of those which have survived have been thumbed almost out of existence. All have features in common with the first one published—Whitney's *A Choice of Emblemes*, 1586—for it was to Whitney that the first set of emblem writers turned for their model.

The title page describes the contents of the *Choice* as 'for the moste parte gathered out of sundrie writers', and the book is, in fact, characterised by a complete absence of originality. Most of the plates are taken from those of Italian and French books which had already been published by Plantin—from Alciati, Hadrian Junius, Sambucus and Paradin—and were printed from the same blocks.[1] It would be unjust, however, to describe the work as no more than a translation, for a comparison of the verses with their originals often shows them to exceed the broadest interpretation of that term; but, whatever the originality of the moralisings, it must be regarded mainly as an anthology. That is in some senses its virtue. Its method was already familiar in other fields; so also to some degree was its material. Apart from all the different non-literary forms in which the fashion was flourishing in England before the publication of Whitney's book, the *Choice of Emblems* fell upon prepared ground because its sources had already reached its readers in their original form. Alciati had drawn his material from Ovid, from Pliny, from Aesop; and in England

[1] H. Green in his edition of Whitney's *A Choice of Emblemes*. 1866. p. 252. has shown that 202 out of 248 woodcuts were printed from identical blocks.

To RICHARD DRAKE *Esquier, in praise of*
Sir FRANCIS DRAKE *Knight.*

THROVGHE scorchinge heate, throughe coulde, in stormes, and
    tempests force,
By ragged rocks, by shelfes,& sandes: this Knighte did keepe his course.
By gapinge gulfes hee pass'd, by monsters of the flood,
By pirattes, theeues, and cruell foes, that long'd to spill his blood.
That wonder greate to scape : but, GOD was on his side,
And throughe them all, in spite of all, his shaken shippe did guide.
And, to requite his paines : *By helpe of power deuine.*
His happe, at lengthe did aunswere hope, to finde the goulden mine.
Let GRÆCIA then forbeare, to praise her IASON boulde?
Who throughe the watchfull dragons pass'd,to win the fleece of goulde.
Since by MEDEAS helpe, they weare inchaunted all,
And IASON without perrilles, pass'de: the conqueste therfore small?
But, hee, of whome I write, this noble minded DRAKE,
Did bringe away his goulden fleece, when thousand eies did wake.
Wherefore, yee woorthie wightes, that seeke for forreine landes:
Yf that you can, come alwaise home, by GANGES goulden sandes.
And you, that liue at home, and can not brooke the flood,
Geue praise to them, that passe the waues, to doe their countrie good.
Before which sorte, as chiefe : in tempeste, and in calme,
Sir FRANCIS DRAKE, by due deserte, may weare the goulden palme.

From Geoffrey Witney: *A Choice of Emblemes 1586*
[slightly reduced]

these were known and widely read. Numbers of classical tales and anecdotes had been retold in prose and verse, and the taste for them had not waned by 1586. The allegorising of classical stories in such works as Abraham Fraunce's *Third Part of the Countess of Pembrokes Ivychurch*, or the description and interpretation of the symbolism attached to the classical gods and goddesses given by Stephen Batman in his *Golden Booke of the Leaden Goddes* (1577) were offshoots of the solid study of the classics which formed the content of a gentleman's education.[1] Whitney is simply picking up those interests again and expressing them in another way. They were a part of the language of Elizabethan England. One of the forms in which they would have been available to the Court was that of Euphuistic prose, another manifestation of the taste for isolated comparisons which is an aspect of the emblem book. It was therefore as a storehouse for Elizabethan commonplaces that Whitney's book was chiefly interesting in his own day, as it is now. From it can be inferred the type of subject which provided the emblem writers with their most suitable material.

In the Preface Whitney describes his emblems as being of three kinds, Historical, Natural and Moral:

Historicall, as representing the actes of some noble persons, being matter of historie. *Naturall*, as in expressing the natures of creatures, for example, the love of the yonge Storkes, to the oulde, or of suche like. *Morall*, pertaining to vertue and instruction of life, which is the chiefe of the three, and the other two maye bee in some sorte drawen into this head. For, all doe tende unto discipline, and morall preceptes of living.

This classification indicates the range of his material but otherwise does little to illuminate it. As Whitney says, the section 'Morall' in fact provides a limbo into which all the rest, unsusceptible of definition, may be relegated. Classification by subject defeated even the author, and it is much more in terms of the relation

[1] For an account of the uses of classical mythology in the English literature of the sixteenth century, see Douglas Bush, *Mythology and the Renaissance Tradition in English Poetry*. 1932. pp. 32 ff.

between picture and text that the different types are to be distinguished from each other. For this approach Whitney gives some help; the book is called *A Choice of Emblemes and Other Devises* and although there is no explicit division to show what he intended to be recognized as 'other devises' it is possible to draw a broad line between the two, and class them as narrative and non-narrative.

By far the majority of Whitney's emblems are narrative; the picture is an illustration of some familiar story which is told in the verse below. Some of the stories belong to the group labelled 'Historical': there is Brutus dying upon his sword, Attilus about to be thrust into 'a tunne with nayles' and the whole account of his capture and death given beneath. Aeneas bears his father away from falling Troy; Brasidas stands holding his false shield. A larger number derive from myth: Icarus falls from Heaven, Niobe's children are slain by bolts from the sky, and Sisyphus, Ixion and Tantalus each suffers his torture. Natural stories, of which there are some thirty, consist mainly in fables from Aesop. A typical example is the fable of blowing hot and cold, where the story is told in a straightforward way ending up with a couplet to point the moral. Often, however, the moral exists only by implication or is summed up in the motto. There is, for instance, the emblem of the lion sick in his den:

> The Lion oulde that coulde not get his praye,
> By swifte pursute as he had done of late:
> Did faigne him sicke, and in his denne did staye,
> And praede on those, that came to see his state;
>   At lengthe, the foxe his dutie to declare,
>   Came to the dore, to knowe howe he did fare.
>
> Who answered, sicke, my oulde beloved frende,
> Come in, and see, and feele my pulses beate:
> To whome, quoth he, I dare not now intende,
> Bicause, these steppes some secret mischiefe threate:
>   For, all I see have gone into thy denne,
>   But none I finde, that have retorn'd againe.[1]

[1] Whitney, op. cit. p. 210.

It is the motto that points the moral: *Fraus meretur fraudem*. In the same way are used the fables of the Fox and the Grapes, the Ant and the Mole, the Dog who dropped his bone into the stream, the Dog in the manger, the Mice playing round a cage of cats. Another group is formed from what were evidently popular witty anecdotes—the usual material of the Jest Book. There is a cut of Washing the Blackamoor, for instance, and another of an old woman gathering skulls on a hill:

> But as shee toil'de, shee stumbled on the grounde;
> Whereat, downe fell the heades within her lappe,
> And here, and there, they ranne abowt the hill:
> With that, quoth shee, no marvaile is this happe,
> Since men alive, in myndes do differ still:
>   And like as theise, in sunder downe do fall,
>   So varried they, in their opinions all.[1]

Another, the story 'of a strange alteration in the world' which resulted from Cupid and Death using each other's bows, is, in fact, labelled *Jocosum*.

Taken all together, these are what constitute the bulk of the book. There are also a variety of non-narrative emblems. Some of these are heraldic devices mostly drawn from Paradin. They include the shirt which Saladin ordered to be borne through the army and which later became the device of Francis II, the garlands of Marcus Sergius, the shield of Marcus Scaeva, a lion bearing a sword, which was the design engraved on the ring of Pompey the great, and all are accompanied by poems describing the achievements of their owners. Among them, too, is the device designated *In Utrumque Paratus* where two hands come out of a cloud, one holding a bricklayer's trowel and the other a sword.

With these non-narrative emblems must be included a number which are not heraldic and yet cannot be classed with the moral tales and fables either. One of the most elaborate of them is the *Medici Icon* which represents Aesculapius seated on a throne with a sceptre in one hand and a staff in the other, and a cock, a dragon, and a dog at his feet. The meaning is explained thus:

[1] Ibid. p. 46.

This portraiture, dothe Aesculapius tell.
The laurell crowne, the fame of physike showes,
The bearde, declares his longe experience well:
The gravitie therewith that alwaie goes.
  The scepter, tells he ruleth like a kinge
  Amongst the sicke, commaunding everiethinge.

The knotted staffe declares the crabbed skill
Moste harde t'attaine; that doth supporte his state:
His sittinge, shewes he must be setled still,
With constant minde, and rashe proceedinge hate:
  The Dragon, tells he doth our age renewe,
  And soone decerne, to give the sicke his dewe.

The cocke, dothe teache his watchinge, and his care,
To visite ofte his pacientes, in their paine:
The couchinge dogge dothe laste of all declare,
That faithfulnes and love, shoulde still remaine:
  Within their brestes, that Physike doe professe
  Which partes, they all shoulde in their deeds expresse.[1]

Here the whole principle of emblem writing, the equating of
pictorial detail with moral ideas, is set forth; the narrative emblems
are merely simplifications of the same method since they are concerned with a single aspect of the subject instead of several. In
another picture this grouping of objects arbitrarily related by a
single connection is seen in even more extreme form: there the
seven golden sentences of the seven sages are represented pictorially and are put all together in a frame each labelled with the
sage's name. Cleobalus' *Keep to the Meane* is indicated by a pair of
scales, Chilon's *Know thyself* by a mirror, a device which is used
again by Peacham for *Philautia* (Self-love), and so on. It is the
presence of designs such as these which distinguished the emblems
as a whole from mere illustrations; there is no essential difference
between the emblem of the old woman picking up skulls and that
made for Sir Francis Drake (reproduced on p. 56). Both are regarded as symbolic. The titles emphasise this by indicating a

[1] Whitney, op. cit. p. 212.

common way of thinking behind them both, and indeed behind them all. Tantalus is the emblem of *Avaritia*, a swallow waking a man is labelled *Garrulitas*, a cock and a lion guarding a church *Vigilantia et Custodia*; these are felt to be just the same in kind as *In Occasionem* (facing p. 18) and *Descriptio Invidia*, the classical figure of Envy herself. This fact is made even clearer in one of the editions of Alciati where the emblems are indexed under the headings Invidia, Avaritia, Mors, Ignorantia, Superbia, etc.[1] The late emblem writers, however, would have made such narrative emblems much more deliberately symbolical by the addition of details of an allegorical non-naturalistic kind.

The *Choice* offered a wide and varied collection of emblems, and subsequent writers had no difficulty in following Whitney's lead. It was an anthology of poems drawn from French and Italian books, and some therefore have contented themselves with direct translation from abroad. It was also an exercise in the vernacular; others consequently spurned the foreign harvest and relied upon their own invention. Though none, with the exception of Peacham, can compare with Whitney in scale, all clearly showed themselves indebted to his work and all follow the lines which he laid down.

II

The next English venture confined itself to one only of Whitney's sources. This was a version of Paradin's *Devises Heroiques* by the unobtrusive P.S. who eluded altogether Francis Meres's observant eye and still remains anonymous. The book contains a number of unframed woodcuts each accompanied by a prose description. Some are of general derivation; there is, for instance, a representation of a jar of water in which one egg is floating on the surface and another lies at the bottom, the motto being *Haud Sidet Inane; an egge being emptie swimmeth aloft*. The text explains that 'by how much the less wisdome there is in a man the more doth he bewray his folly by his selfe love and ambition'.

[1] Lyons. 1550.

The main concern, however, is with coats of arms and crests belonging to the French courtiers, to the Roman Emperors, or more generally, referring to a classical story. The familiar designs to illustrate the motto *Festina lente*, the dolphin and anchor of Augustus, and the crab and butterfly of Vespasian are both there. Sometimes a single symbol is enough to conjure up the whole story; for instance one device presents the golden fleece with the motto *Pretium non vile laborum*: *he reaped no small reward of his labours.*

The chief interest of the book lies in its demonstration of the wide range of things that in the sixteenth century were capable of concrete representation. In the crudest possible way it states the quick leap to imagery made by the Elizabethan mind. *Omnis caro foenum*: *all flesh is grass* is immediately pictured; *Caelitus impendet*: *the sword of God's wrath hanging over our heades*, produces the image of a sword suspended from the clouds; *In utrumque paratus*: *readie for both*, two hands, one holding a sword and the other a trowel. No abstraction was far removed from particular examples, and Elizabethan English is vivid and alive for this very reason. It can express ideas in abstract and general terms but there is an underlying wealth of concrete reference which enables the writer to move naturally from the general to the particular, from an abstract idea to a closely realised image.

The only reason for a closer inspection of the work of P.S. is that Shakespeare is thought to have had access to the devices of Paradin, either in the original or in this English version, and to have made use of them in *Pericles*. Of the devices borne by the knights in the tournament which takes place in the play, three can be found in Paradin, with their mottoes. They are the wreath carried by the third knight, the inverted torch of the fourth, and the touchstone of the fifth, which is reproduced on the plate opposite. The evidence that Paradin was Shakespeare's actual source for these is no less, and no more, convincing than evidence of such a kind can ever be. He certainly did not invent them; they are heraldic commonplaces, and, indeed, his only recorded attempt at invention was a failure as the impresa he made was so

DEVISES. 17

Nutrifco, & extinguo.

I nourish, and I extinguish.

The Salamander lying in the fire, was the badge or Cognizance of Frances king of France. Which worme, Plinie writeth, is of such a cold nature that it quencheth the fire. Like as. Others write that he liueth, & is nourished

DEVISES. 217

Sic ſpectanda fides.

So is faith to be tried.

The goodnes of gold is not onely tryed by ringing, but also by the touchstone : so the triall of godlines and faith is to bee made not of wordes onely, but also by the action & performance of the deedes.

[slightly reduced]

From P.S.: The Heroicall Devises of M. Claudius Paradin 1591

obscure that nobody understood it.[1] But he could easily have found the same devices elsewhere; the touchstone and the torch, for instance, also occur in Whitney. There is no book except Paradin's, however, which contains as many as three out of the six and it seems reasonable to conclude, therefore, that Shakespeare with the unabashed economy of great genius made use of it.[2]

Another emblem book which was French in its origin was the translation of de la Perrière's *The Theatre of Fine Devices* by Thomas Combe. The only known copy is dated 1614, but Combe was one of the emblematists cited by Meres in 1598 and the book was entered on the Stationers' Register in 1593, so that it must have been published some time between those dates. The emblems are concerned with incidents rather than with heraldic designs and are set in frames in the manner of Whitney. Combe adds a preface of his own entreating the reader to 'requite the Translators

[1] Lord Rutland's Impresa for a tilt in 1613. 'Item 31 Martii, to Mr Shakespeare in gold about my Lorde's impreso, xliiij s; to Richard Burbage for paynting and making yt, in gold xliiij s.' See E. K. Chambers, *William Shakespeare*. 1930. Vol. II. p. 153.

[2] The sources are discussed at length in Henry Green's *Shakespeare and the Emblem Writers*. 1870. pp. 156–86. His results may be summarised as follows: For the first, second and sixth device he finds no exact source; there is a near approach to the first in Reusner's *Emblems*, Frankfort. 1581. and a French parallel for the motto but not the device of the second; the sixth cannot be traced at all. The remaining devices are to be found in Paradin, and the mottoes are identical except for a slight difference in the wording of the fourth. The fourth and fifth are also printed by Whitney, who derived them from Paradin, and Green thinks that he was the more likely source of the two. The shadowy nature of evidence brought forward to establish sources of this kind need not be stressed; the variety of possibilities makes the certainty of any one of them very doubtful. The fourth device, for instance, appears in Symeoni's *Tetrastichi Morali* and in Vaenius' *Amorum Emblemata*, and it is described by Samuel Daniel in his translation of Giovio's *Worthy Tract*, where the modification in the wording of the motto is also to be found. Green's whole book is an attempt to prove Shakespeare's debt to emblem books, and he drew countless parallels of wording and imagery with small regard for context or method. It is as likely as not that Shakespeare was acquainted with the work of Whitney, but to maintain that there was necessarily always direct influence is to make peculiar to the emblem writers themes and images which were the common property of the age. It is also doubtful whether this part of *Pericles* is by Shakespeare at all; but the author is plainly indebted to the emblem writers for his material as neither Gower nor Twine, the two sources, records a tournament.

pains by reading and observing, and thou shalt double his deserts in thine owne profit'.

After these translations appears the first English emblem book that professed independence of foreign models. This is *Sacrorum Emblematum Centuria Una* in Latin and English by the 'laborious and learned Dr. Willet'. Enough has already been said of its author and his intentions; of the book it is easy to say too much. Any one of the emblems will show well enough its level as poetry:

Emblem 84. Res crescunt concordia.

> The Bees by swarmes abroad doe flye,
>   And worke together all:
> Refresht they be with pleasant crye
>   And thicke on flowers fall.
> So without wrath we should agree
>   Beeing knit faste in one minde:
> If peace among the wicked bee
>   Much more it should us binde.[1]

All the verse in the *Centuria* has this home-made air. It reads like a translation, and indeed it seems probable that of the two versions of each emblem the Latin was written first; it is certainly the more accomplished. Willet, inspired perhaps by the division suggested in Whitney's preface, divides his emblems into three classes. After a preliminary five of dedication and commemoration, appear thirty-one 'Emblemata Typica sive Allegorica' consisting mainly of religious symbols such as Noah's Ark. Next follows a group of 'Emblemata Historica' or incidents from the Bible; and the book ends with what is its liveliest section, 'Emblemata Physica a rerum natura sumpta'. This contains, for example, a spirited picture of the Elephant, with a moral much in the manner of Dr. Watts:

> Of beastes most great in might
> The Elephant call by right
> Whose picture to thy sight
> is set forth here.

[1] Willet, op. cit. sig. K.1ʳ.

EMBLEME VI.

Most men do vſe ſome colour'd ſhift,
For to conceal their craftie driſt.

Masks will be more hereafter in requeſt,
And grow more deare than they did heretofore:
They ſcru'd then onely but in play and ieſt,
For merriment, and to no purpoſe more:
Now be they vſde in earneſt of the beſt,
And of ſuch Maskers there abound ſuch ſtore,
    That you ſhall finde but few in any place,
    That carrie not ſometimes a double face.
B

From Thomas Combe: *The Theatre of Fine Devices 1614*

His taile as cedar tall,
His bones of iron all,
No gun maketh him to fall,
    but he doth escape.

The trees doe not him hide,
The fields scarce meate provide,
Nor rivers drinke, with mouth wide
    for flouds he doth gape.

The Lord his power to show
Hath placed this beast below
That we to God might bow,
    of so great strength.[1]

This type of emblem drawn from natural history perhaps took the place of the mediaeval bestiary; at any rate it is a very simple taste for the marvellous that is being satisfied here, and the one positive quality that can be ascribed to Willet's verse, for all the solemnity of its lengthy title, is such a simplicity. The *Centuria* demonstrates the extent to which the emblem could become elementary, and though its author has a place among the emblem writers for his profession of originality, a place among the poets he could scarcely claim.[2]

[1] Emblem 89. sig. K.3ʳ.
[2] Willet's book is not dated, but it cannot have been written later than 1592 and the *D.N.B.* gives the date of publication as 1591; the most definite evidence of the time of composition is in Emblem 83 which is dedicated to Richard Vaughan, Rector of Dunmow, who held that parish only from February 1591 to August 1592. A full account of the Emblems can be found in *Studien zu den Anfängen der Puritanischen Emblemliteratur* by Irma Tramer, Berlin, 1934. Miss Tramer describes the work of both Willet and Wither and points out that Willet used the Calvinist translation of the Old Testament, the *Testamenti Veteris Biblia Sacra* of Immanual Tremellius and Francis Junius, and not the Vulgate, as the source of his Biblical quotations. She also suggests that the pictures so clearly before Willet were those in the illustrated Bibles and lists those of Holbein, Virgil Solis, Symeoni, Tobias Stimmer, and Pierre Vase, as well as the emblems of Alciati, Paradin and Whitney as possible sources of the pictures which in Willet's mind, though not in fact, clothed the naked emblems. For a seventeenth century account of Willet, see Clement Barksdale: *A Remembrancer of Excellent Men.* London. 1670. pp. 53–71. 'Dr Andrew Willet from Dr Peter Smith.'

Besides the printed books, a number of manuscripts[1] were made for presentation to noble patrons, and the fact that court circles encouraged such presentations shows the kind of milieu in which the emblem fashion flourished at the end of the sixteenth century. Most of these manuscripts remained unpublished, and no doubt many more were made than have survived. In form and content they have the same characteristics as the printed books, their devices being for the most part borrowed from Continental sources and their poems made by the donor himself. Thomas Palmer, for instance, an Oxford Catholic, dedicated a volume of two hundred emblems to the Earl of Leicester in which woodcuts from editions of Alciati and Aneau supplied the majority of the pictures but 'poosees' by Palmer accompanied them. In another volume, which he presented as a new year gift to Lord Burleigh in 1598, he showed more originality and made a collection of 'vegetable emblems' designed, coloured, and in the main invented by himself. Leicester was also the recipient of a gift of emblems from Geoffrey Whitney; the manuscript has since disappeared, but as it was the origin of the *Choice* published later by the Plantin Press, where Whitney refers to it as his 'first edition', it, too, must have been based on Continental models. Another manuscript emblem book of which the contents derive largely from foreign authors was that made by Abraham Fraunce and dedicated, together with an essay on rhetoric, to Sir Philip Sidney. Fraunce's interest in emblems was later to manifest itself in a critical work on the subject, but it is significant that he should here already have associated them with the arts of rhetoric. The dedication to Sidney emphasises this association, for the *Arcadia* was regarded by writers on rhetoric as a treasury of figures and tropes.

A presentation manuscript slightly different in interest was made by Francis Thynne for Sir Thomas Egerton.[2] Here there are no pictures and the verse is poor. The material is derived from Pliny and Ovid, and, as Thynne himself says, it was 'partlie drawen out

---

[1] For an annotated list of MSS. see bibliography. pp. 234 ff.

[2] *Emblemes and Epigrames* by Francis Thynne. Ed. by F. J. Furnivall for E.E.T.S. 1876.

of historie and partlie out of physicall philosophie, but tending
to Moralitie, and for the moste parte endinge in necessarie precepts
and perswation unto virtue'. It is probable that some were also
drawn out of Whitney: the judgement of Paris, Prometheus, the
dog taking revenge upon the stone that had been thrown at him,
the story of Death and Cupid, are only some of the parallels: but
if so, Thynne borrows nothing from Whitney's verse. Although
the emblems are naked ('for soe I doe terme them because they are
not clothed with engraven pictures'), Thynne has them always
very clearly before his eye: the emblem entitled 'God slowlie
punisheth', upon the theme 'the mills of God grind slowly, but
they grind exceeding small' begins:

> What doth the waightie millstone meane,
>   not turned by the wynde?
> Of heavenlie god it signifies
>   the nature and the kynde.[1]

It is this feature which distinguishes the emblems from the
epigrams that follow. Those rarely have any pictorial reference
and aim purely at verbal wit; the emblems, however, are firmly
based on their imaginary pictures. In theme they show very little
of the interests expected of a man who was to be appointed two
years later to the post of Lancaster Herald. One called the *Ensignes
of the Clergye* appears to be his own invention:

> Thow doest demaund of me,
>   why this right hande doth houlde
> the slipperie Ele, which turnes himself
>   in circle manifoulde;
> And whye the guelye arme
>   in midst of Sheild is placed,
> Of Asured cullour, whose bright shine
>   the firmament hath graced.[2]

The 'persuasion to virtue' is much in evidence. The moral is drawn
conspicuously at the end, and each emblem has its point summed

[1] Op. cit. p. 31.   [2] Ibid. pp. 37-8.

up in the title—*Art the Antidote against Fortune, Labour quencheth Lecherie, Flatterers, Our Betters or Enemies not to be Provoked with Wordes*. This last is illustrated by the story from Pliny of the Strymonian cranes who carry a stone in their beaks when they cross Mount Taurus in order that they may remain silent and not betray their presence to the eagles; it had already done good service in Euphuistic prose. Thynne's emblems must be classified with those of Wither and Willet in their moral concern: the reiterated didacticism and the kind of virtue inculcated, *Diligence obtaineth Riches, Pleasures to be Eschewed, Vane Ostentations*, suggest the values of the Puritan middle class. Technically, however, the collection represents an attempt to do what Peacham was afterwards to do with far greater skill and success.

Whitney, P.S., Thomas Combe, and Andrew Willet make up the sum of the emblem writers whose work was published before 1600 but their methods persist beyond the end of the century and with them must be included two others, Henry Peacham, the younger, whose *Minerva Britanna or A Garden of Heroical Devises* was published in 1612, and H.G., the author of the *Mirrour of Maiestie or The Badges of Honour conceitedly emblazoned*, 1618. There is no conclusive evidence as to the identity of H.G. but in all probability he was Sir Henry Godyere, the friend and correspondent of Donne. Of the two, Peacham is the more interesting both as a man and as a maker of emblems.

Peacham's father was the author of a book of rhetoric, *The Garden of Eloquence* (1577), and it was perhaps this paternal example rather than any deference to a general fashion which inspired the sub-title of *Minerva Britanna*. Henry, who was born in 1576, early showed a passion for drawing; according to his own account he had practised it 'ever naturally from a child', and though his abilities were hardly equal to his enthusiasm, this gift enabled him to produce his own illustrations for his emblem books and may perhaps have directed his attention to the convention in the first place. His designs, if not in themselves particularly distinguished, at least form a much more adequate complement to his verses than second-hand plates could ever have provided, and

10

EMBLEME XXXIX.

To be a soldier good indeed,
Must of a Captaine good proceed.

Suppose a heard of Buckes should go to warre,
And by a lusty Lyon they were led:
On th'other side, if that a Bucke compare
To beare the standard as the Lyons head;
That onely Lyons force surpasseth farre,   (bred.
With those his Bucks, whose courage he hath
    So valiant leaders cause faint cowards fight,
    A coward Captaine mars the soldiers might.

Let

From Thomas Combe: *The Theatre of Fine Devices 1614*

allowed him also full freedom of invention.[1] Moreover, Peacham was a man of considerable versatility of mind and his wide range of accomplishments were of a kind peculiarly well suited to the writing of emblems. Consequently his emblem books are much more fully an expression of his personality than are those of any other emblem writer: for most, the fashion provided a casual occupation, for Peacham it was almost a profession.

Both *Minerva Britanna* and his manuscript emblem books belong to the early stages of Peacham's career. On leaving Cambridge he had attempted to win preferment at Court, and to this end he presented two emblem books in manuscript to the King and his son. *Minerva Britanna*, in which some of these designs were used again, was published not long after. The emblem books did not, however, bear all the fruit expected, and after the death of Prince Henry, Peacham left England and went abroad, visiting the Low Countries. There he had an opportunity of studying Dutch painting and engraving and of learning more about the art for himself; an engraving of Princess Elizabeth's eldest son dates from this period.[2] He also turned soldier for a brief space, serving under Prince Maurice of Nassau. Later he settled down as a schoolmaster at Wymondham in Norfolk where he led a strenuous life which he found wearisome and profitless:

> *Windham:* I love thee, and I love thy soile,
> Yet ever loath'd that never ceasing toile
> Of thy faire Schoole, which whiles that it was free,
> My selfe the Maister lost my libertie.[3]

---

[1] The one independent drawing of any interest made by Peacham is a representation of the supplication scene in *Titus Andronicus*, which is the first known illustration to any play by Shakespeare. The purpose for which he made it remains obscure, but it is of some interest to scholars because the text which accompanies it contains divergences from those of the Quartos and Folio. The document is preserved in *Harley Papers*. i. f. 159ᵛ. For reproductions and a full account see E. K. Chambers, *The Library*. 4th Series. Vol. V. p. 327, and *William Shakespeare*. O.U.P. 1930. Vol. I. p. 312.

[2] Frontispiece for *Prince Henry Revived*, 'from Utrecht', 1615.

[3] *Thalia's Banquet*. 1620. Epigram 30.

Drudgery seems not to have been much to his taste in any form and all his books spring from the impulse of the moment: they include courtly poems and elegies, prose pamphlets on topical or political issues, one of which relates directly to his experiences as a soldier, and anecdotal little volumes of essays in which he embodied, as he expressed it, 'one man's experience of his age'.[1] Peacham knew always how to turn an occasion to good account, and if he possessed no single gift in any high degree he was exceptionally skilful at using the many with which he had been endowed in a minor way to their best advantage.

Two of Peacham's books have particular interest in connection with his emblematic activities. In many he makes passing references to the art of emblem writing, but in these two some definite instructions on methods of personification are given. One, *The Gentleman's Exercise*, is a handbook for painters and was, characteristically, Peacham's first publication.[2] It contains one long section devoted to the treatment of allegorical themes and another on the understanding and practice of heraldry. In it Peacham shows how 'according to truth to portract and expresse *Eternitie, Hope, Victorie, Pietie, Providence, Vertue, Time, Peace, Concord, Fame, Common Safetie, Clemencie, Fate*, etc. as they have been by Antiquitie described either in Coines, Statues, or other the like Public Monuments', and also 'the manner of expressing and figuring *Flouds, Rivers*, all sorts of *Nymphes; the Muses, Plants, Windes, Faunes* and *Satyres*, the *Seasons* and *Monthes* of the *year*'. The other is *The Compleat Gentleman*: here, however, it is not so much Peacham's work as that of 'a very good hand' who after his death enlarged the sections on heraldry that is relevant.

---

[1] For what is known of Peacham's biography see M. C. Pitman, 'Studies in the Works of Henry Peacham'. Summaries of Theses in *The Bulletin of Historical Research* (Univ. of London). XI. 1934. pp. 189–92.

[2] First published as *The Art of Drawing with the Pen* 1606. Enlarged and printed as (*a*) *The Gentleman's Exercise* 1612, and (*b*) *Graphice* 1612 (two issues differing only in the title page). Reprinted 1634 and subsequently with *The Compleat Gentleman*. I have derived this bibliographical information from M. C. Pitman's unpublished thesis on Peacham. Quotations are from *The Gentleman's Exercise*. 1612.

Since Peacham had already shown himself well versed in that science, this editor, who has been identified as Thomas Blount,[1] was mostly engaged in bringing up to date the numerous coats of arms which Peacham himself had described and illustrated; but he also made a contribution of his own which is one of the most interesting parts of the later editions of *The Compleat Gentleman*. It can safely be regarded as representative of general opinion, for nothing was further from any of Blount's writing than the idiosyncratic; most of his work was compilation or translation, acknowledged or unacknowledged. The addition is a whole chapter of 'Directions for Painting or Colouring of cuts and painted pictures in Watercolours'. It consists of an account of the significance of colours, some practical hints on painting along the lines of Peacham's *The Gentleman's Exercise*, and, finally, instructions on the colouring of classical and allegorical figures. This is, in effect, a catalogue of abstractions susceptible of personification, with a brief description of the clothes and emblems appropriate to each. Among the personifications are three drawn directly from *The Faerie Queene*, which must have remained a source-book for personified figures throughout the seventeenth century. Blount is doing rather more thoroughly, and at the same time more briefly and more dogmatically, what Peacham had already done in *The Gentleman's Exercise*, and both accounts provide much useful information upon contemporary sources and methods of personification. The discussions in *The Gentleman's Exercise* have moreover a direct bearing upon Peacham's *Minerva Britanna*, as he refers to them for authority more than once.

It was in books which were many-sided in their interest that the most adequate means of expression for a personality such as Peacham's lay. His claim to be remembered rests chiefly on *The Compleat Gentleman*, a book of courtesy which had for its object the fashioning of a man 'absolute in all the most necessary and commendable qualities concerning Mind or Body that may be required in a person of Honour', and in which, consequently, his own manifold accomplishments could find full scope. In it he

[1] The translator of Estienne's *The Art of Making Devises*. See above. p. 14.

stresses in the true Renaissance spirit the active end of learning which was so characteristic of himself:

> For since all Vertue consisteth in Action, and no man is borne for himself, we adde, beneficiall and usefull to his Country: for hardly they are to be admitted for Noble, who (though of never so excellent parts) consume their light, as in a darke Lanthorne in contemplation, and a Stoicall retirednesse.[1]

He was at home in many of the fields of learning he covers, and the chapters on style in speaking, writing and reading, music, statues and medals, poetry, travel, and war have the additional value of being based upon their author's own first-hand experience. His own comment on the book: 'I have pleased myself', is the measure of its success. For the same reasons the emblem book also provided an excellent medium for him. In it the number and diversity of his interests, the quickness rather than profundity of his intelligence, and the fertility of his mind could be given full play, and his unobtrusively graceful style adds the same charm to his verse as is reflected in the prose of The Compleat Gentleman.

The emblem form seems to have had an irresistible attraction for him. Minerva Britanna was the only collection of emblems that he published, but it was by no means his first experiment with the fashion, nor perhaps his last.[2] It was, rather, the outcome of constant preoccupation of his mind which creeps out both in his frequent references to them in his prose and also in his use of emblems in his verse. The Period of Mourning, an elegy on the death of Prince Henry, for instance, is composed of six visions in imita-

[1] The Compleat Gentleman. 1634. p. 2. All references are to this text unless otherwise stated.

[2] Peacham says in The Compleat Gentleman. ed. cit. p. 228. that 'our English wits' are equal to the Italians in the invention of Impresas and Emblems and that he had himself made a collection of the devices of Tiltings of Sir Philip Sidney, the Earl of Essex and others which he had intended to publish but found the expense too great. Whether this collection was made before or after the publication of Minerva Britanna it is impossible to tell. He also refers in a note to Epigram 70 in Thalia's Banquet to 'a second volume of Emblemes, done into Latin verse with their pictures', upon which he had been working.

tion of those of du Bellay, culminating in a scene in Elysium in which all the heirs apparent who met with untimely deaths are introduced, each with his manner of dying specified in an Impresa, 'so sweetly limned as by an Angel's hand'. *Thalia's Banquet*, too, contains a group of 'Impresas', brief epigrammatic poems without illustrations such as this for William Byrd:

> A Swan set dying, singing, and the *Word*,
> In golden letters, *Never such a bird*.[1]

These are informal emblems and are scattered casually through Peacham's verse but they show the persistence of his interest in the convention.

Before the publication of *Minerva Britanna* Peacham had presented emblem books to the King and Prince Henry. He made three manuscripts altogether, two in pen and ink, one of which was for James, and a coloured one for Prince Henry. All are based on '*Basilikon Doron*, his Majesties Instructions to his dearest Sonne Henrie the Prince'. Prince Henry's passion for emblems in tournaments was well known, and the gift was 'gratiously accepted'; 'limned in lively colours', it must certainly have seemed a considerable improvement upon the King's rather tedious moralising. The emblems are in Latin, each picture being accompanied by a quatrain based upon some part of the King's 'Instructions', supported by quotations from the classics. They are not identical in the three manuscripts; sometimes Peacham provides new pictures, sometimes modifies the details; but a few occur in all three and finally reappear in *Minerva Britanna* with no alterations at all. The figure of *Philautia*, Self-love, for instance, remains quite unchanged from beginning to end.

A particular interest is given to Prince Henry's book by the presence of coloured plates. Peacham was never a very good artist: his instructions in *The Art of Drawing* quite outrun the merits of his performance; but he uses his medium here with at least a moderate degree of success. The pictures are of various kinds, the best being those which treat of heraldic subjects or

[1] Op. cit. Epigram 97.

allegorical figures where the design is necessarily fairly simple. It is not their artistic qualities so much as the light they throw on the symbolical use of colour which makes the pictures interesting, and since some of them were later transferred to the plain *Minerva Britanna*, it is an interest that is not confined to the manuscript alone. The emblem, *Constantia*, for instance, represents an old man bearing the world on his back: he is dressed in blue shot with silver, the colour of faithfulness.[1] *Sancta Fides*, a woman leaning upon a cross, is also dressed in blue. *Hilaritas* is represented by a woman riding upon an improbable-looking elephant; she wears green with yellow sleeves, the colours of youth and joy. Anger is in red and purple. Peacham's sense of the significance of colour is much more marked than that of any other emblem writer and is still present in *Minerva Britanna* although the book could not, of course, be printed in colour. It obviously formed an integral part of his emblems and he frequently refers to it without considering any interpretation necessary: Deceit wears a golden coat, and Choler carries a shield charged with flames upon a crimson field. In the emblem of Inconstancy, however, the meaning is explained:

> INCONSTANCIE with fickle foote doth stand,
> Upon a *Crab*, in gowne of palie greene,
> A shining Cressaunt shewing in her hand,
> Which, as her selfe, is changing ever seene;
> 　The cullour light, she borrows from the Sea,
> 　Whose waves continue, never at a stay.[2]

Most of the personifications in *Minerva Britanna* were, in fact, drawn from sources in which colour was important. Some of the figures were transferred directly from the illuminated *Basilikon Doron*, and nearly all the rest were copied from the *Iconologia* of Caesar Ripa in which there were notes indicating the colours appropriate to each figure.

The interest of the manuscripts does not go beyond the pic-

---

[1] For details about the symbolical use of colour and its significance see M. Channing Linthicum, *Costume in the Drama of Shakespeare and his Contemporaries*. 1936.
[2] *Minerva Britanna*. 1612. p. 147.

74

tures. The text consists only of Latin quatrains and quotations from the classical authors or from King James himself. In *Minerva Britanna*, however, the moralisations are done into English verse. This book, which Peacham also dedicated to Prince Henry, contains a large collection of emblems, in part gathered from the usual classical and contemporary sources and in part original, besides some which had already been used in the manuscripts. They consist of woodcuts enclosed in ornamental borders and poems of about two verses in length. The woodcuts are Peacham's own. They may have been copied from foreign models—the lute, for instance, in *Basilikon Doron* is imitated fairly closely from Alciati—but they are not, as were Whitney's, printed off identical blocks. Peacham drew the designs himself and, though crude and simple in outline, they make his points effectively. The portrait of *Dolus* in Plate 16 (p. 109) has a guilelessness which recalls Archimago:

> Sober he seemed and very sagely sad.

The other figures often have a vitality which makes not very good drawing convincing. Peacham's verse, too, is undistinguished but adequate for the purpose for which it is needed here. Lines such as these show the best that he can do:

> ETERNITIE is young, and never old:
> The circle wantes beginning and the end:
> And uncorrupt for ever lies the gold:
> And heaven her lightes for evermore did lend,
> The Heathen thought, though heaven and earth must passe,
> And all in time decay that ever was.[1]

Occasionally his poetry manages to startle by its success with an isolated phrase, and his justness of sentiment sometimes gives it a grace and a cadence which is quite independent of its technical merits. On the whole, the verse shows at best advantage in its context, as a contributory factor to the emblem book, and has little to recommend it outside that framework.

In *Minerva Britanna* the range of subject is wide. The classical

[1] Ibid. p. 141.

stock-in-trade is represented in emblems of Diana and Actaeon, Adonis killed by the boar, Hercules with a distaff, and Ganymede flying upon an eagle. An emblem of Priam sacrificing at an altar as Troy falls is dedicated to Peacham's tutor at Cambridge:

> When *Priam* saw his Citie set on fire,
> At once and drowned, in his Peoples blood,
> To pacifie the heavens enkindled ire,
> (Since humane helpe doth fail to do him good:)
>> *Creusa* warnes him to the Altar flie
>> Although he were assured there to die.
>
> The case is every christians in distresse,
> Who to the Lord, himself should recommend,
> As who can best the wrongfull cause redresse,
> And patiently t'abide, what he shall send:
>> Fall'n into the handes of foes, our freedome thence,
>> Or glorious death, to crowne our innocence.[1]

Other material common to the emblematists is included, for Peacham drew plenty of help from his predecessors. There are fables—the story of the fool who sawed off the branch of a tree with himself on it, the tale of the two friends and the bear (Plate 11), which is told in Peacham's most lively manner, the incident of Cupid and Death, here retold with an acknowledgement to Whitney; symbolic animals—Pegasus prancing in the corner of an emblem of Bacchus, the inevitable Phoenix—this time paying a compliment to the Earl of Salisbury:

> Th' Arabian PHOENIX heere, of golden plumes,
> And bicie brest, upon a sacred pile
> Of sweetest odors, thus himselfe consumes;
> By force of PHOEBUS fiery beames, the while,
>> From foorth the ashes of the former dead,
>> A faire, or fairer, by and by, is bred.
>
> You, you (Great Lord) this wondrous PHOENIX are,
> Who wast your selfe in Zeale, and whot desire,
> Of Countries good, till in the end your care
> Shall worke your end, as doth this PHOENIX fire.

[1] *Minerva Britanna.* 1612. p. 65.

11

TWO frendes there were that did their Iourney take,
And by the way, they made a vow to either,
What ere befell, they never would forsake,
But as sworne brethren, liue and die togeither:
    Thus wandring thorough deserts, here and there,
    By chance they met, a great and vgly *Beare*.

At whome, amazed with a deadly feare,
One leaues his frend, and climbeth vp a tree:
The other, falles downe flat before the *Beare*,
And keepes his breath, that seeming dead to be,
    The *Beare* forsooke him, (for his nature's such,
    A breathles bodie never once to touch.)

The beast departing, and the daunger past,
The dead arose, and kept along his waie:
His fellow leaping from the tree at last,
Askt what the *Beare*, in's eare did whispring say,
    Quoth he, he bad me, evermore take heede,
    Of such as thou, that failst in time of neede.

From Henry Peacham: *Minerva Britanna 1612*
[slightly reduced]

But while you are consuming in the same,
You breede a second, your immortall Fame.[1]

Trees—the laurel and the vine, symbolising the proper union of art and learning with wealth and prosperity, the myrtle and the pomegranate for friendship between neighbours, and the cypress, which Peacham has included instead of the usual palm-tree to illustrate the motto *Nitor in adversum*. Many other emblems are adaptations from common knowledge. In one picture a camel crouches on the ground under the burden of the last straw while anxious merchants attempt to raise him; in another there is a game of football in progress, the movement of the ball typifying the capriciousness of worldly wealth. These are all examples with which readers of emblems would have been entirely familiar, and Peacham often adds a reference to an original in the margin.

Another type of emblem which Peacham uses extensively and which is often of his own invention is what may be termed the diagrammatic emblem. It is of the same type as Whitney's emblem of the Seven Sages in which a number of different symbols are assembled together to represent a single idea. 'Filial piety', for example, is represented in *Basilikon Doron* by a bird holding a skull in its claw, with a plant twining round beneath it; 'the search for knowledge' by an eye, a heart, an open book and a green leaf. In themselves, seen separately, the parts of the picture are wholly incongruous but clamped together by the idea to which they all contribute, they show only that limited aspect of themselves which will not conflict with the rest. When the unifying idea is forgotten or unexplained, the whole appears nonsense. A poem which begins:

A poysonous Serpent wreathed up around
In scalie boughs, a sharpe two-edged Sword,
Supported by a booke upon the ground,

[1] Ibid. p. 19. The Phoenix did noble service in and out of emblem books. Its peculiar method of reproduction made its application almost unlimited. With the motto *Nascatur ut Alter*, it was used with particular appropriateness as the symbol of the mother of Edward VI who died willingly in childbirth. It appears as *Unica semper avis* in Whitney. p. 177.

is meaningless until the application of each image is defined and
limited by the next line:

Is worldly wisedom grounded on GODS word.[1]

Like Paradin's *Devises*, these emblems provide a comment on
another aspect of Elizabethan poetry—its use of imagery. The
beauty of an Elizabethan lady is recorded in a number of images
each of which, in itself, has little or no connection with the others,
just as Peacham could juxtapose disparate objects, and even
represent them pictorially, without any apparent conflict once
their relationship was accepted in the mind. Rosalind's eyes are
'sapphires set in snow';[2] Warner's mistress is described in three
images which are quite incompatible with each other:

> My mistress is a paragon,
>   The fairest fair alive:
> Atrides and Aeacides
>   For fair less fair did strive.
> Her colour fresh as damask rose,
>   Her breath as violet,
> Her body white as ivory,
>   And smooth as polished jet,
> As soft as down: and were she down
>   Jove might come down and kiss
> A love so fresh, so sweet, so white,
>   So smooth, so soft, as this.[3]

This is a method like that of Peacham when he symbolises a happy
marriage by a dove perched on an olive round the branches of
which hangs a gold ring, or the wisdom of Solomon by a book,
an eye and a heart, and a cedar crossed with hyssop:

> For from the Cedar, saith the text, he knew
> Unto the hyssop, all that ever grew.[4]

[1] *Minerva Britanna.* 1612. p. 2.   [2] Lodge, 'Rosalynde'. 1590.
[3] William Warner, 'My Mistress'. 1592. Printed by Norman Ault, *Elizabethan Lyrics.* 1925. p. 153. This characteristic of Elizabethan poetry is most
obvious in the love poems because conventional language was there more
highly developed, but it can be seen elsewhere also. Compare, for example,
John Dennys's 'The Anglers Song'. Norman Ault, op. cit. p. 429.
[4] *Minerva Britanna.* p. 40.

Finally, a large group of emblems which must be singled out in *Minerva Britanna* for separate consideration are the personifications. These almost all derive from the *Iconologia* of Caesar Ripa, an anthology of engraved figures drawn from Egyptian, Latin, Greek, and contemporary Italian writing, painting and sculpture, intended for the use of 'Oratori, Predicatori, Poeti, Formatori d'Emblemi, & d'Imprese, Scultori, Pittori Disseguatori, Rappresentatori, Architetti, & Divisatori d'Apparati'. The book was first published without cuts in 1593, at Rome. In 1603 it was re-issued, this time with engravings to illustrate many of the figures described in the text, and in this form it reached England and soon became a source-book for Jacobean personification.[1] For the masque writers it was a guide for costume; and Peacham derived several of his directions for the representation of the moral qualities in *The Gentleman's Exercise* from it, and copied the figures which interested him most into *Minerva Britanna*. His Truth, a naked woman gazing at the sun, holding a book and a palm in her hand and treading down the world with her foot, Inconstancy, Learning,[2] a 'comely dame, in years' with an open book on her knee and a sceptre in one hand which symbolises her 'power and sovereign might' and is surmounted by a shining sun to expel blind ignorance, derive the details of their symbolism and even of their posture from Ripa. It was Ripa, too, who provided Peacham with models for his representation of the four humours: the figure of Melancholy, for instance, with his mouth bound up as 'the sign of silence', has an owl and a cat for companions, rests his foot upon a cube, 'the which him plodding constancie affords' and carries a book and a sealed purse to show

[1] Other editions appeared during the century and it was translated into French but not into English until 1709. The new engravings with which it was then published show the trend of eighteenth century interest. The figures are no longer like those which appeared in Inigo Jones's sketch book but each holds her symbol as if it were intended to add to the design rather than to the meaning of the picture. In its original form, however, it was the standard work for allegorical design.

[2] *Minerva Britanna*. p. 134; p. 147; p. 26. Peacham's plates may be compared with Ripa's designs for the same figures. *Iconologia* . . . Padua. 1611. pp. 529, 244 and 128.

that avarice is his characteristic quality.[1] Other designs from the same source are the figures of Felicity, Repentance with her fish, Matrimony, Virtue, Eternity, Favour and Fortune.[2] The two presentations of *Capriccio* or the unstaid mind in Plate 12 show how closely Peacham followed the detail of his original: in both, Instability is personified by a youth dressed in various colours with plumes in his hat, a pair of bellows in one hand with which he is blowing into his own ear, and a spur in the other.[3] Peacham also drew upon the *Iconologia* for some of the figures described in *The Gentleman's Exercise*. Matrimony, for example, is there typified as a youth standing in the stocks and bearing a yoke on his neck and 'the fruitful quince' in his hand, exactly as Ripa had portrayed him.[4] For the personifications in the manuscripts of *Basilikon Doron*, however, he has either relied upon his own resources or looked to the older emblem books. *Gula* comes from Alciati, but none of the others appears in any of the books which Peacham declares himself to have known.

It was not to Ripa only that Peacham turned for his personifications. *The Faerie Queene* also supplied him with models and he drew upon Spenser both for the directions he gave in the *The Gentleman's Exercise* and occasionally, too, for the designs for the emblem books. Some of the borrowings are acknowledged, some not. It is not very easy to ascertain whether Spenser occupied the same kind of position as Ripa as an authoritative source book of personified figures for masques and decorative work of all kinds; but certainly both Peacham and Blount, in his additions to *The Compleat Gentleman*, appear to regard him in that light, and include his personifications with those of Alciati and the classical authors. In Peacham's directions for expressing the months, the painter is instructed to portray August 'as our Spencer describeth him',[5] and Fear is to be presented as 'he is described by our excellent Spencer (to ride) in Armour, at the clashing whereof he

[1] *Minerva Britanna.* pp. 126–9.
[2] Ibid. p. 25; p. 46; p. 132; p. 35; p. 141; p. 206; p. 153.
[3] Ibid. p. 149.   [4] *The Gentleman's Exercise.* 1612. p. 168.
[5] Ibid. p. 135. Cp. *The Faerie Queene.* VII. vii. 37.

12

From Henry Peacham: *Minerva Britanna 1612*

From Ceasar Ripa: *Iconologia 1611*

looks deadly pale as afeared of himself'.[1] Blount does not acknowledge his authority at all, but he undoubtedly drew some of his
material word by word from *The Faerie Queene*. Envy, for
instance,

> All in a kirtle of discoloured say
> He clothed was, ypainted full of eyes,

is noted as in 'a kirtle of discoloured say full of eyes' [2] and the
descriptions of Faith, Hope and Charity:

Fidelia in white garments with a cup of gold.

Hope in blew with a silver anchor.

Charity in yellow robes, on her head a tyre of gold, with precious
stones, her chair ivory [3]

owe all their details to Spenser's description of the three sisters
in the House of Holiness. Another of Peacham's figures, Dissimulation, 'a Lady wearing a visard of two faces, in a long Robe
of changeable colour, in her right hand a Magpie, the poet *Spenser*
described her looking through a lattice', seems to arise out of a
confusion between Suspect and Dissemblance, one of the pairs
in the Masque of Cupid.[4] When Peacham came to produce the
emblem books, Ripa, whose plates could serve as copies, was far
more useful and it is from the *Iconologia* that the majority of the
personifications are derived. But there are likenesses to Spenser,
particularly in the coloured *Basilikon Doron*, and the purpose to
which Peacham read *The Faerie Queene* is evident enough from
the references in the *The Gentleman's Exercise*. In one emblem in
Minerva Britanna, Pallas is caught in a net by Avarice and Dissimulation. Avarice is represented as carrying a bag and Dissimulation here has two faces. Neither of these figures appears in
Ripa, and Peacham's avowed knowledge of the Masque of Cupid
makes it probable that he drew them from Spenser. There are

[1] Ibid. p. 27. Cp. *The Faerie Queene*. III. xii. 12.

[2] *The Faerie Queene*. I. iv. 31. *The Compleat Gentleman*. 1661. p. 167.

[3] Ibid. p. 166. Ripa has a similar figure of Charity with her babes hanging at
her breast, but she is dressed in red and has no chair or doves.

[4] *The Gentleman's Exercise*. p. 114. Cp. *The Faerie Queene*. III. xii. 14.

other possible reminiscences of *The Faerie Queene*: *Philautia*, for instance, a woman dressed in purplish red and holding a mirror in one hand, a snake in the other, might well be a picture of Lucifera; and *Gula* is drawn in much the same way as Spenser drew him except that he is dressed in a yellow suit instead of Spenser's vine leaves; but the essential type characteristics, the long neck and vast paunch, are identical in both.

In its personifications, as in its linking of ideas in the diagrammatic emblems, Peacham's work has some interesting connections with Elizabethan and Jacobean poetry. Before considering these, however, something must be said of the remaining emblem book of the early group, H.G.'s *The Mirrour of Maiestie*. Its author [1] is described with some asperity by Sir Tobie Matthew:

> Sir Henry Goodyear was ever pleasant and kind, and gave me much of his sweet conversation; and he would ingenuously confess whensoever in discourse he thought I had the better reason of the two. But if his constancy had been as great as his nature was good, he had been much happier in both worlds. [2]

Sir Henry is known to have been something of a poet and was appointed by James I a Gentleman of His Majesty's Privy Chamber: these are his qualifications as author of a book of verse the origin and destination of which was the Court.

In general make-up *The Mirrour of Maiestie* is handsome enough. The cuts are clear and well designed, and there is no trace of that confusion of figures which sometimes occurs in Whitney's more

---

[1] The identification of H.G. with Sir Henry Godyere was first suggested by W. C. Hazlitt, *Poetical Miscellanies*. See H. Green. Facsimile Reprint of *The Mirrour of Maiestie*. Holbein Society, 1870. and B.H. Newdigate, T.L.S. October 24, 1936. Some account of Godyere is given by H. J. C. Grierson, *The Poems of John Donne*, O.U.P. 1912. Vol. II. p. 144. He was a friend of Donne, who used to stay with him at Polesworth in Warwickshire, and also of Michael Drayton; his cousin Anne Godyere, who married Sir Henry Raynsford, was probably the lady who inspired Drayton's *Idea*. Poems by Godyere are printed by Grierson. op. cit. Vol. I. p. 433. Another poem ascribed to him is printed in A. Latham, *Poems of Sir Walter Ralegh*. 1929. p. 112. His work is also found among the prefatory poems to *Coryats Crudities*.

[2] Sir Tobie Matthew. *A True Historical Relation of the Conversion of Sir Tobie Matthew to the Holy Catholic Faith*. Ed. A. H. Mathew. 1904. p. 86.

13

From Sir Henry Godyere: *The Mirrour of Maiestie 1618*

overcrowded plates. Thirty-one engravings of the coats of arms
borne by the King and Queen and the more conspicuous officers
of state are matched by thirty-two emblems, two for the King and
one for each of the others. Here for the first time is an attempt to
distinguish in the designs themselves between the heraldic device
and an emblem proper, but the difference is still only superficial.
The change is no more than a transference of the old elements
into a new setting—heraldic devices are put into a context. The
emblem for Prince Charles in Plate 13 is an example of what
H.G. conceives an emblem to be, and in it the main features of the
device still remain, a naturalistic background being added merely
to the familiar motif of the heraldic eagle. Some plates are in
appearance, at least, less closely connected with the designs for
badges; the plate of Pegasus and the Nine Muses seems for instance
much less close to its heraldic counterpart. But the difference lies
mainly in the subject-matter, which certainly is more complicated: in treatment Pegasus retains the formal, essentially static.
quality of the heraldic design.

H.G. wrote two Epithalamia, a congratulatory poem to the
Prince, and other occasional verse of no great distinction. The
poems in *The Mirrour of Maiestie* have little to recommend them;
they do their work adequately, but with immeasurable dullness.
This, for instance, is the poem which accompanies the picture
of Pegasus:

> Heere *Phoebus* and the *Sacred Sisters* sit,
> Chiefely attending *Harmonie*, and *Wit*:
> Who stay to heare the dying Swans to sing
> Sad *Epods*; riding on the *Thespian* Spring
> Heere the *Wingd-Horses* hoofe digs up that *Well*
> Whence gurgle streames of *Art*, and Sacred *Skill*.
> *Divines* (like *Pegasus*) divinely mooue
> In Man, springs of profound, and precious loue
> To heav'nly *Wisedome*; who t'ech passing by,
> Poynts out the path-way to *Eternitie*;
> And whilst You doe your noble thoughts confine
> To what *Divines* preach, You become Divine.[1]

[1] Emblem 24. p. 47.

The plate and subject were promising enough to have inspired a better poem in almost any other emblem writer; but H.G. had neither Willet's naïve enthusiasm nor Peacham's gift of graceful compliment. He found the necessity of offering appropriate flattery to every one of the 'Noble Personages ranckt in the Catalogue' rather hampering than otherwise. It limited his material and forced him to neglect the best of what usually constituted an emblem book—stories from Jest Books and Bestiaries and the more lively aspects of mythology—for subjects of this kind:

> *Joue, Phoebus,* and *Minerua* were assign'd
> To be the three chiefe ornaments of mind.
> *Joue* figur'd *Prouidence, Minerua, Wit,*
> *Phoebus, Content*; and all that purchas'd it.[1]

The plates certainly improve upon the verse but as soon as *The Mirrour of Maiestie* is regarded as anything more than a picture-book its mediocrity becomes conspicuous.

[1] Emblem 26. p. 51.

Chapter 4

EMBLEMS IN ELIZABETHAN
LITERATURE

CONTEMPORARY discussions of the nature and function
of emblems do not throw much light upon their relation to
Elizabethan literature in general. In Italy emblem writing had
developed into a highly specialised science with rules and distinctions as finely drawn as those which had prevailed in the convention of courtly love, and consequently even those critics who
made it their business to pronounce upon the theory of emblem
writing began to approach their task in the humble spirit of an
amateur. For instance Paolo Giovio, who evolved the five rules
for making devices, complained that reasoning upon such a subject was like entering a vast sea from which there could be no easy
issue, and in England both the emblem writers themselves and the
professed critics showed considerable agility in evading their re-
sponsibilities. Peacham and Whitney both explained that they
might have written more upon the topic had they wished to but
that the continental critics had forestalled them; Thynne re-
treated behind the figures of Giovio and Claude Mignault, one of
Alciati's editors; and the criticism of Abraham Fraunce and of
N.W. occupies itself mainly with repeating once again the narrow
distinctions and definitions of the supersubtle Italians and their
French commentators.[1]

Taken as a whole, however, these discussions at least raise one
important point about the incidence of the emblem form. In all
contemporary criticism, emblems are connected, explicitly or
implicitly, with two main interests, interest in decoration and
interest in rhetoric. From the very beginning it had been uncertain whether the form derived from Egyptian hieroglyphics or
from the Greek anthology, whether, that is, its pictorial or its

[1] See below, Appendix 2, on Lord Shaftesbury's *Second Characters*. p. 241.

rhetorical side was of prime importance. This doubt resulted in a dual classification: emblems were associated by some critics, notably Abraham Fraunce, with insignia, arms, symbols and hieroglyphics, and by others, for instance by John Hoskins in his *Directions for Speech and Style* with allegories, similitudes, fables and poets' tales.[1] The dichotomy is of course false, for the whole essence of the emblem method is that in it picture and word are intimately combined; but the two sides do none the less exist, though they exist in conjunction and not independently of one another, and it was inevitable that the particular interests of the critic or poet or artist should lead him to emphasise one at the expense of the other. The application of the emblem form accordingly became two-fold. On the one side it was regarded as an aid to the mastery of rhetoric, the concern then being exclusively with the text; on the other as a collection of heraldic or allegorical *motifs* useful to painters, sculptors, embroiderers and the like: the picture was then the main object of interest, although, if the medium allowed, the motto might also be incorporated. In these two ways the emblem entered Elizabethan literature, being used now as a source of verbal wit and of rhetorical devices generally, now as a source of imagery. There was, of course, no reason why the emblem form should not also be employed in its entirety; it was so employed in the Masques where the picture could actually be presented before the eye, and in dramatic or narrative poetry where description replaced a visible design. But since it had this dual nature, it is hardly surprising to find that it was often split into its two parts and put to whatever purpose an author had in mind.

It is the pictorial element which probably constitutes the main interest of the emblem form today. For contemporary readers, however, the rhetorical interest of the text could be just as great

[1] John Hoskins, *Directions for Speech and Style*. c. 1599. Ed. Hoyt H. Hudson. Princeton. 1935.

14

And what is beate vpon ſo oſt, and ſayd,
Reioyce ye Righteous, and againe Reioyce ;
D 3

And

16. The impediments of *Chriſtian* converſation.

THe *Cittizens* for moſt part Hacknies hire,
   And none ſo ſoone as they,their horſes tier.
Which riſeth hence; With full career they Ride;
And in their Innes the beaſts to th' Rack are tied
Meateles vndreſt ; yet are they ſwitcht, and ſpurrd,
If on their way they haue a whit demurrd.
But cauſe they provender with-hold them from,
They grow vnable (through) to bring them home.
Like vnto theſe are ſome ; thoſe *Chriſtians* ſad,
Who looke not on the *Goſpell*, which makes glad ;
But on the *Rigour* of the *Law*, their eyne
Doe fix, and on their *faults* their ſoules to pine ;
Conſidering not what *Chriſt* for them hath payd,

From Thomas Jenner: *The Soules Solace 1626*

as the decorative and allegorical interest supplied through the pictures. In books on eloquence an emblem was treated as a distinctive figure of rhetoric: in Hoskins's *Directions for Speech and Style*, for example, it is classified as a kind of similitude. It was, for him, one of the different means by which writing may be 'varied', an aid to literary success. Puttenham too classed it among literary devices, and what was suggested in theory was undoubtedly put into practice.[1] The emblem book in fact became a useful source book for writers. Lyly used Alciati's *Emblematum Liber* as an anthology of rhetorical figures, and derived a number of his similes from it.[2] Conversely the images introduced by preachers into their sermons were collected and published in emblem form. A volume entitled *The Soules Solace or Thirtie and One Spiritual Emblems*, which first appeared in 1626 and was reprinted twice in the seventeenth century, contains pictures based on verbal illustrations used in sermons; these pictures were accompanied by an explanatory poem. Each poem is initialled M.A., M.W., etc., after the divine from whose sermon the image was drawn, and consists in a description of the picture followed by an explanation of its moral significance. That there were three editions of *The Soules Solace* suggests that the collection was read widely as a guide to godliness, and priests may have used it in the same way as Lyly used Alciati, as a collection of ornaments with which to 'vary' their sermons. The existence of such a book at least indicates how far images in prose were regarded as independent decorations capable of being detached from their contexts and studied as examples of different types of rhetorical figures. Doubtless the schoolboys who attended divine service and took notes upon the sermon for Monday's lessons, were expected to observe the preacher's use of images. Hoskins's copy of *Arcadia* with its metaphors marked M shows the same principle in practice.

The rhetorical uses of the emblem were not confined to the

[1] Puttenham. *The Arte of English Poesie.* 1589. Ed. G. Willcock and A. Walker. 1936. pp. 102–8.
[2] See *Euphues.* Ed. Maurice Croll and Harry Clemons. London. 1916. Introduction and notes to the text.

professional writer or speaker. As witty conceits they appealed also to another type of reader. The would-be gentleman is advised by Peacham to study them as a help to conversational success:

> In your discourse be free and affable, giving entertainment in a sweete and liberall manner; and with a cheerefull courtesie seasoning your talke at the table among grave and serious discourses, with conceits of wit and pleasant invention, as ingenious Epigrams, Emblemes, Anagrams, merry tales, wittie questions and answers.[1]

As rhetorical figures they were also valued by schoolmasters, and emblem books had a place in the seventeenth century schoolboy's satchel in company with such helps to style and syntax as Erasmus's *Adagia* and Baldwin's *Moral Philosophy*, which Nashe had already complained to have been 'all snatcht up for painter's posies'.[2] They helped to provide material for the school theme and the means by which 'to flourish and adorn it neatly with rhetorical tropes and figures'. Charles Hoole, in his book on what he describes as 'this despicable but comfortable employment of teaching school', recommends, among other text-books, Alciati's *Emblems* for the use of the fourth and fifth forms, Reusner's *Symbols* in the fifth, and Valerius in the sixth.[3] These, quite independently of their pictorial charms, contributed to the already huge bulk of commonplaces with which the child's head must by this time have been stored: memorising of sentences began in the lowest forms and the youngest scholars had to repeat the text after the sermon or 'some little pious sentence which was then delivered'. Further, although it is not in this capacity that they were specified by Hoole, they may also have been used as picture books for teaching: the *Orbis Sensualium Pictus*, 'A World of things obvious to the senses drawn in pictures' of J. A. Comenius, which was translated by Hoole in 1658 and recommended by him for teaching purposes, is closely allied to them. The educational theory

[1] *The Compleat Gentleman.* 1634. p. 225
[2] Nashe, *Have with you to Saffron Walden* 1596. *Works.* Ed. McKerrow. Vol. III. p. 20.
[3] *A New Discovery of the old Art of Teaching Schoole.* 1660. 'A Note of Schoole-Authors.'

behind this book is one that was constantly reiterated both outside and inside school, that 'Men are more led by the eye than the ear'. Comenius' arguments in support of his thesis are of considerable interest for they anticipate the psychology of Locke:

The ground of this business, is, that *sensual objects be rightly presented to the senses*, for fear they may not be received. I say, and say it again aloud, that this last is the foundation of all the rest: because *we can neither act nor speak wisely, unless we first rightly understand all the things which are to be done, and whereof we are to speak. Now there is nothing in the understanding, which was not before in the sense. And therefore to exercise the senses well about the right perceiving the differences of things, will be to lay the grounds for all wisdom, and all wise discourse, and all discreet actions in one's course of life.* Which, because it is commonly neglected in Schools, and the things that are to be learned are offered to Scholars, without being understood or being rightly presented to the senses, it cometh to pass, that the work of teaching and learning goeth heavily onward, and affordeth little benefit.[1]

He was insistent that by his method 'the Scare crows may be taken away out of Wisdome's Garden'. Accordingly, the *Orbis Pictus* was illustrated with copper plates the poor quality of which was later to be deplored ungratefully by Evelyn. However, they served their purpose and the frequent reprints suggest that the book was put to a practical use. It resembles the emblem books first in the principle of instruction by pictures and secondly in some of its contents. It includes, for instance, nine personifications of moral virtues of the kind found in emblem books. *Ethica* is a version of the choice of Hercules:

> *This* Life *is a* way
> *or a* place divided into
> two ways, *like*
> Pythagoras's letter Y.
> *broad* I.
> *on the left-hand track*;
> *narrow 2*
> *on the right*;

[1] Hoole's translation of the author's preface. Text from the edition of 1672.

that belongs to Vice 3
this to virtue 4
　　Mind, Young man 5
imitate Hercules:
leave the left-hand way,
turn from Vice.
the Entrance 6 *is fair,*
but the End 7
is ugly and steep down.
　　Go on the right hand,
though it be thorny 8.
no way is
unpassable to vertue,
follow
whither virtue leadeth.

The numbers refer to numbers on the picture. Another cut shows Prudence with a serpent, and Opportunity flying away behind; other stock figures such as Temperance and Justice are also included.

The insistence on the part of so enlightened and so great a teacher as Comenius upon the value of pictures in education may well have led those influenced by his system to utilise the plates as well as the texts of the school emblem books. But the main use of the emblematic picture was decorative not pedagogic. Just as the rhetorical aspects of the form had been isolated by those interested in the art of eloquence, so the pictorial aspects were seized upon by those concerned with decoration, and craftsmen of all kinds saw in the emblem books a valuable addition to their collections of patterns. The designs of Alciati and Whitney were found to slide easily into the medium of embroidery; the broader outlines of Peacham's woodcuts needed only slight modifications to be followed in the plasterwork of ceilings and panels. An interest in the emblematic had long been present in decoration; indeed, as was pointed out in Chapter 2, in England the essential features of the emblem book appear there before they are found in literary form, and certain subjects akin to, or even identical with, the themes in the emblem books occur frequently among the devices used. The Nine Worthies, the Four Seasons, the Four Elements, the Four Evangelists, the Five Senses, the Three Theological Virtues, all had to make their appearance sooner or later on the ceilings or panels of houses just as they had appeared in other forms in the past. Time, Peace and Plenty, Faith with her cross and cup, Charity with her babes, for instance, are among the figures modelled in relief on the panels and ceilings of Boston House at Brentford.[1] The most popular sources of these designs were pattern books engraved in the Low Countries [2] but some craftsmen looked for their material closer at hand and found it in an emblem book. Peacham's *Minerva Britanna* provided the figures on the ceiling of a gallery at Blickling Hall in Norfolk;[3] others were set in the plasterwork panels of a house in Houndsditch which has since been destroyed. The devices chosen for these panels went beyond the usual personifications, and besides Temperance and Hypocrisy, the craftsman chose Peacham's symbol of wisdom, the sword with the serpent wreathed around it, and his emblem of Priam at the altar.[4] These figures were in all probability gilded and coloured, as Peacham himself had originally intended them to be. His woodcuts are particularly well suited to this purpose; their broad outline and simplicity of design have already the characteristics of sculpture, and there was no necessity for any serious alteration to be made in order to adapt them for practical use; it was only a matter of transference.

Peacham's emblems differ from the rest in that they are his own and are therefore immediately recognisable. It is impossible, however, to establish definite sources for most of the designs which

---

[1] 1623. For reproductions see M. Jourdain, *English Decoration and Furniture of the Early Renaissance.* 1924. Figs. 159–61. p. 119.

[2] Numbers of these have been traced to their originals by M. Jourdain, *English Decorative Plasterwork of the Renaissance.* 1926. pp. 8 ff.

[3] Blickling Hall was built in 1619–20. Peacham became a schoolmaster at Wymondham a few miles away after his return from the Netherlands in 1614 and he may perhaps have had some personal connection with its decoration.

[4] Essex House, Gravel Lane, Houndsditch. For reproductions of the ceiling and of Peacham's plates see M. Jourdain, *English Decorative Plasterwork.* Plates 23–5. p. 18.

appear in decoration. A few in any group can almost always be traced to Whitney; but Whitney's work was avowedly an anthology, and the debt may, therefore, be due to one of its sources rather than to *A Choice of Emblemes* itself. On no occasion does it appear to have been the only pattern book used, and all that can be said with certainty is that a number of the emblems which were printed by Whitney made their way, through some channel or other, into the decorative arts. There was, for example, a bedstead in a Leicestershire house which had emblematic devices with Latin mottoes painted in its panelled compartments, six of which seem to have been almost identical with Whitney's designs.[1] Again, the painted emblems which decorate the walls of a small room, probably built as an oratory, at Hardwick House [2] may owe something to Whitney. The collection has every appearance of being considerably later than the *Choice*, and although one emblem can be exactly paralleled in Whitney and several others are to be found in Wither, they have as a whole a distinctly metaphysical turn, and the old fables and myths so common in the earlier emblem books are replaced by images of this kind:

A Painter painting a Woman.	*Dic mihi qualis eris.*
A Globe borne by a crab	*Sic orbis iter.*
A man rowing towards a town	*Et tamen aversor.*
A ship anchored to a whale	*Nusquam tuta fides.*

The last two are interesting in a wider connection. Milton's image of the 'Pilot of some night-foundered skiff' was not, it seems, necessarily bookish in origin, while the Waterman—an image previously used by Fulke Greville [3]—reappears (full use being made

[1] The bedstead, which contained 29 panels in all, is described, but unfortunately not reproduced, in a note in *The Gentleman's Magazine*. Vol. 81. 2. 1811. p. 416.

[2] The house of Elizabeth Drury whose death was commemorated by Donne in the *First* and *Second Anniversary*. The emblems date from the reign of James I and are reproduced in Cullum, *The History of Hawsted and Hardwick*. 1813, pp. 160–5.

[3] *Caelica*. Sonnet LXI; date of composition uncertain; probably between 1577 and 1586. *Poems and Dramas of Fulke Greville*. Ed. G. Bullough. 1928, p. 110.

of the moral implications of the motto), as By-Ends' grandfather in *The Pilgrim's Progress*. Whether connections can be established with any particular emblem books or not, the way in which images slip from emblem books into decoration and from decoration into literature is a significant comment on the place they occupy in the literature of the seventeenth century.

Emblem books were useful also to embroiderers and tapestry makers. How many of the more commonly repeated designs in embroidery and textiles were emblematic is a matter of opinion. Flowers, for instance, are said each to have had their own significance, and there are extant some octagonal panels worked by the Countess of Shrewsbury which contain devices taken from herbal books and enclosed within a border inscribed with a motto.[1] The mottoes are not mere labels but have a reference to some quality in each flower. In general, however, there seems no good reason for inferring sorrow whenever the columbine makes its appearance or fidelity whenever a sunflower is represented in a border. The patterns given in such handbooks for embroiderers as *The Needles Excellency* [2] include a variety of flowers and also such designs as a man holding a cup, a woman holding a flower, or the heraldic lion and unicorn supporting the rose and thistle crowned, which are emblematic in the sense that they are not naturalistic and are capable of moral or political interpretation; but they do not on that account necessarily bear an emblematic significance. Flowers, as such, are not at all common in the emblem books; Whitney gives a Tudor rose, but it is a rose with a scarab in it and the point of the emblem is the 'scarabee' not the flower in itself. The sunflower, however, which makes its first

[1] For reproductions, see Mary Symonds and Louisa Preece, *Needlework through the Ages*, 1928. p. 174. Plate L. Cp. 'A Nosegay always sweet' (? by William Hunnis) in which lavender, rosemary, sage, fennel, violet, thyme, roses, gillyflowers, carnations, marigolds, pennyroyal, cowslips, are all introduced with emblematic meanings, although it is plain that these are entirely arbitrary and are chosen more for the sake of alliteration or other poetic advantages than for any connection they may have with the flowers. The poem, which was written before 1576, is quoted by Ophelia in the mad scene in *Hamlet*. For the text of it see Norman Ault, *Elizabethan Lyrics*. p. 65.

[2] *The Needles Excellency*. 12th edition, London. 1640.

appearance in English emblem books in the work of Thynne, typifying there the duty of a good subject towards his king, was used frequently; it occurs also in Wither and later became popular among the writers of religious emblem books. The rose, too, was often employed emblematically because it was closely associated with politics.[1] But there is no sharp line to be drawn between what is, and what is not, consciously of the emblem kind. Elizabethan decoration was universally emblematic and wherever the needle could penetrate the tendency to personification and allegory finds expression. When it was the custom to present gloves with a set of verses accompanying them, it was only appropriate that they should be embroidered with a row of hearts transfixed by arrows or a border of phoenixes renewing love in their own ashes. Books were bound in embroidered covers; hangings bore appliqué figures of the virtues and vices; carpets were woven in emblematic designs; and clothes, not only in tournaments but on ordinary occasions, carried devices, or conveyed symbolical meanings through their colours and design. The portraits of Queen Elizabeth offer well-known examples of this: in a painting at Hatfield the lining of her dress is embroidered with eyes and ears to signify vigilance, her left sleeve bears a serpent, the symbol of wisdom, and in her hands she holds a rainbow with the motto *Non sine sole iris.*

When the needle aspired to something more elaborate, emblem books offered suitable material. Some of Whitney's emblems were used as models for the designs on a jacket which is said to have belonged to Queen Elizabeth.[2] It is a tight-fitting short coat made of silk, and embroidered all over with a tendril pattern of leaves, flowers and fruit. Within the leaves are enclosed various animals, birds, and fish worked in the same black silk outline stitches, and also a few distinct emblems. The child Hercules, for instance, appears riding on a crocodile with snakes in either hand; there is a man piping to an ape in a tree, a lion watching a burning

[1] M. B. Huish, *Samplers and Tapestry Embroideries.* 1913. p. 66.
[2] Now in the Victoria and Albert Museum (T. 80. 1924). For a reproduction of the coat as a whole see M. Jourdain, *English Secular Embroidery.* 1910. p. 144.

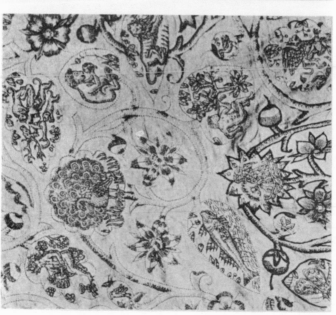

15

From Geoffrey Witney: *A Choice of Emblemes 1586*

Detail from an embroidered coat, late 16th Century
[reduced a third]

house, a flying fish caught between a bird and a sea monster; the pelican in her piety, Actaeon the prey to hounds, Bacchus with his drum. Two of these, Bacchus and the pelican, are faithful copies of plates in Whitney; and the device of Actaeon is presumably derived from the same source, although there is some modification of the design. There are signs, too, that the embroiderer found a model for some of the animals there; the swan is almost identical with that on the shield of the emblem of the poet, and the outline of the kite is very close to one of the 'Greedie Kytes' in another of Whitney's designs.[1]

Whitney's collection was also used by tapestry makers. In the four tapestries of the Seasons which were made for Hatfield House in 1611 or soon after, twenty-nine out of the hundred and seventy emblems which form the borders can be traced to Whitney's *Choice*. The centre of each tapestry is occupied by the figure of a god set against a background of landscape in which the various occupations appropriate to the season are represented. The emblematic medallions round the edges contain designs mainly of a heraldic kind but among those from Whitney are Occasion, Justice, Ulysses and the sirens, and the ass which thought that the worship paid to the shrine on its back was directed to itself. A few, such as the image of a winged cherub blowing a heart with bellows, or the hand from a cloud hammering a heart, the motto being *Cor contritum Gratium Deo*, belong to the convention of religious emblems which was later to flourish in England in the work of Quarles and Christopher Harvey.[2]

The links between emblem books and the decorative arts are also reflected in the hybrid form, the Masque. As Jonson said, Masques were 'Court Hieroglyphics'. The figures found in the emblem books are there dramatised and transplanted into a new setting.[3] Ripa was used extensively by Jonson as a source for his

[1] Whitney, *A Choice of Emblemes*. pp. 126 and 170.
[2] For a full account and pictures of these Tapestries, see an article by A. F. Kendrick, *Walpole Society Annual*. II. 1912–13. pp. 89–97.
[3] For an account of the Masque and the Impresa see Allardyce Nicoll, *Stuart Masques and the Renaissance Stage*. 1937. Chapter VI.

detailed stage directions. In *The Masque of Queens*, Good Fame is openly acknowledged to be the property of Ripa:

Here the Throne wherein they sate, being *Machina versatilis*, sodaynely chang'd: and in the Placē of it appeard *Fama Bona*, as she is describ'd, in Iconolog. di Cesare Ripa, attired in white, with white Wings, having a collar of Gold about her neck, and a heart hanging at it: which *Orus Apollo* in his Hieroglyp. interprets as the note of a good fame. In her right hand she bore a trumpet, in her left an olive branch, and for her state, it was as Virgil describes her, at the full, her feet on the Ground, and her head in the Clouds.[1]

And there are many others. Nor did Ripa influence Jonson only; his figures continued to appear as long as Masques were written. Carew in *Coelum Britannicum* 1634 represents Eternity in a modified form of Ripa's and Peacham's design:

His garment was long, of a light blue, wrought all over with stars of gold and bearing in his hand a serpent bent into a circle, with his tail in his mouth.

Another familiar figure in the same Masque is Occasion:

Tyche her head bald behind and one great lock before; wings at her shoulders, and in her hand a wheel.

This was not by any means her first appearance among the hieroglyphics of the Court; Robert White's *Masque of Cupid's Banishment*, 1617, had presented her in a rich garment embroidered with silver and a crimson mantle to compensate for her baldness.[2]

Emblems entered the masques in ways other than through personifications. The scene was often painted with small emblem-

---

[1] Ben Jonson, *Works*. Ed. Herford and Simpson. Vol. VII. 1941. p. 305. Cp. Ripa, op. cit. 1611. pp. 154-5: Fama Buona. Donna con una tromba nella mano dritta, & nella Sinistra con un ramo d'oliva, haverà al collo una collana d'oro, alla quale sia per pendente un cuore & haverà h'ali bianche a'gl'homeri.

La tromba significa il grido universale sparso per gl'orecchi de gl'huomini.

Il ramo d'oliva mostra la bontà della fama, e la sincerità dell' huomo famoso per opere illustri, pigliandosi sempre l'olivo, & il frutto suo in buona parte; . . .

Il cuore pendente al collo, significa, come narra Oro Apolline ne i suoi leroglifici, la fama d'un huomo da bene. . . .

[2] J. Nichols. Progresses of King James I. 1828. Vol. III. p. 285.

atic designs arranged in much the same fashion as they were in the engraved frontispieces of books. In Shirley's *The Triumph of Peace*, 1633, in which the characters are almost realistic except for their names and their clothes, there is a direction for the back-cloth which is to have in one of its smaller compartments 'a sharp-sighted eye' and in another 'a golden yoke', the hierogly-phics of Justice and Law. Sometimes the characters would bring emblems with them; the twelve Nymphs in *The Masque of Blackness* carried fans 'in one of which were inscribed their mixt names, in the other a mute hieroglyphic expressing their mixt qualities'. Ocyte and Kathare (swiftness and clear-ness) presented emblems of a pair of naked feet in a river, Notis (moist) and Psychrote (cold) 'a Salamander simple', Euphoris and Aglaia (fruitfulness and brightness) a golden tree laden with fruit. Ben Jonson explains that he preferred this method of symbolisation to that by means of Imprese 'as well for strangeness as relishing of antiquity, and more applying to that original doctrine of sculpture which the Egyptians are said first to have brought from the Aethiopians'. This is clearly the method of the emblem writers set out before the eye. The twelve nymphs, representing each a single idea, are grouped in pairs, and a picture is then evolved to represent their 'mixt qualities'.[1]

These connections of the emblem books with the various uses of rhetoric and of decoration are significant partly for what they suggest about the nature of the emblem books themselves, and partly for the light they throw upon the aims and methods of contemporary literature. In so far as they provided assistance for such a number of different activities and could be used to supply the needs of preachers or teachers or craftsmen, they cannot be regarded as belonging only to the sphere of literature. When they were read for themselves alone and not for any im-mediate practical purpose, or when they entered the drama or

[1] An analysis and interpretation of Jonson's symbolism is made by D. J. Gordon, 'The Imagery of Ben Jonson's The Masque of Blacknesse and The Masque of Beautie'. *Journal of the Warburg and Courtauld Institutes*. Vol. VI. 1943. pp. 122–41.

the narrative poem, they did not lose those extra-literary associations. There was in fact a very much closer relation between
literature and decoration and between literature and rhetoric in
the sixteenth century than has ever existed since; and the way in
which craftsmen used the emblem books to supplement the
pattern books provided for their particular trade points simultaneously to the literary nature of contemporary decoration and
to the decorative nature of contemporary literature. This fact can
be further emphasised if one considers which designs out of the
whole of Whitney's *Choice* before him a craftsman selected as the
most suitable. There are plenty of engravings in Elizabethan
emblem books which might well have had their place in *The
Needles Excellency*, plenty of formalised devices in Peacham which
the plasterworker could have copied and repeated as a pattern.
But it is not these, or not these alone, which are chosen. Subjects
seemingly so unpromising as Bacchus, Actaeon, Priam at the
altar are taken and transferred to walls, tapestries, clothes. If
decoration was so literary, it was almost inevitable that literature
itself should be closely allied with the content and technique of
the decorative arts. In the same way the rhetorical devices found
in the emblem books are imitated in poetry and prose.

This versatility accounts perhaps for the appeal of the emblem
books to the adult mind of the sixteenth century. It was not,
necessarily, a more childish age than the nineteenth, and yet when
the Victorians attempted to recapture the emblematic method
they were successful only when they wrote for children. At first
sight, the Victorian emblem book does not appear much unlike
its predecessor. It is instructive, it points a moral, it has pictures.
But it is much more elementary. The difference is that whereas
Peacham and Whitney made books out of what could be seen
all round them in other contexts, and what they made could be
restored to those contexts, the Victorian is drawing his material
only from the world of ideas. His book offers a collection of over-
simplified moral precepts; the books of Whitney and Peacham
are rooted in design. It remains, in fact, the great merit of the
Elizabethan emblem books that they could be set in such a variety of

contexts with so little alteration and that while a courtly Euphues was poring over one emblem book to find witty ideas with which to enliven his conversation, his wife was embroidering his coat from another. That factor could not be recaptured, and it was that which gave the Elizabethan emblem books their distinctive quality.

II

When the emblem form entered literature it brought with it all its rhetorical and decorative connotations. The links between the emblem books themselves and the literature of the later sixteenth and early seventeenth centuries are too numerous and too varied to make any comprehensive account of the relationship either possible or useful. Parallels between Shakespeare's *Pericles* and Paradin's emblems, or those between the design of the Waterman in Hardwick House and Fulke Greville's *Caelica* and Mr. By-Ends' ancestors [1] could be multiplied endlessly—indeed the form was so characteristic of its age that there are very few poets of the period in whose work the matter, if not the manner, of the emblem books cannot somewhere be traced. The material upon which they drew was never their peculiar prerogative; it was easily accessible and could equally well be drawn upon by others for other purposes. The manner was inherited from past traditions in allegory and found its way into poetry and prose quite independently of the specialised adaptations of it made by emblem writers. The form cannot, therefore, be regarded as one whose influence can be pinned down and precisely defined; nor should its importance be overstressed. Probably its greatest value for the Elizabethan poet or prose writer was a purely general one: emblems embodied and gave currency to certain conventions in allegory and imagery which were accepted without difficulty by readers and which could, therefore, be used as a natural part of their technique by poets concerned with much wider and more serious themes. Certainly emblems were useful in this way to dramatists. Shakespeare, Jonson, Chapman, Webster all found some place for them in their plays. Jonson in *Cynthia's Revels*

[1] See above, pp. 62 and 92.

99

uses the whole method satirically; Shakespeare in *As You Like It*
defines and criticises Jaques's sentimental mediocrity as a moralist
by the introduction of one of the stock images of the emblem
books. The First Lord describes how he came upon Jaques gazing
at a dying stag weeping into a stream—the picture he draws of the
scene can be paralleled in the engravings of Symeoni and Otho
Vaenius—and in answer to the Duke's enquiry:

> But what said Jaques?
> Did he not moralise this spectacle?

all the various applications which Jaques had given it are listed.
Point is given to the satire by the use of the technical word 'moralise' which directs the listeners' attention to the emblem writers
and their methods. Both Chapman and Webster also make it an
important element in their dramatic technique, and indeed often
include emblems for the rhetorical interest they had for the
audience rather than for any more precise dramatic purpose.
Flamineo's tale of the crocodile in *The White Devil*, and Chapman's elaborate images with their careful point by point comparisons with the object they describe, appear to be insertions for
their own sake. Webster can make very successful dramatic use
of the form at times. Vittoria's account of her dream of the yew
tree in the churchyard is emblematic in method, and is at the
same time an organic part of the play. The same is true of the
treatment of the emblem of the stag in the same play:

Monticelso	Here is an Embleme nephew pray peruse it:
	'Twas throwne in at your window.
Camillo	At my window?
	Here is a Stag my lord hath shed his hornes,
	And for the losse of them, the poore beast weepes—
	The word, *Inopem me copia fecit.*
Monticelso	That is,
	Plenty of hornes hath made hime poore of hornes.
Camillo	What should this meane?
Monticelso	Ill tell you, 'tis given out
	You are a cocould.[1]

[1] John Webster, *The White Devil*. II. 1. 319–26. *Works*. Ed. F. L. Lucas. 1929.
Vol. I. p. 130.

Yet, though examples of this kind could be multiplied, the emblem, even as used by dramatists like Chapman and Webster who rely upon it so much, was never more than an adjunct, one device among many. It could not be said to colour their whole technique. There is one Elizabethan poet, however, for whom an exception must be made—Spenser. The emblematic method is, in a greatly simplified way, Spenser's method, and the emblem books can be most profitably related to his poetry because the bearing they have upon it is central. This is true also of two later authors, George Herbert and Bunyan, but by the time they began to write the technique of the emblem had altered in certain ways and its influence upon them is of a rather different kind. It is Spenser who is the poet of the type of emblem that has so far been considered, the emblem which has such distinct and well-defined rhetorical and decorative associations.

An interest in the methods of the emblem writers is reflected throughout Spenser's poetry. His first published work, the anonymous 'Visions of Petrarch and du Bellay' in *A Theatre for Worldlings* has already been mentioned among the early appearances of the form in England,[1] and in his later poems Spenser continued on the path he had chosen then. The 'Visions' were revised and joined to a set of twelve original sonnets entitled ' Visions of the Worlds Vanitie ' which are further examples of the same type of poem. The theme of the world's vanity is presented in a series of concrete illustrations, each followed by an interpretation, showing how the greatest depends upon, or may be destroyed by, the least: the little fish called Remora can wreck a great ship, the cedar of Lebanon is brought low by 'a little wicked worm perceived of none', the crocodile needs the help of a little bird. All these examples are the familiar material of the emblem books, though Spenser may well have derived them from other sources. Taken separately each is an emblem, lacking, it is true, a picture but otherwise cast in the usual form of description followed by interpretation and moral; collectively they form a series of *exempla* for a single theme, and the whole set is concluded by a

---

[1] See above, p. 51.

sonnet commenting in general terms upon the insecurity of human achievement. 'The Ruines of Time' makes similar use of emblems to illustrate a single theme, but here the main part of the poem is concerned with the general treatment of the subject and the 'tragical pageants' are introduced at the end to exemplify the effects of mutability in human experience. Again the subjects can be traced to emblem books, and the method is undoubtedly emblematic.

A rather different manifestation of Spenser's interest in the form appears in *The Shepheardes Calender*. Here 'Emblems' are provided for the shepherds at the end of each Eclogue. These are not emblems in the same sense as the poems just mentioned; they are tags in Latin, Greek, or Italian, which sum up the moral of the whole Eclogue or the arguments of each of the shepherds. E.K., who interprets them in his Glosse, calls them Poesies; they are, in effect, what in an emblem proper was generally termed the Motto. Diggon's Emblem, for instance, at the end of the September Eclogue on the abuses in the church, is *Inopem me copia fecit*, which E.K. says is an emblem 'much used of the author'. It was also a motto much used by emblem writers, though Spenser here gives it his own interpretation and makes it the moral of Diggon's story of his downfall. Apart from this use of mottoes, *The Shepheardes Calender* is not particularly emblematic except when fables are introduced. The tale of the Oak and the Briar with its clearly expressed moral:

> Such was thend of this Ambitious brere,
> For scorning Eld.[1]

and accompanying mottoes in Italian appropriate to old Thenot and to Cuddie, the scorner of age, closely resembles Whitney's treatment of similar material in the *Choice*.

These examples suggest that Spenser had an interest in the emblem form at an early stage in his poetic development and show that he was experimenting with it then. They would, how-

[1] 'Februarye Eclogue', pp. 237–8. Spenser, *Works*. Ed. E. de Selincourt. p. 426. All quotations are made from this edition.

ever, have no particular significance if he had not made a fuller and more fruitful use of the method later on. For the 'Visions' are merely experiments, not even very successful experiments, and in *The Shepheardes Calender* he has adopted one element only of the make-up of the emblem book, and has used it for purposes of his own. There is some historical interest in the fact that a great poet shows himself conscious of the existence of the form and aware that it has some literary potentialities well before it had actually made its appearance in English literature; but what really matters is that Spenser afterwards made it an integral part of his poetry. These early experiments bore fruit later in his imagery and in his allegorical method. Furthermore, in all Spenser's poetry description is linked with decoration in a way that has already been hinted at in the discussion of the relations between emblem books and the decorative arts in the early part of this chapter. It is these three aspects of Spenser's poetry, its imagery, its allegorical method, and its decorative quality, which give his early use of emblematic material in the 'Visions' and *The Shepheardes Calender*, an importance that it would not otherwise possess.

Spenser's use of imagery is emblematic in the sense that the image and its significance are clearly distinguished from each other, and the likenesses are established point by point between them. These may be implicit rather than explicit, but there is no attempt at identification or fusion of the image with its object. Naturally such a use of imagery is marked by a preference for simile rather than metaphor; it is also largely visual. *The Faerie Queene* offers countless examples of these characteristics, and they are also present in the minor poems:

> So all the world, and all in it I hate,
> Because it changeth ever too and fro,
> And never standeth in one certaine state,
> But still unstedfast round about doth goe,
> Like a Mill wheele, in midst of miserie,
> Driven with streames of wretchednesse and woe,
> That dying lives, and living still does dye.[1]

[1] 'Daphnaida' 428–34. *Ibid.* p. 532.

The mill-wheel forms a picture and comparisons between it and
the world are indicated by the vocabulary of every line, though
the two are never identified. The most remarkable example of
emblematic imagery in Spenser's poetry, however, is his use of
the two swans in *Prothalamion*, for the whole poem is built round
them. The swan was often used by emblem writers as the symbol
of the poet: the sweetness of its dying note symbolised the
beauty of the poet's song, its whiteness was the badge of his
sincerity.[1] But in *Prothalamion* the swans symbolise marriage in
general, and the two brides for whose wedding the poem was
written in particular. They are never identified with the brides
but provide the means by which the marriage celebrations can
be allegorically presented. They appear floating beautifully and
majestically on the river, they are crowned with garlands by the
nymphs, the water is strewn with flowers, and the waterfowl
make a procession to follow them.

> At length they all to mery *London* came

where 'two gentle Knights of lovely face and feature' were wait-
ing for them, who

> forth pacing to the Rivers side,
> Received those two faire Brides, their Loves delight.

—the swans have become the brides, and the poem ends. There
is no elaborate series of comparisons by which the swans are
likened to the ladies but the image nevertheless is emblematic
from the beginning. In all the details of their presentation the
swans reflect the qualities and virtues of the brides. A picture is
made but it is not only a picture. Spenser's account of their first
appearance well illustrates the method he is using:

> With that, I saw two Swannes of goodly hewe,
> Come softly swimming downe along the Lee;
> Two fairer Birds I yet did never see:
> The snow which doth the top of *Pindus* strew,
> Did never whiter shew,

[1] e.g. Whitney, *A Choice of Emblemes*. p. 126. 'Insignia poetarum.'

Nor *Jove* himselfe when he a Swan would be
For love of *Leda*, whiter did appeare:
Yet *Leda* was they say as white as he,
Yet not so white as these, nor nothing neare;
So purely white they were,
That even the gentle streame, the which them bare,
Seem'd foule to them, and bad his billowes spare
To wet their silken feathers, least they might
Soyle their fayre plumes with water not so fayre,
And marre their beauties bright,
That shone as heavens light,
Against their Brydale day, which was not long:
Sweet *Themmes* runne softly, till I end my Song.[1]

If the only point of all this is to establish that the swans are white, the method seems unnecessarily laboured. But the word-play is emblematic not descriptive, and through it Spenser is defining the beauty and goodness of the two brides, not describing the appearance of the swans. The whiteness is the whiteness both of their purity and of their 'beauties bright': it has an ethical and aesthetic significance as well as a visual one.

The swans are emblematic. They are also decorative. In his treatment of the natural world Spenser was constantly reaching out towards the effects of embroidery and sculpture. He found a mode of expression in which formality appears spontaneous and artifice natural. The descriptions in *The Faerie Queene* are always of this kind:

And over him, art striving to compaire
    With nature, did an Arber greene dispred
    Framed of wanton Yvie, flouring faire,
    Through which the fragrant Eglantine did spred
    His pricking armes, entrayld with roses red,
    Which daintie odors round about them threw,
    And all within with flowres was garnished,
    That when myld *Zephyrus* amongst them blew,
Did breathe out bounteous smels, and painted colors shew.[2]

This is, of course, Art striving to compare with Nature, but it is

[1] *Prothalamion*. Stanza 3. Ed. cit. p. 601.
[2] *The Faerie Queene*. II. v. 29. p. 93.

Nature herself who leads the way. In the Garden of Adonis the trees of their 'owne inclination' make an arbour:

> Which knitting their rancke braunches part to part,
> With wanton yvie twyne entrayld athwart,
> And Eglantine, and Caprifole emong,
> Fashioned above within their inmost part.[1]

or there is an arboret 'with painted blossoms dressed', a porch 'archt overhead with an embracing vine', trees 'with leaves apparelled And deckt with blossoms white and red'. Everywhere Nature fulfils the canons of art; plants are twined and woven 'in wreathings intricate', plains are 'mantled with green', mountains 'high-reared', seas 'heaped'; she is indeed 'the art of God.'

This kind of perception is not, of course, confined to Spenser. The associations with embroidery may belong only to his poetry, but its patterned outline is shared by all Elizabethan description. The same quality is reflected in the work of Drayton. In *Poly-Olbion* the motion of a river winding its way through the painted fields and curled groves is so described as to create the effect of ornament as well as of progression:

> *Ouze*, having *Ouleney* past, as shee were waxed mad,
> From her first stayder course immediatly doth gad;
> And in Meandred Gyres doth whirle herselfe about,
> That, this way, here, and there, backe, forward, in, and out,
> And like a wanton Girle, oft doubling in her gate,
> In Labyrinth-like turnes, and twinings intricate,
> Through those rich fields doth runne, till lastly in her pride,
> The Shires Hospitious towne, shee in her course divide,
> Where shee her spacious breast in glorious bredth displayes;
> And varying her cleere forme a thousand sundry wayes,
> Streakes through the verdant Meads. . . . [2]

The movement is basically the same as that of Spenser's trees when they make an arbour; always there is the effect of making a pattern, of seeing the natural object in a frame, as part of a

---

[1] *The Faerie Queene.* III. vi. 44. p. 175.
[2] Michael Drayton, *PolyOlbion.* Song XXII. ll. 17–27. *Works.* vol. IV. Ed. J. W. Hebel. Oxford. 1933.

design. Indeed Spenser in *The Faerie Queene* has a philosophical discussion of the purpose and process of growth in the world which suggests the character of the general ideas underlying this way of looking at the activity of nature. When Mutability demands sovereignty over all created things on the ground that all are subject to change, Nature counters her claim with the argument that although

> all things stedfastnes doe hate
> And changed be: yet being rightly wayd
> They are not changed from their first estate;
> But by their change their being doe dilate:
> And turning to themselves at length againe,
> Doe worke their own perfection so by fate:
> Then over them Change doth not rule and raigne;
> But they raigne over change, and doe their states maintaine.[1]

This is an impressive answer, and it effectually silences Mutability, who is 'put down and whist', while Jove is 'confirmed in his imperial see'. Part of its impressiveness derives from precisely this view of the patterned activity of natural things, and depends upon the force of the word 'dilate'. Nature as the art of God is always achieving the effects of art. Movement and growth are thought of as processes which have for their first end not self-fulfilment but the achievement of design, and are conceived less in terms of evolution than of pattern. It is this principle which is set up against Mutability and her pageant of supporters, and defeats them the more completely because it exists not in spite of them but to include them. It is this principle too, which underlies much Elizabethan poetry. Ideas culminate in images and personifications which embody a whole process of thought, rather than in a conclusion which stands as the last step in an argument; indeed the whole structure of Elizabethan lyric poetry is worked out so as to 'dilate' a theme rather than develop it. And in the same way, in description, moving objects are made to display themselves at the same time as they progress, and they convey not only the process of movement but its quality.

[1] *The Faerie Queene.* VII. vii. 58. p. 406.

One of the most characteristic expressions of this habit of thinking is heraldry. An organic part of the social life of the Elizabethans, it was also an organic part of their poetry. Battles in *The Faerie Queene* are always heraldic, and are curiously static despite their apparent fury. A duel between two knights takes place not in consecutive action but in a series of positions. The opposing sides are stiffly balanced and blow is given for blow in formal alternation:

> With that they gan their shivering speares to shake
> And deadly points at eithers breast to bend.[1]

The imagery perpetually suggests two supporters for a shield. Knights fight like 'two Mastiffs' or like 'a Beare and Tyger'; Guyon meets Pyrochles

> Like as a Lyon, whose imperiall powre
> A prowde rebellious Unicorne defies.[2]

Even the wounds are heraldic:

> Wyde was the wound, and a large lukewarme flood,
> Red as the Rose, thence gushed grievously.[3]

However much the content appears to be concerned with action, the treatment, quite apart from the specific heraldic vocabulary, always retains something of the fixed unmoving quality of a heraldic image. Once more movement is framed and formalised. The whole character of this kind of description is perhaps best summed up in Drayton's comment upon a tapestry in *Mortimeriados*. Here Isabella and Mortimer are engaged in the truly Elizabethan occupation of 'devising upon the pictures' contained in a room in Nottingham Castle. Among the rest there is

> A counterpoynt of Tyssue, rarely wrought,
> Like to *Arachnes* web, of the Gods rape,
> Which with his lifes strange history is wrought,
> The very manner of his hard escape,
> From poynt to poynt, each thing in perfect shape,

[1] *The Faerie Queene.* IV. ii. 14. p. 221.   [2] Ibid. II. v. 10. p. 91.
[3] Ibid. II. viii. 39. p. 110.

16

O F simple looke , with countenance demure ,
  In golden coate , lo heere *DECEITE* doth ſtand ,
With eies to heauen vpcaſt, as he were pure ,
Or neuer yet , in knaü:ry had a hand ,
  Whoſe nether partes , reſemble to our ſight,
  The figure of a fearefull Serpent right.

And by his ſide , a Panther cloſe you ſee ,
Who when he cannot eaſily catch his pray ,
Doth hide his head, and face , with either knee ,
And ſhew his back , with ſpots beſpeckled gay
  To other Beaſtes : which while they gaze vpon ,
  Are vnawares , ſurprized every one .

Simulatores et callidi provocant Iram Dei
Neque clamabunt cum vincti fuerint , morietur in tempeſtate anima
corum , et vita eorum inter effœminatos .

Abhominatio Domino eſt omnis illuſor .

From Henry Peacham: *Minerva Britanna 1612*

As made the gazers thinke it there was done,
And yet time stayd in which it was begun.[1]

In this general relationship between Elizabethan poetry and the decorative arts the emblem books have their place, for they are one of the means by which connections recognised through critical study can be explicitly established.

Finally, Spenser's general methods of allegory may be considered in relation to the emblem method. The detailed similarities between his personified figures and those of Peacham have already been pointed out; but there is also a likeness in Spenser's whole manner of presentation and whole treatment of allegory which goes beyond sources and cross-references. Certainly a number of figures in *The Faerie Queene* such as Occasion and the Seven Deadly Sins had appeared previously in Alciati or in other emblem books. Certainly, too, Peacham derived figures for his books from Spenser, but these parallels are less important than the general allegorical principles which Spenser shares with the emblem writers. The figures in *The Faerie Queene*, like those of Peacham and Whitney, all have their qualities externalised: the Prince meeting Ignaro 'guessed his nature by his countenance', and Dissimulation's character is made apparent in exactly the same phrase. Guyon, finding a lady in distress, says 'Thou

the image art
Of ruefull pitie, and impatient smart'.[2]

Anamnestes and Eumnestes earned their names 'by their properties', and Munera was so called, 'her name agreeing with her deeds'. They are all recognisable by their outward appearance, and Spenser's way of describing that appearance is the way of the emblematist. He presents them through emblematic detail until their meaning is clear. Often they enter carrying some significant object in their hands as a symbol of their functions. Prays-desire has a poplar branch, Excesse a golden cup, Grief carries a pair of

[1] Michael Drayton, 'Mortimeriados'. 1596. ll. 2388-94. *Works*. Vol. I. Ed. J. W. Hebel. Oxford. 1931.
[2] *The Faerie Queene*. II. i. 44. p. 74.

pincers, Murder a bloody knife, Displeasure 'an angry wasp in a vial', just as in *Minerva Britanna* Temperance bears her bit and bridle, Repentance her fish, and Fame her trumpet. Sometimes the figures are summed up in one feature, as, for instance, the Porter at the gate of the Temple of Venus, who is the classical Janus given an ethical twist:

> His name was *Doubt*, that had a double face,
> Th' one forward looking, th' other backeward bent.[1]

Others are longer and more elaborate, but the method remains the same. Envy and Detraction, Occasion, Ignaro, Slander, Ate, are all set forth in a catalogue of significant details; they resemble the figures which appear in the long allegorical scenes, in the House of Pride, the Cave of Mammon or the Masque of Busyrane, for whom names and a single adjective are enough, and merely accumulate more external characteristics by which to be identified. They are 'to each unlike, yet all made in one mould'.

The mould was the presentation of the human being as an expression of an abstract quality. Unlike Bunyan, Spenser is not generally concerned to describe the doubting man or the envious woman but Doubt itself and Envy itself. He is more interested in the quality than in the character. There are exceptions, notably the heroes of each book who represent virtue in action and in so doing take into their own persons the virtue they represent. They themselves are human beings, but the world in which they move is peopled by figures of a different kind. With the Red Cross Knight goes Una, his counterpart in more abstract terms, with Guyon, the Palmer, with Artegall, Talus; they meet Envy and Doubt, Occasion, Fury and Slander. The difference between the two types is pointed out by Alma when Guyon attempts to speak to one of her maidens:

> Straunge was her tyre, and all her garment blew,
> Close round about her tuckt with many a plight:
> Upon her fist the bird, which shonneth vew,
> And keeps in coverts close from living wight,
> Did sit, as yet ashamd, how rude *Pan* did her dight.

[1] *The Faerie Queene.* IV. x. 12. p. 261.

When addressed she is silent and hangs down her head. Guyon, child of his age, ought to have deduced what she stood for from her symbolic blue dress and her bird, but Alma has to explain:

> She is the fountaine of your modestee;
> You shamefast are, but *Shamefastnesse* it selfe is shee.[1]

She is not merely a bashful woman, but the idea of bashfulness. The person is absorbed into the attribute, and is only incidentally interesting as a person. Such is the nature of the majority of the characters in *The Faerie Queene*, and as such they must weaken the persuasiveness of the allegory for all except the most philosophically-minded of readers. Bunyan's method, by which an abstract quality is always seen as a part of human nature and never merely as an idea, is without question the more successful.

Even when Spenser presents a character first as a human being and only secondly as an abstraction, he will abandon it and transform it into a personification. In the story of Malbecco and Hellenore such a transformation takes place. Malbecco at the beginning is a man, a jealous husband 'old and withered like hay', blind in one eye, avaricious and suspicious, who keeps his wife Hellenore locked up in a castle. The scene in which Paridell, the knight who has succeeded in gaining entrance to the castle, flirts with Hellenore during supper from his advantageous position on Malbecco's blind side, is reminiscent of a fabliau in its realistic treatment. Hellenore escapes with her lover, Malbecco pursues her and eventually finds her, now deserted by Paridell, living with the satyrs. Preferring even this to the 'hard restraint and jealous fears' of his company, she will not return to him, and he is attacked by the satyrs, flees from them, and finally reaches a cave under an overhanging rock:

> Into the same he creepes, and thenceforth there
> Resolv'd to build his balefull mansion,
> In drery darkenesse, and continuall feare
> Of that rockes fall, which ever and anon
> Threates with huge ruine him to fall upon,

[1] Ibid. II. ix. 40, 43. p. 116.

That he dare never sleepe, but that one eye
Still ope he keepes for that occasion;
Ne ever rests he in tranquillity,
The roring billowes beat his bowre so boystrously.

Ne ever is he wont on ought to feed,
But toades and frogs, his pasture poysonous,
Which in his cold complexion do breed
A filthy bloud, or humour rancorous,
Matter of doubt and dread suspitious,
That doth with curelesse care consume the hart,
Corrupts the stomacke with gall vitious,
Croscuts the liver with internall smart,
And doth transfixe the soule with deathes eternall dart.

Yet can he never dye, but dying lives,
And doth himselfe with sorrow new sustaine,
That death and life attonce unto him gives.
And painefull pleasure turnes to pleasing paine.
There dwels he ever, miserable swaine,
Hatefull both to him selfe, and every wight;
Where he through privy griefe, and horrour vaine,
Is woxen so deform'd, that he has quight
Forgot he was a man, and *Gealosie* is hight.[1]

He has become the type of figure who might now easily inhabit the Cave of Mammon or join the throng of abstractions which crowded after the procession in the House of Busyrane. The single eye and the suspicious temperament which once characterised him as a man are seen now as symbols of Jealousy—emblematic of watchfulness and melancholy. He bears the same relation to his former self as did Shamefastness to Guyon: he has become an abstract idea.

That Spenser could make such a transformation at all is in itself significant. If he can move from one plane of allegory to another in the presentation of a single figure, it is hardly surprising to find similar changes of method in *The Faerie Queene* as a whole. Recently there have been attempts to disintegrate the poem; the different allegorical methods have been attributed to

[1] *The Faerie Queene.* III. x. 58–60. pp. 199–200.

different dates of composition, and the shifts from one type of presentation to another interpreted as changes of plan.[1] There is much to encourage this point of view. *The Faerie Queene* was composed over a long period of time, and at best Spenser's strength as a poet cannot be said to lie in his powers of construction. He had a preference for diversity: in *The Shepheardes Calender* he chose to put together a very odd assortment of material, in *Mother Hubbard's Tale* he complicates the satire and weakens the force of the poem as a whole by shifting his ground three times. But *The Faerie Queene* is a deliberate attempt to combine different types of allegory, not an accidental one. It lacks unity only because it is incomplete, not because it is varied. In the emblem books it is possible to see a number of different kinds of allegory in simplified forms. Whitney's and Peacham's anthologies include anecdotes, parables and fables, personifications, objects treated symbolically; all are equally capable of moralisation. A reader familiar with the *Choice of Emblems* would be prepared to adjust himself to the extraordinary transformation of Hellenore's husband; he has only to turn over the page from one mode of allegory, that known as *Jocosum*, the moralised anecdote, to another, the personification. And Spenser moves easily among the different kinds; he is allegorising in the manner of his age.

[1] See Janet Spens, *Spenser's Faerie Queene.* 1934. and Josephine Waters Bennett, *The Evolution of 'The Faerie Queene'.* Chicago, 1942.

Chapter 5

QUARLES AND HIS FOLLOWERS

I

THE emblem books of the kind popularised in England by Francis Quarles and those who wrote like him, Christopher Harvey, John Hall and Edmund Arwaker, require a method of approach more specifically literary than that made to their predecessors. They were using a new set of conventions and they were using them in a new way. Links with the decorative arts are no longer to be found; instead there is much greater concentration upon the poems accompanying the pictures, and for the first time the emblem book begins to lay claim to some serious consideration of its merits as literature. Quarles and Christopher Harvey especially saw in their material the potentialities of a real poetic form; they were not content simply to describe and interpret the the picture before them, but attempted also to base varieties of poetic effect upon it. The poems they produced were lyrical, or dramatic, or narrative, instead of merely didactic. They changed their metre and their stanza form to suit each new subject. In fact, they set out to be poets and must be estimated as such.

In one sense Quarles succeeded. His work was popular. Over two thousand copies of his *Emblemes* and *Hieroglyphikes of the Life of Man* were printed for the first combined edition in 1639 and another three thousand at least were issued in the subsequent year.[1] Edition followed edition through the seventeenth century and into the early part of the eighteenth; and although there were no reprints between 1736 and 1777 the changes in literary taste never banished Quarles's name and effected only a temporary obscurity of his work. Johnson ignored him, Pope disparaged him, and Walpole remarked that Milton had had to wait until the world

[1] G. S. Haight, 'The Publication of Quarles's Emblems'. *The Library*. Vol. XV. 1934–5. pp. 97–109.

17

*Oh that my wayes were Directed
to keepe thy Statutes. Ps-119-5-*
W. Simpson Sculp.

From Francis Quarles: *Emblemes 1635*

had done admiring him;[1] but the world, although it ceased to have any use for emblem books as such, was never quite done with its admiration for Quarles. He escaped the oblivion into which the rest fell because his emblems were valued more highly as poetry than the others were. Indeed, when towards the end of the eighteenth century a critic in *The Gentleman's Magazine* took it upon himself to rehabilitate Quarles, whose memory, he said, had 'hitherto been almost totally neglected, or when called to remembrance solely for the sake of being associated with Black-more or some such worthy, as a synonymous and cant term for a blockhead',[2] it was neither the religious nor the emblematic aspect of the work which interested him, but the versification. For this he had the highest praise. The themes were 'too hallowed for the hands of a poet', in fact 'the grand defect of Quarles is his subject', but for all that the book 'bears many incontestable proofs that Quarles was a great master of versification. In these Emblems we find almost every species of metre the English Language affords; and however deficient the meaning, the ear at least has seldom reason to be offended.'[3] This opinion would hardly be endorsed to-day, for Quarles's poetry, full of variety as it is from the purely metrical point of view, has very little rhythmical scope, and the ear, if not offended, is certainly wearied by the monotony of the obvious and inevitable, but it does at least indicate where the interest of his work must lie. Christopher Harvey is also to be judged as a poet, though his emblems have not the same merits nor did they ever achieve the same popularity as Quarles's.

There enters then into the emblem books of this new type a literary factor which had not before been present. At the same

[1] Letter to George Montagu. Aug. 25, 1757. *The Letters of Horace Walpole.* Ed. P. Cunningham, 1891. Vol. III. p. 99.

[2] Pope's couplet was evidently not easily forgotten:

> The Hero William, and the Martyr Charles,
> One knighted Blackmore, and one pensioned Quarles.

'The First Epistle of the Second Book of Horace Imitated'. ll. 586-7. *The Poems of Alexander Pope.* Vol. IV. Ed. John Butt. 1939. p. 227. Pope's other tribute to Quarles is quoted below, p. 131.

[3] *The Gentleman's Magazine.* Vol. 56. ii. 1786. p. 666 and p. 926.

time a wholly new field of material was discovered. The type of
emblem which Quarles adopted was entirely different from that
hitherto known in England. The nearest approach to it had been
the polyglot edition of the *Amorum Emblemata* of a Dutch painter
Otto Vaenius or Otto Van Veen, whose work has already been
mentioned in connection with the emblems of Philip Ayres.[1]
This book was printed first in 1608 in a number of different
languages, the version intended for English readers being in Latin,
Italian and English. The emblems, engraved in ovals by Cornelius
Boel, represent the adventures of Cupid; sometimes alone, sometimes accompanied by a host of fellow Cupids. He is shown
playing blind man's buff, plucking roses from a thorny bush,
shooting at the human heart, watching a bear lick its cub into
shape. Such emblems belong to a distinct literary convention
which found its chief exponents in Holland in Daniel Heinsius and
Vaenius. It appears in England at the end of the seventeenth
century in the *Emblemata Amatoria* of Ayres. It is not in its secular
form, however, that it made any deep impression upon English
emblem writers, but in its adaptation for religious ends. By a
simple transference the whole idiom was absorbed into a devotional framework: Cupid became the Infant Jesus or Divine Love
seeking the human soul, personified in Anima a young maiden.
The necessary adjustments were so slight that Vaenius easily transformed his *Amorum Emblemata* into *Amoris Divini Emblemata*.[2]
Numbers of works of this kind were published under the direction
of the Jesuits who saw in them the potentialities of an educational
method. Their own great emblem book, the *Imago Primi Saeculi
Societatis Jesu*, celebrating the first hundred years of the Society's
history, which was published by Plantin in 1640, gave further
sanction and stimulus to the already widespread publication of
devotional emblem books for Catholics.[3]

[1] See above, p. 45.
[2] The whole genre is discussed at length by Mario Praz. Op. cit. Chapter III,
and is related by him to the Ovidian conceit. He traces the transference of
secular imagery to religious uses in Vaenius.
[3] The book represents the Society in five different phases of its activity,
nascens, crescens, agens, patens and *honorata*, and each section contains prose,

To this new fashion Quarles turned his attention. It is now known that his *Emblemes* (later to be so enthusiastically admired for their religious teaching by eighteenth century evangelical ministers) were derived from two of the books sponsored by the Jesuits—Herman Hugo's *Pia Desideria* published in 1624 and the anonymous *Typus Mundi*, 1627.[1] Both these works have for their theme the search of the human soul for holiness. The plates of *Pia Desideria* are mainly representations of the adventures of Anima and the Infant Jesus: they show Divine Love making his creatures of clay while Anima looks on and wonders, Divine Love sitting in judgment while Justice brings the guilty human soul before him, Divine Love stretching out a rescuing arm to Anima who is shipwrecked and almost lost in the stormy waters. Those from *Typus Mundi* have greater variety and include such scenes as the temptation of Eve, or the triumph of the Devil who is enthroned at the top of the world while below him one harpy with shears clips the wings of Faith and another, 'double fraud', symbolised by a woman with two faces, drives Justice from the earth. These two sets of plates were re-engraved with a few minor alterations and provided the content of Quarles's book. The thefts were unacknowledged, but one of them did not pass unnoticed in his own day, for in 1686 a clergyman, Edmund Arwaker, made a new translation of *Pia Desideria* because, he said, 'Mr. Quarles only borrowed his Emblems to prefix them to much inferiour sense'.[2] In the main Quarles's debt to his sources was pictorial.

[1] The first, *Pia Desideria Emblematis Elegiis et Affectibus SS Patrum illustrata*. By Herman Hugo, S. J. Antwerp. 1624. was the source of Books III–V of the *Emblemes*. Books I and II derive from *Typus Mundi in quo eius calamitates et pericula nec non divini, humanique amoris antipathia, emblematice proponuntur a RR. C.S.I.A.* Antwerp. 1627. (Rhetoribus Collegii Societatis Iesu Antwerpiae). Professor Praz and Mr. G. S. Haight are responsible, each independently, for establishing Quarles's debt to *Typus Mundi*.

[2] *Pia Desideria: or Divine Addresses*. London. 1686. Quarles himself was the object of piracy of a similar kind when twenty-two of the engravings of the

poems, orations and emblems. These last are surrounded by elaborate baroque scroll-work and are finely engraved. Although not concerned with the adventures of the two holy children, these emblems show the importance which the Jesuits attached to the method in general.

Such likenesses as exist between his verse and the Latin of the
originals are chiefly limited to the inevitable parallels which must
arise from the use of identical engravings and mottoes. Occasionally he translates closely: the opening lines of Emblem II, Book V,
for instance, are plainly derived from Hugo's:

> Scire cupis, mea lux, quibus intus amoribus urar?
> Quantaque flamma tui pectora nostra coquat?

> How shall my tongue express that hallow'd fire
> Which heav'n has kindled in my ravisht heart!

The first emblem in the same book owes its rhetorical structure to
a similar effect in the original. On the whole, however, Arwaker
was right in his claim that Quarles was not to be regarded as a
translator. His debt to the Jesuits was a large one since their books
gave him the material he needed, but the use to which he put it
was his own.[1]

Quarles's work occupies an important place in the history of the
emblem convention in England, for it introduced both new
themes and a new method of allegorising them. Whitney and the

---

[1] The whole question of Quarles's sources has been investigated by
G. S. Haight, 'The Sources of Quarles's Emblems.' *The Library*. Vol. XVI.
1936. pp. 188–209. He has established that all but 10 of the 79 emblems originate
in the two Jesuit books and he discusses the modifications of the Invocation
and of Plate 6 in Book V, in both of which the topography is altered to suit
Quarles's own circumstances. Roxwell, where Quarles lived, Finchingfield, the
home of Benlowes, and Hilgay, that of Phineas Fletcher, are all marked out
together upon the globe in the emblem V. 6. The *Emblemes* were dedicated
to Benlowes, and Mr. Haight concludes that it was from these two that the
suggestion that Quarles should illustrate the Jesuit engravings first came. The
changes in other plates are discussed at length and they seem to have been
made mainly for the purpose of adapting them to the poems and of avoiding
inconsistencies between the free versions which Quarles had made and the
pictures of the original. Small figures are introduced to illustrate particular
lines and occasionally a fundamental change takes place, as in I. 9. where the
new figure of Fortune attempts to influence the motion of the rocking globe
upon which Cupid and Pluto are poised. For changes in another plate (IV. 6.)
Mr. Haight tentatively suggests a political significance.

Emblemes were used as illustrations to an English version of Juan de Castaniza's
The Christian Pilgrime in his Spiritual Conflict and Conquest, published in Paris.
1652.

Elizabethan emblem writers had found the content of their books in what was already well known and easily accessible to their readers; they used fables from Aesop, natural history from Pliny, anecdotes drawn from the general store of classical legend. Quarles, on the other hand, is offering something unfamiliar, new and curious. In his presentation of the adventures of Amor and Anima he is no longer treating subjects that are matters of universal knowledge, nor has his material the same objective nature as that of the earlier emblem books. His symbols represent the individual experience of the human soul in its search for sanctity, and their significance is psychological. Amor and Anima between them embody the subjects of religious contemplation, and the poems accompanying the emblems both explain the symbolism and explore the states of mind it suggests. In Plate 17, for example, Anima, dressed like a pilgrim, picks her way with difficulty through the maze which symbolises the world. Here is the human soul on its way to the celestial city, and the poem is a lament, put into the mouth of the pilgrim, on the difficulties and dangers of the journey. In another emblem the subject is the aspiration of the human soul—Anima, chained to the world, is attempting to leap up to her God—in a third it is the bondage of the soul and Anima, imprisoned within a skeleton, laments 'Who shall deliver me from the body of this death?' In this fashion Quarles objectifies and allegorises religious themes. His pictures and their accompanying poems attempt to present and define ideas which are personal and psychological.

Naturally the allegorical method must change with the material. The whole is still emblematic in that the ideas find literal expression in the pictures: Anima, contemplating the body of this death, is seen actually imprisoned in the skeleton; she wishes to flee away from the world and her arms are transformed into the wings of a dove; she thinks of the brevity of human life and an hour glass and sundial are set before her. But the singleness and simplicity of the older emblems has been replaced by an elaborate symbolical composition in which every detail has some special significance and in which no one element is sufficient in itself. The engravings are made up of a number of emblematic figures taking part in a scene which is itself allegorical. In the plate opposite, for example, a game of bowls is in progress. The Devil is urging on the two gamesters, Cupid and Mammon, who are competing for a fool's cap proffered by Fortune. The meaning of the episode is explained in the lines:

> The world's the Jack; the Gamsters that contend,
> Are *Cupid, Mammon.* That juditious Friend,
> That gives the ground, is *Sathan*; and the Boules
> Are sinfull Thoughts: The Prize, a Crowne for Fooles.
> Who breathes that boules not? what bold tongue can say
> Without a blush, he has not bould to day?
> It is the Trade of man; And ev'ry Sinner
> Has plaid his Rubbers; Every Soule's a winner.[1]

Personifications are seen in action, and their behaviour can be interpreted allegorically. In this particular plate one, at least, of the figures is familiar. Fortune, or Occasion, who is to reward the players, was a favourite *motif* of the earlier emblem books. By Whitney she was pictured standing upon a wheel, holding a razor in one hand, 'by which she armies can divide', and a flying scarf in the other. Her feet were winged and her head bald except for a long strand of hair in front—for Occasion slips by and must be seized instantly or she will escape. Represented like this, she had been interesting enough in herself and required no other excuse for her presence; it was she, and the idea she embodied, that formed the subject of the emblem.[2] In Quarles her appearance is much the same, she has all the recognisable features, the wheel, the forelock, the scarf, but she has become only one element in a composite picture. A fool's cap relevant only to this particular occasion is substituted for her emblematic razor, and the subject of the emblem is not Fortune alone but a whole episode of which she is a contributory part. In the same way in other emblems the older personified figures are used to build up an allegorical scene:

---

[1] *Emblemes.* I. 10. The text of the quotations is from the first edition. 1635.
[2] Whitney. Op. cit. p. 181. For a reproduction of the plate see above, p. 18. An account of the origin and history of the concept of Occasion is given by E. Panofsky, *Studies in Iconology.* New York. 1939. pp. 71–2.

18

From Francis Quarles: *Emblemes 1635*

Fraud expels Justice from the earth, Night and Day turn away from the sighing soul.

Quarles's emblems are, in fact, much more deeply concerned with action. They adopt the single personified figure or the single emblematic object of the earlier emblem books only to make them part of an episode symbolising some experience of the soul. Paradin's thunderbolt, for instance, once in itself 'a sweet Moral symbol', now becomes a weapon in the hands of the enraged Amor as he threatens a terrified Anima:

> O whither shall I flee? what path untrod
> Shall I seeke out, to scape the flaming rod
> Of my offended, of my angry God? [1]

Quarles also uses isolated single images as a means of reinforcing the point of the main action. In one emblem Anima is holding a mariner's compass towards Amor, the subject of the poem being a detailed comparison between the 'arctic needle' and the human soul upon the text *I am my beloved's and his desire is towards me*. In the background the theme is repeated in the engraving of the sunflower turning towards its sun. Another plate shows the human soul trapped in the snare of death as it flees from temptation and sin. A spider sitting in her web in one corner of the picture can hardly be supposed to be taking any part in the pursuit, but her presence gives further point to Quarles's moralising on the subject of snares:

> A world of dangers, and a world of snares:
> The close Pursuers busie hands do plant
> Snares in thy substance; Snares attend thy want;
> Snares in thy credit; Snares in thy disgrace;
> Snares in thy high estate; Snares in thy base;
> Snares tuck thy bed; and Snares arround thy boord;
> Snares watch thy thoughts; and Snares attache thy word;
> Snares in thy quiet; Snares in thy commotion;
> Snares in thy diet; Snares in thy devotion;
> Snares lurk in thy resolves; Snares, in thy doubt;
> Snares lie within thy heart, and Snares, without;
> Snares are above thy head, and Snares, beneath:
> Snares in thy sicknesse; Snares are in thy death. [2]

[1] *Emblemes*. III. 12.   [2] Ibid. III. 9.

The point of the main emblem again lies in the presentation of a scene, and the single image of the spider underlines its meaning.

Quarles's emblems were not confined to the book that bears their name. Their success induced him to invent 'a second service', the *Hieroglyphikes of the Life of Man* which appeared three years later. Its publication coincided with that of another work on precisely the sames lines; Robert Farlie's *Lychnocausia or Lights Morall Emblems*, but each seems to have been wholly independent of the other. Both books have the same central theme, the comparison of man's life with that of a burning candle. Quarles confines himself solely to that single conception; the candle, set in an urn, stands prominently in the centre of each picture, and other contributory themes are grouped round it. The first plate represents it unlit, the accompanying motto being, *Sine Lumine Inane*. The poem elaborates the motto:

> The Lamp of nature lends
> But a false light, and lights to her owne ends.
> These be the wayes to Heav'n; These paths require
> A light that springs from that diviner fire,
> Whose humane soule-enlightening sunbeames dart
> Through the bright Crannies of th' immortall part.[1]

The subsequent plates represent the gift of light to the candle when a hand holding a flame stretches out from the clouds, the dangers that beset the soul, the blasts of sorrow which puff at it, and the doctor who trims the flame almost to extinction. Time and Death argue over their prey (see the plate in the frontispiece to this book); the accompanying poem is in the form of a dialogue:

> *Time* Behold the frailty of this slender snuffe;
>   Alas, it hath not long to last:
> Without the helpe of either Thiefe, or puffe,
>   Her weakness knowes the way to wast:
> Nature hath made her Substance apt enough
>   To spend it selfe, and spend too fast:
>   It needs the help of none,
>   That is so prone
>   To lavish out, untoucht; and languish all alone.

[1] *Hieroglyphikes.* 1638. Hieroglyphike I. p. 3.

Death Time, hold thy peace, and shake thy slow pac'd Sand;
    Thy idle Minits make no way:
Thy glasse exceeds her how'r, or else does stand,
    I can not hold; I can not stay;
Surcease thy pleading, and enlarge my hand
    I surfet with too long delay:
      This brisk, this boldfac'd light
      Does burn too bright;
Darkness adornes my throne; my day is darkest night.[1]

The last seven emblems embody the seven Ages of Man: the
candle shortens inch by inch, and the sign of the Zodiac above it
indicates the passage of the years symbolised in the different
seasons. Plate 20 (p. 132) represents man at twenty. The ground
is strewn with flowers to emphasise that

    Youths now disclosing Bud peeps out, and showes
      Her *Aprill* head;
      And, from her grass greene bed,
    Her virgin Primerose early blowes.

The youth on the horse at the back is hunting:

    His downie Cheek growes proud, and now disdaines
      The Tutors hand;
      He glories to command
    The proud neckt Steed with prouder Reynes:
The strong breath'd Horne must now salute his eare,
With the glad downefall of the falling Deare.

The hunting scene might well be regarded simply as a restate-
ment in realistic unsymbolical terms of the moral implied by the
gradual shortening of the candle, but it is in itself emblematic:
blossoms fall, the horse gallops unheeded away. The last verse
draws all the images together into relation with the original
candle theme:

    Proud Blossom, use thy Time; Times headstrong Horse
      Will post away;
      Trust not the foll'wing day,
      For ev'ry day brings forth a worse:
    Take Time at best; Beleeve't, thy daies will fall
From good, to bad; From bad, to worst of all.[2]

[1] Ibid. VI. p. 23.   [2] Ibid. X. p. 39.

Farlie's *Lychnocausia* shares the same theme but offers a quite uncoordinated treatment of it. The book consists of fifty-eight emblems on the subject of light. Its cuts are unusually primitive and its poems very undistinguished, but it has some interest as a statement in quite elementary terms of the symbolism of darkness and light which so much preoccupied seventeenth century minds. The light is distinguished from the candle in which it is lodged just as is the soul from the body; the light of the candle is measured beside the light of God and is seen to be a fraction of the Divine Light; light is compared with darkness both as a setting for, and as a symbol of, the actions of men:

> For men in day time maskt with vizards goe
> Of truth and faith making an outward show,
> But when they can nights secret silence find;
> Before the lamp they do unmaske their mind.
> Happy is he whom sun and lamp sees one,
> Whose honest still though witness there be none.[1]

The reiterated theme of Sir Thomas Browne that, were it not for the darkness, 'the greatest part of the creation had been left unseen and the stars as invisible as on the fourth day when they were created or there was not an eye to behold them', finds expression here in:

> No glory could I shew wer't not the night
> If sable clouds did mantle in heavens light . . .
> The more nights fogge doth maske the spangled spheare
> The more in darkness doth my Light appeare.[2]

In another poem, light is the 'Aeterni lux verbi', and the poem ends with an exhortation to the priests, to whom,

> the word of light
> Is trust, advance your torches in the sight
> Of mortals, show them who in darknesse dwell
> The narrow way that leads to Heaven, from Hell.[3]

Candles do not provide the only symbols; lights of other kinds have their place too, though they occur more rarely. 'Hero's

---

[1] *Lychnocausia*. Emblem 5.   [2] Ibid. Emblem 23.   [3] Ibid. Emblem 6.

19

From Robert Farlie: *Lychnocausia 1638*

bright lampe', for instance, and Diogenes' lantern are among the deviations from the main image; there is too an engraving of a ship, representing 'Nauplius his lights', which is followed by the story of how Nauplius hung out false lights to lure the Greek fleet to destruction. In this fashion Farlie isolates some of the complexities involved in contemporary thinking upon the theme of darkness and light and presents them in pictorial form. The emblems are simple, but each in its small and fragmentary way contributes towards the building up of the great symbolical conception which that theme became for the seventeenth century. These ideas formed the content of the minds who thought in terms of the 'candle of the Lord', and who knew the poems of Vaughan, the *Nox nocti indicat scientiam* of Habington, and the prose of Sir Thomas Browne. *Lychnocausia* may now provide candles only for students of literary history, but it does at least illuminate the ordinary levels of mind upon which poetry builds.

Before turning from the *Emblemes* and *Hieroglyphikes* of Quarles to the work of other emblem writers of the same type, something must be said about their poetic qualities. The enormous enthusiasm with which his books were received in their own day and the extent of his reputation afterwards require some explanation, and although there can be no doubt that the popularity of the *Emblemes* and *Hieroglyphikes* was greatly in excess of their merits, a little of it at least must be attributed to Quarles's genuine abilities as a poet. Other factors also contributed to his success. The subject, though to eighteenth century eyes a 'grand defect', certainly accounts in some measure for his appeal. So also do the pictures. Quarles had caught the moment when the illustrated book was at a premium. Where forty years before John Harington had been able to list the number of picture books in England in one sentence, William Marshall now engraved as many in a year.[1] Even the most insignificant little volumes had their emblematic title pages and more ambitious publications were often illustrated with full page plates. The profession of printseller had grown up as an independent occupation, and an interest in prints began to

[1] See above, pp. 54-5.

be one of the accomplishments of a gentleman. In the year that the *Emblemes* were first published, 1635, two other books of the same type were put on the market, Wither's *A Collection of Emblemes* and Heywood's *The Hierarchie of the Blessed Angells*, which contained engraved pictures, poems and descriptions of emblems suitable for each order of Angels borrowed from various emblem writers. Indeed the state of the book trade at this time is set out with considerable satiric force in one of the commendatory poems in *Lychnocausia*:

> I need not praise thy Booke: No more to tell,
> Then that it Pictures hath, will make it sell:
> Bookes, gaudy, like themselves, most do now buy,
> Fine, trim, adorned Bookes, where they may spy
> More of the Carvers than th' Authors skill,
> And more admire the Pencill, than the Quill:
> Pamphlets, whose Outsides promise, they may finde
> What may their Eyes feed, rather than their minde:
> Nay nowadayes who almost doth behold,
> One booke without a gaudy Liv'ry sold?
> E'ne poetry it selfe is at a stay
> For all its Feet, if Carvers mak't not gay.[1]

Quarles evidently had found the secret of the best seller. Yet other books with both pictures and a religious subject did not do so well, and to these two attractions a third must be added—the popular appeal of the style. Quarles's powers as an author seem to have been just those which the process of writing for the market-place would develop; there was a happy coincidence of the man and the moment. He had an epigrammatic style, an eye for parallels, a trick of taking the reader into his confidence; he had a fondness for compound epithets which looked impressive and yet could easily be reduced to their simple parts, and thus afforded the reader a pleasant sense of intellectual achievement without overmuch intellectual effort. All these were gifts likely to win popularity for their possessor. In the emblem convention Quarles found a form in which he could use them to the best advantage. At the same time it was a form which successfully obscured his

[1] From a poem by John Hooper in Robert Farlie's *Lychnocausia*, 1638.

defects. Obviousness is an asset rather than a handicap in emblem writing; the picture supplied the central theme, and the more points of likeness the author can find, the more often he can repeat the theme in a different way, the better the emblem will be. Furthermore, the picture supplies also the requirements of structure and the poet can rely upon its support instead of having to create a support within the poem for himself. For all these reasons it was to be expected that the emblem form would contribute largely to the success of Quarles's poetry.

Quarles's method of moralising his emblems was a thorough one. The plate on page 33, for instance, represents the human soul shipwrecked in the sea of the world and Divine Love coming as the rescuer. From all possible points in this incident Quarles draws a moral. The body is the ship, the heart the seaman's card, the will the unfaithful pilot, prayer the rope, hope the anchor . . . the list continues almost without end. Each parallel fastens upon a single aspect of the central idea, and no attempt is made to develop that idea as a whole. It is accepted from the outset and remains always an external support:

> The world's a Sea; my flesh, a ship, that's man'd
> With lab'ring Thoughts, and steer'd by Reason's hand.[1]

The bucket (repentance), the pump (his eye), the plummet (conscience), the cargo (corruption) all reinforce the original comparison, but they cannot at any point be said either to illuminate it or to justify it. It remains as arbitrary as it was at the beginning. The result is an admirable emblem but a bad poem.

The poetic style itself through which this is done has the same obviousness and facility. Quarles relies upon every kind of rhetorical device—antithesis, accumulation, repetition, contrast—to stretch out his material to its utmost limits. The use of repetition to make up for the tenuousness of his thought in the passage on life's snares quoted above on page 121 is one example of this resourcefulness. Antithesis is another fruitful method; in this passage he is describing the deceptiveness of the world:

[1] *Emblemes.* III. 11.

Whose fruit is faire, and pleasing to the sight,
But sowre in tast; false, at the putrid Core:
Thy flaring Glasse is Gemms at her halfe light;
She makes thee seeming rich, but truly poore:
  She boasts a kernell, and bestowes a Shell,
  Performs an Inch of her faire promis'd Ell:
Her words protest a Heav'n: Her works produce a Hell.[1]

By the time the last line of the stanza is reached, the antitheses
have degenerated into a series of expected opposites and their
intended effect is accordingly lost. Such verbal facility as this is
inevitably its own undoing; the critical reader cannot fail to see
how little lies below the surface. The vocabulary, too, suffers
from the same defect: it is wide, but commonplace. It abounds in
the phrases and figures of speech recommended by handbooks
on the art of rhetoric. It makes, for instance, very full use of the
compound epithet, a device mentioned by Thomas Blount in
The Academie of Eloquence as being fashionable for both poetry
and prose in the mid-seventeenth century. Blount gives a list of
suitable models:

> The Quiver-bearing Meads.
> The Wool-ore-burthened Sheep.
> A horror-strucken minde.
> Sence-distracting grief.
> Soul-subduing graces.
> An un-Sun-seen cave.
> Love-distilling tears.
> Liver-scalding lust.
> Marble-hearted cruelty.
> Time-beguiling pleasure.
> Corner-haunting lust.[2]

In Quarles's poetry similar and identical phrases are extensively
used; he talks of the 'down-ripe fruit', 'hot-mouthed passion',
'human soul-enlightening Sunbeams', and even packs them all
together in close concentration:

[1] *Emblemes.* I. 7.
[2] T. Blount, *The Academie of Eloquence.* London, 1654. pp. 47–8.

... Wry-mouth'd disdaine, and corner-haunting lust,
    And twy-fac'd Fraud; and beetle-brow'd Distrust;
    Soule-boyling Rage; and trouble-state sedition;
    And giddy doubt; and goggle-ey'd suspition.[1]

Quarles's readers had, of course, a rhetorical training behind them
which gave writing of this kind a merit and an interest quite
independent of its poetic quality. An age which printed *sententiae*
in quotation marks and scratched little pointing hands beside the
witty phrases in its books naturally delighted in poetry so consciously inlaid with the colours of rhetoric. Its devices were
easy to identify; its examples suffered little from being detached
from their context. It is not difficult to understand the reasons for
Quarles's popular appeal nor to see why his *Divine Fancies*, a
volume of epigrams and emblematic poems, was recommended
for use in the upper forms of schools as an aid to the composition
of English verse.[2] The style has so many superficial attractions.

Yet for all its facility and fluency, Quarles's poetry is not wholly
without merit. It is in some ways unlike the contemporary modes
of expression. For his own generation the conclusions reached by
thinking were rarely isolated from the process of thinking: the
metaphysical poetry and rhetorical prose of the early part of the
seventeenth century reveal through their structure and imagery
a constant movement of the mind, a stretching out for ideas which
are undefined and only half related to the main subject. Nothing
is seen as wholly objective or wholly complete. In such qualities
Quarles's poetry has no real share in spite of its apparently 'metaphysical' interests. He lacked indeed those powers of intelligence
and feeling which could have created such effects; he had instead,
however, gifts which brought to his work effects of a different
kind. The best of Quarles looks forward to Restoration and
Augustan poetry. His strength lies in a power of detachment, in
a command of lucid phrase and forceful epigram. In the *Emblemes* he can often clinch what he has to say with epigrammatic
neatness:

[1] *Emblemes.* V. 14.
[2] See Foster Watson, *The English Grammar Schools to 1660*. London. 1908.
p. 481.

And he repents in Thornes, that sleeps in Beds of Roses,[1]

and

   That blast that nipt thy youth, will ruine thee;
   That hand that shook the branch will quickly strike the tree.[2]

and

   And what appear'd in former times
   Whisp'ring as *faults*, now rore as *crimes*.[3]

It is this kind of wit, rather than the metaphysical kind, which is responsible for Quarles's greatest successes in his poetry. In the *Emblemes* and *Hieroglyphikes* it is too often weakened by an emptiness of content and by the labouring of ideas when the parallels are set out too fully, but it none the less remains his outstanding virtue there. It is also the strength of his other work. Quarles's best poem outside his lyrics in the emblem books, perhaps his best poem altogether, is *Argalus and Parthenia*,[4] a long narrative work in couplets, which, while reflecting in its material his emblematic interests, is characterised also by a notable poise and satirical skill. The story derives from Sidney's *Arcadia*, and Quarles presents it in all its Elizabethan emblematic details. He describes the armour of Argalus with its knots of woman's hair, the battle with Amphialus, the trappings of Parthenia when she disguised herself as the Knight of the Tombs; an elaborately planned masque is introduced to celebrate the wedding of the lovers; the familiar forms of Time and Occasion make their appearance, and the illustrated editions included a picture of Envy with her snaky locks in the two scenes where the villain, Demagoras, is at work. Yet, unlike Sidney, he is selfconscious in his handling of the story: from time to time he comes forward and with the same gift for showmanship which he afterwards manifested in his treatment of the pictures in the emblem books comments upon the action. He speaks as an independent observer rather than as the narrator of the tale:

[1] *Emblemes.* I. 7.   [2] *Hieroglyphikes.* XIV.   [3] Ibid. XIII.
[4] *Argalus and Parthenia.* 1629. Plates were added in the edition of 1656 and afterwards.

And here my Muse bids draw our curtains too.
'Tis unfit to see what private Lovers do.
Reader, let not thy thoughts grow over rank,
But veil thy understanding with a blank.
Think not on what thou think'st; and if thou canst
Yet understand not what thou understandst.

This spirit of critical detachment pervades the whole poem and is the foundation of Quarles's burlesque style. Parthenia's beauty, for example, is celebrated in a manner very remote from that of the original:

The curious Painter wisely doth displace
Fair *Venus*, sets *Parthenia* in her place.
The pleader burns his books, disdains the Law,
And falls in love with whom his eyes ne'er saw.
Healths to the fair *Parthenia* fly about
At every board, whilst others more devout,
Build Idols to her and adore the same,
And *Parrots* learn to prate *Parthenia's* name.

The portrait of Demagoras begins as a mere caricature of the stage villain but ends as a serious satirical portrait which in its psychological interest looks forward to Dryden:

Perverse to all; extenuating what
Another did, because he did it not:
Maligning all men's actions but his own,
Not loving any, and belov'd by none;
Revengeful, envious, desperately stout,
And in a word, to paint him fully out,
That had the Monopoly to fulfil
All vice, the Hieroglyphick of all ill.

Quarles's couplets have not the consistent epigrammatic brilliance of those of his successors, but their merits are sufficiently striking to show where his natural abilities lay. Though Pope despised Quarles and mocked at the whole emblem fashion,

where the pictures for the page atone
And Quarles is sav'd by Beauties not his own,[1]

[1] *The Dunciad* (1742). Book I. ll. 139–40. *The Poems of Alexander Pope.* Vol. V. Ed. James Sutherland. 1943. p. 280.

it is yet not unlikely that he learnt something himself from Quarles's verse. The mock-heroic style of *The Rape of the Lock* may have owed something to the tone of *Argalus and Parthenia*, and when Quarles writes of the nature of man in the *Hieroglyphikes* it is impossible not to be reminded of Pope's 'glory, jest and riddle of the world':

> Even such was Man (before his soul gave light
> To his vile substance) a meer Child of night,
> Ere he had life, estated in his Urne
> And markt for death; by nature, born to burn:
> Thus liveless, lightless, worthless first began
> That glorious, that presumptuous thing, call'd Man.[1]

No other emblem writer deserved the same success as Quarles, for no one else had the same variety and originality of manner. His faults were doubtless many but it is not only the pictures which atone for them.

II

Quarles's borrowings did not escape the notice of his contemporaries, and others began to use the same sources. Edmund Arwaker's attempt to improve upon the rendering of *Pia Desideria* in the *Emblemes* appeared in 1686, and before that Christopher Harvey had published anonymously, and also without any acknowledgement of its origin, a version of another Jesuit emblem book, Benedict van Haeften's *Schola Cordis*.[2] Arwaker's book added very little to the stock of emblem literature since its contents had already been popularised by Quarles, nor can the author's claim that he was bettering the work of his predecessor be substantiated by his text. He maintained that Hugo had been 'a little too much of a Poet, and had inserted several fictitious stories in his Poems, which did much to lessen their gravity, and very ill became their devotion'; and therefore, in spite of his censure of Quarles's freedom, he replaced as many of the classical allusions as he could with ones to the Bible and pruned away any passages

---

[1] *Hieroglyphikes.* I. Cp. *An Essay on Man.* Ep. II. ll. 1–18.
[2] Antwerp, 1629.

20

Proles tua, Maia, Iuventus.

will Marshall sculpsit.

From Francis Quarles
Hieroglyphikes of the Life of Man 1638

which he thought too frivolous or otherwise unsuitable for the
Anglican reader, such as Hugo's lists of perfumes and flowers.
The result is a work that seems calculated to send even 'the
Religious Ladies of our age', for whom it was chiefly intended,
hastening back to Quarles's more lively if less accurate version.
The verse is entirely monotonous. Where Quarles achieved variety
of metre and structure, Arwaker can proceed only in lifeless
couplets:

> Shall my just grief be querulous, or mute,
> Full of *Disease*, of *Physick* destitute?
> I thought thy Love so constant heretofore,
> That Vows were needless to confirm me more:
> And dost thou now absent, and slight my pain!
> What fault of mine has caus'd this cold Disdain? [1]

When Quarles treats this theme he presents it in the form of a
dialogue between Physician and patient, Christ and the sick soul,
and the ambiguities involved in the interplay between the
allegorical and literal meanings are made doubly effective by the
dramatic form:

> *Jes*: How old's thy grief?   *Soul*: I took it at the fall
> With eating fruit.

Where Quarles can be rhetorical, dramatic, didactic, or lyrical
by turns, at one moment urging the soul with all the persuasiveness of a preacher's art to return from the paths of wickedness,
at the next elaborating a scene between the guilty Anima and
Justice in which Christ dramatically intervenes to save the now
repentant sinner, Arwaker presents each emblem from exactly
the same point of view. Every one of his poems is a pious lament
by the suppliant soul. He has one theme and one method of
handling it: at best it is a dull method and, although he had some
competence as a translator, his versification was not sufficiently
skilful to infuse much life into the unvarying monotone of the

[1] *Pia Desideria: or Divine Addresses*. London. 1686. p. 17. I have considered it
unnecessary to reproduce a plate from Arwaker since his material is already
well represented in the engravings reproduced from Quarles.

soul's 'divine addresses'. Christopher Harvey, on the other hand, was a better poet and more happy in his choice of a source. He lighted upon a different type of Jesuit emblem book, one which had not before been offered to English readers, and he had therefore the interest of novelty as well as the advantages of greater literary ability.

Van Haeften's *Schola Cordis* belongs to a group of emblem books which is closely associated with the convention of Amor and Anima but which has for its centre of interest and the main subject of its pictures not their experiences but those of the human heart. This theme had been developed in various different ways by Jesuit and Benedictine writers. In one series Christ is seen entering the heart and slowly making it a fit place for His habitation; in another the heart is represented as going through a period of trial and purification at the hands of Amor and Anima. It is to this second type that the *Schola Cordis* belongs. It contains fifty-five engravings accompanied by meditations in Latin prose upon the shortcomings and sufferings of the heart. Harvey owed to his source the plan of his book and its plates but little else. His *Schola Cordis*, first published in 1647, follows the sequence of the original faithfully until the end when he rejects such pictures as those which show the crucifixion of the heart or the refuge of the heart in the wounded side of Christ, and reduces the number of emblems in consequence to forty-seven in all. The book traces the separation of the heart from God and its final return to Him. It opens with the Infection of the Heart: Eve, standing beneath the Tree of Knowledge, offers her heart to the serpent. There follows a series of emblems depicting the condition of the fallen heart, its darkness, its vanity, its covetousness, its hardness, its insatiability. Finally after an appeal from Christ:

> Returne O wanderer, returne, returne.
> Let me not alwayes wast my words in vaine
> As I have done too long. Why dost thou spurn
> And kick the counsells that should bring thee back again.[1]

[1] *Schola Cordis*. London. 1647. Ode 11.

the heart does return, and Amor and Anima begin to test, purify and prepare it for heaven. Plate 25 on page 166 shows one of these trials taking place: the heart is weighed and found wanting. Afterwards it is sounded for its depth with a plummet, tested with a spirit level for its uprightness, and falling far short in every trial is in the end replaced by a new heart.

In all these emblems there is much the same kind of literalness as characterised the plates of Quarles. The heart is pictured as actually going through all the different processes, being burnt on the sacrificial altar, washed in a fountain of blood, ploughed and sown with the good seed, crushed flat beneath a press; or it is endowed with an ever open eye in accordance with the text, *I sleep but mine heart waketh*. The poetry, too, is given an emblematic shape. For 'The Ladder of the Heart' the ten lines of each verse are arranged in a scale of increasing length,[1] in 'The Flying of the Heart' they are designed to resemble wings:

> Oh that it were once winged like the Dove,
> That in a moment mounts on high,
> Then should it soone remove,
> Where it may ly
> In love.
> And loe,
> This one desire
> Methinks hath imp'd it so,
> That it already flies like fire
> And ev'n my verses into wings doe grow.[2]

Like Anima when she expressed similar sentiments in Quarles's *Emblemes*, the heart in the engraving has grown wings and is flying up into heaven. These emblems, in fact, show the same mixture of literalness and symbolism as had pleased the readers of Quarles; and although in the third edition Harvey went so far in acknowledging his authorship as to describe it as 'by the author of the *Synagogue*', the book was later ascribed to Quarles and frequently republished with the *Emblemes* and *Hieroglyphikes*.

---

[1] Ibid. Ode 37.   [2] Ibid. Ode 38.

Harvey learned his poetic art chiefly from Herbert and Quarles; he seems also to have read Donne:

> Thou hast not been content alone to sinne,
>   But hast made others sinne with thee,
>   Yea made their sinnes thine owne to be
> By liking, and allowing them therein.[1]

It was to Herbert, however, that he owed most in both form and style. His first book of devotional poetry *The Synagogue*, which was published in 1640, is confessedly 'in imitation of Mr George Herbert' and has for its subtitle *The Shadow of the Temple*. Its short lyrics on the various people and objects associated with the Church are treated emblematically in the manner of Herbert. The poem on the *Sexton*, for instance, begins:

> The Churches key-keeper opens the door,
>   And shuts it, sweeps the floor,
> Rings bells, digs graves, and fills them up again;
>   All Emblemes unto men,
> Openly owning Christianitie,
> To marke, and learn many good lessons by.[2]

and the different functions of the Sexton are then developed independently. This structure with its statement at the outset of several aspects of the subject and subsequent elaboration of each is reminiscent of that of Herbert. Herbert, too, had been acquainted with emblem books of the type of *Schola Cordis*, and had even made their theme the basis of one of the poems in the *Temple*.[3] In style, also, the association of Harvey with Herbert is very close. The patterned poems in *Schola Cordis* follow his example, and the 'Flying of the Heart' is, in fact, a close imitation of Herbert's 'Easter Wings'. There are extensive verbal borrowings throughout Harvey's work. The opening stanza of 'Resurrection or Easter Day':

[1] Ode 14. Cp. Donne, *A Hymne to God the Father.*
[2] *The Synagogue.* 3rd. edition, 1657. p. 23.
[3] i.e. 'Love unknown.' See below, pp. 164–7.

Up and away,
  Thy Saviour's gone before.
Why dost thou stay,
  Dull soul? Behold the door
Is open, and his precept bids thee rise,
Whose pow'r hath vanquish't all thine enemies.

is typical of his close application to Herbert's technique. The difference is that whereas Herbert in using an emblematic structure and simple language succeeds in making out of them complex poetry, Harvey in imitating his master's simplicity fails to achieve his subtlety. As an emblem book, however, Harvey's *Schola Cordis* is second only in literary merit to that of Quarles. He achieved considerable variety in metre and in treatment. Some of his poems are lyrical, others dramatic and direct. Ode 8, for example, opens with:

What have we here? An heart? It lookes like one,
  The shape, and colour speake it such . . .

which is very different from the lyrical tone of Christ's appeal in 'Returne O wanderer, returne, returne'. Some are in dialogue form. Harvey could be rhetorical too in the manner of Quarles though without that vitality which was Quarles's salvation; he could be metaphysical:

Lord, if I had an arme of pow'r like thine,
  And could effect what I desire,
    My love-drawn heart, like smallest wyre,
Bended and writhen, should together twine,
    And twisted stand
    With thy command.

Occasionally, even, he could be epigrammatic. His poetry in fact added much to the already considerable attractions of a devotional subject.

For the literary merits of the remaining emblem book of this kind, John Hall's *Emblems with Elegant Figures*, there is little to be said. It is a collection of twenty-eight emblems with engravings, and was published the year after Harvey's *Schola Cordis*. Although

he seems to have used no one particular foreign source, Hall undoubtedly found his material in continental work of the kind
already used by Quarles and Harvey. In some of the plates the
exploits of Amor and Anima form the central theme, in others
Amor appears only to point the moral of the picture, in others
again it is the heart that takes the centre of the stage. In one plate
Anima holds up a heart to heaven and it is filled from a chalice
poured down from above; the accompanying text is *Inebriate my
heart, O God, with the sober intemperance of thy love*. In another, the
heart is held by two Cupids beside the banks of a river, while
Hall laments his departure from Cambridge and lack of success
as a poet in London, in verse that well explains his failure:

> Now I am fal'n, and now
> Under my care's must either break or bow;
> And that great Fabrick of *Leucenia*,
> Which should to th' last of time my name conveigh,
> Must lie unperfit, and dismember'd so,
> And be at most a monstrous Embryo.[1]

The texts are drawn almost exclusively from St. Augustine. The
plate opposite, for example, represents the unlearned rising and
taking heaven by violence, while Amor expounds the moral of
this to the wise: heaven is for them inaccessible

> Yet may a modest ignorance
> Unto so great an height advance,
> And of such sparkling beauties gain a glance.[2]

This is one of Hall's more successful emblems; and undoubtedly
the Elegant Figures were a great asset. The poems sometimes fail
to explain the meaning of the plates, and are themselves of such
small merit as to make the book negligible as literature, but it is
evident from the example reproduced here that the pictures did
in some measure offset the limitations of the text.

Enough has been said of this group of emblems to make it
plain that they brought much that was alien to the habits of

[1] Op. cit. p. 78. [2] Ibid. p. 30.

21

*The unlearned rise and take heaven by
violence; and we with our learning
without affection, behold! where we
wallow in flesh and blond!* Aug.Conf.
lib. 8. cap. 8.

V
Ain curiosity! yee lead
   The mind in mazes, make her tread
A-side, while that she toyles and is not fed.

O empty searchings! do I care
   If I can slice yon burning sphere
To the least atoms, and yet near come there.

Though I can number every flame
   That fleets within that glorious frame;
Yet do not look on him that can them name,

Though I can in my travell'd mind
   The earth and all her treasures find
Yet leaving pride swolne into hills behind.

Though I can plum the sea, and try
   What monsters in her womb do lie;
Yet n'ere a drop full from my frozen eye.

Am I the better, though I could
   All wisdome with a breath unfold,
And a heart boundless as the Ocean hold?

No not a whit unless that he
   By whom these glorious wonders be
Lead me and teach mine eyes himself to see.

From John Hall: *Emblems with Elegant Figures 1648*

[slightly reduced]

thought of their readers. In their themes, in the conventions on which they were based, they were obviously more suited for the expression of Catholic than of Protestant religious ideas; their closest affinities in English literature are with Crashaw. For this reason their lasting success, not as emblem books but as religious books, is not a little remarkable. Both the *Emblemes* and the *Schola Cordis* were accepted in Victorian Nonconformist homes where any explicit Roman influence would presumably have been anathema. That remained unnoticed, however, and the reason is perhaps to be found in the very fact that the material *was* alien— even to the writers themselves. The pictures may remind the reader of the more extravagant passages in Crashaw, but the poems never do.[1] The treatment of the themes, however they may be represented in the engravings, remains essentially Protestant.

[1] Lines like these are in closer accord with the sensuous qualities of the plates of the Jesuit emblem books than is any of the poetry of Quarles and Harvey:

> What did Their weapons but with wider pores
> Inlarge thy flaming-brested Lovers
>   More freely to transpire
>   That impatient Fire
> The Heart that hides Thee hardly covers.
> What did their Weapons but sett wide the Doores
> For Thee: Fair, purple Doores, of love's devising;
> The Ruby windowes which inricht the EAST
> Of Thy so oft repeated Rising.
> Each wound of Theirs was Thy new Morning;
> And reinthroned thee in thy Rosy Nest,
> With blush of thine own Blood thy day adorning. . . .

'To the Name above every Name, the Name of Jesus'. ll. 211–22. *The Poems of Richard Crashaw*, Ed. L. C. Martin. Oxford, 1927. p. 239.

Crashaw's poetry was, of course, often emblematic in its imagery and structure, as such poems as 'The Weeper' and some of the 'Divine Epigrams' in *Steps to the Temple* show. *Carmen Deo Nostro* contains a number of plates, probably designed by Crashaw himself, which are also emblematic. They include such designs as a heart hinged and padlocked, which is accompanied by both a motto and an epigram (Martin. p. 235), a Pieta with emblems of the passion (p. 284), and a portrait of S. Mary Magdalen with a winged heart, which is flaming and weeping (p. 308), accompanied by an epigram:

> Loe where a WOUNDED HEART with Bleeding *Eyes* conspire,
> Is she a FLAMING Fountain or a WEEPING Fire!

It is significant that, with the possible exception of Hall, none of the writers in this group invented their pictures; the material was imported from abroad, and in their handling of it the emblem writers show that same asceticism of temperament which led English translators of Continental devotional books to expurgate those passages which, though theologically blameless, might in sentiment offend their readers.[1] Neither Harvey nor Quarles lingers long over the physical; both are too much preoccupied with the moral and intellectual potentialities of each theme to find space for luxuriant detail. Consequently, the raptures, ecstasies, and sighs of the devout soul in the presence of its Lord never became for them an interest absorbing in itself. Many of Quarles's emblems are based on quotations from the Song of Songs, but even there it is the expression of moral ideas rather than the creation of sensation that is the main concern. The conventions of Amor, Anima and the Searching Heart certainly lent themselves to the development of a religious eroticism with which the English Protestant mind has very little sympathy. But these possibilities were ignored, although the framework of the convention was still preserved. Harvey and Arwaker were both of them Anglican priests, and the popularity of their work, and of Quarles's, shows that the convention could be modified so as to appeal to Protestant readers.

The work of this group of poets represents the English share in what was the main branch of religious emblem-writing on the Continent in the seventeenth century. Some religious emblem books, however, were written that do not spring from these particular conventions, and in which Amor, Anima, and the experiences of the Heart have no place. In England such books were mainly devotional works in prose which included emblems as part of a whole scheme of meditation, but there is one exception that deserves mention here, George Wither's *A Collection of Emblemes Ancient and Modern*. This collection, published in an impressive folio in the same year as Quarles's *Emblemes*, belongs in

[1] See Helen White, *English Devotional Literature (Prose) 1600–1640*. Univ. of Wisconsin Studies. 1931. pp. 238–9.

one sense to the earlier tradition of emblem books, for its subjects are the familiar ones of the Elizabethan form of the convention; but in another, in its treatment of those subjects, it belongs to the group which has been discussed in this chapter. It seems, therefore, best to consider it in this place.

Wither was by no means a negligible poet, although, towards the end of his lifetime and afterwards, he became the butt of critics and wits. To Pope he was 'wretched Withers',[1] to an anonymous critic of the early eighteenth century, 'the worst of bards',[2] and even in his own day Sir John Denham is reported by Aubrey as having implored the King to spare Wither's life after his capture by Royalists in the Civil War 'for that whilest G.W. lived he (Denham) should not be the worst poet in England'.[3] The plea had its effect, and Wither survived to add more weight to Denham's argument. From the enormous waste of lifeless poetry which he produced, it seems that there was some justice in Denham's jibe. Wither's pastorals are dull with all the dullness of the late Elizabethan manner; his satires lack point and wit. Nevertheless, his emblems are, as Lamb said, characterised at least by 'a hearty homeliness of manner and plain moral speaking',[4] which gave them considerable success as emblems, even though their ultimate value as literature might not be very high. The folio of 1635 must have been an expensive work, but fifty of the emblems were later made accessible in a cheaper form by the piracy of Nathanial Crouch who reproduced plates and poems under the title of *Delights for the Ingenious*, without the least mention of the author.[5] A few more were also reprinted without plates in Wither's *Remains* in the hope that 'those who did read

---

[1] Pope. 'The Dunciad' (1742). Book I. l. 296. Ed. cit. p. 291.

[2] *The Gentleman's Magazine.* Vol. 8. Sept. 1738. p. 484.

[3] Aubrey, *Brief Lives.* Ed. Clark. 1898. Vol. I. p. 221.

[4] Lamb, 'On the Poetical Works of George Wither'. 1818. *Works.* Ed. E. V. Lucas. 1903. Vol. I. pp. 181–4.

[5] *Delights for the Ingenious, in above Fifty Select and Choice Emblems, Divine and Moral, Ancient and Modern.* Collected by R.B. for Nathanial Crouch, 1684. The plates are bad copies of de Passe's engravings and the poems to each are given in full. William Marshall's frontispiece is also copied. A Lottery is included, and an Epistle to the Reader signed R.B. (i.e. Robert or Richard

them heretofore either *negligently* or in *sport* only, will peruse them to better purpose'.

Wither's *Collection* consists of four books of fifty emblems each. The pictures had appeared originally in a Dutch emblem book published some twenty years earlier, Gabriel Rollenhagen's *Nucleus Emblematum Selectissimorum*, and Wither, according to the account he gives in his Preface to the Reader, had considered them so well executed, but the verses attached to them 'so meane', that he had decided to give them a worthier setting and to reproduce them with his own moralisations. There was, however, a long delay in obtaining the plates from Holland and the book did not, therefore, appear until 1635 when the type of emblem it offered had become somewhat old fashioned. Nevertheless, the engravings made by Crispin van de Passe are admirable, and the suspension of publication until the plates could be sent over from Holland was more than justified in that it gave to the book the rare distinction of illustrations by a highly-skilled professional engraver. Whatever the limitations of the poetry and the content of the book, the pictures are uniformly excellent.

Wither's poetry was written for the middle-class reader of a puritanical turn of mind. The author maintains that he takes little pleasure in '*Rymes, Fictions* or conceited *Compositions*' for their own sake, and uses only so much of them as may '(without darkening the matter, to them who most need instruction) . . . stirre up the *Affections*, winne *Attention*, or helpe the *Memory*'. Throughout, the emphasis is laid on painful industry and honest care: the Puritan virtues of diligence and thrift are those most repeatedly praised and held up for imitation. The affinities of Wither's emblem book are, in fact, with the popular guides to godliness: its ethic is Puritan, its doctrine frankly anti-Catholic:

Burton, a pseudonym used by Crouch) is made up of parts of Wither's Address to the Reader and his Apology for the Lottery. Whether this was the first pirated edition I do not know. A sixth edition, entitled *Choice Emblems, Divine and Moral, Ancient and Modern, or Delights for the Ingenious*, was printed for Edmund Parker in 1732.

22

From George Wither: *A Collection of Emblemes 1635*
[reduced a third]

It is not mumbling over thrice a day
A Set of *Ave Maries* or of *Creeds*,
Or many houres formally to *pray*;
When from a dull *Devotion* it proceedes:
Which *God* respects. . . .
We ought not, therefore, to regard, alone,
How *often*, but how *Well*, the *Worke* be done.[1]

In spite of this bias, however, Wither's emblems possessed one
feature which the true Puritan would hardly have expected to
find there—a Lottery. This was a device not unknown to emblem
books,[2] though Wither's original had not possessed one, and its
appearance in this collection is therefore the more surprising. Of
the propriety of his addition Wither had, it is true, some doubts
and found it necessary to apologise for it at length. His considered
opinion was, however, that Lotteries were to be excused on the
same grounds as pictures which, though in themselves unim-
proving and capable of catching the reader only 'in a spirit of
levity and childish delight in trifling objects', might none the less
be a means of leading his curiosity to discover the hidden lesson
beneath. This laudable purpose was fully achieved in the form
the Lottery took in Wither's book. The plate opposite shows how it
was designed to work. A pointer spun round on each of the two
charts would determine which emblem fell to the player's lot; by
it he was directed not only to the page where a picture and thirty
lines of moral instruction were to be found, but also to another
place where the special application of his emblem to everyday
life was set out in a short, easily remembered stanza. Thus for
the emblem of the death's head a further moral was provided:

Let such, as draw this *Lot*, have care,
For *Death*, and *Sorrow*, to prepare
All times to come, lest one of these,
Their persons, unexpected, seize:
For them, or some of theirs, to slay,
Pale Death, drawes neerer, ev'ry day.
Yet, let them not disheartned bee:

[1] *A Collection of Emblemes.* p. 25.
[2] There is, for example, a Lottery in the Jesuit, J. David's *Veridicus Christi-
anus.* Antwerp. 1601.

For, in their *Emblem*, they shall see,
Death may (though, in appearance, grim)
Become a *blessing* unto them.[1]

The Lottery was designed by Wither to be used as a parlour game, or what he called a 'Moral Pastime', and it obviously had something of the same appeal as a Fortune-teller at a party. If its message happened to be peculiarly appropriate to the one who drew it, the fact merely added to the general amusement, and to the success of the book's purpose :

For, if any who are *notoriously Guiltie*, shall by drawing their *Chances* among other Companions, be so fitted with *Lots*, (which may now and then happen) that those *Vices* be therby intimated to the by-standers, of which the world knowes them guilty; they do therin make their own *Libels*; and may (I hope) bee laughed at without my blame.

This interest in driving home the moral lesson far outweighed Wither's interest in the meaning of the pictures, and these he often treats in a highly cavalier fashion:

. . . little care I take
Precisely to unfold our *Authors* minde;
Or, on his meaning, *Comments* here to make.
It is the scope of my Intention, rather
From such perplext *Inventions* (which have nought
Of Ancient *Hieroglyphick*) *sense* to gather
Whereby some usefull *Morall* may be taught.[2]

The reason for this airy dismissal of the original sense lies partly in the fact that the pictures were imported from Holland and some of them seemed to him exceptionally obscure, but it is mainly due to Wither's consciousness that his material belongs to a tradition now obsolete. He introduces the emblems by such phrases as 'in former times' or

Our Elders, when their meaning was to show
A *native speedinesse* (in Emblem wise)
A picture of a *Dolphin-fish* they drew. . . .[3]

The subjects, in fact, were similar to those of Whitney but Wither

---

[1] *A Collection of Emblemes.* p. 55.   [2] Ibid. p. 67.   [3] Ibid. p. 72.

does not find them nearly so interesting in themselves. He does not conceal his impatience with the plates and is anxious to get to what he regards as the real business of his book, moral improvement:

> To seeke out the *Author* of every particular *Emblem* were a labour without profit: and I have beene so far from endeavouring it, that I have not so much as cared to find out their meanings in any of these *Figures*; but applied them rather to such purposes as I could think of at first sight.

The result is that for most readers Wither offers overmuch of Lamb's 'plain moral speaking' and too little explanation of the symbolism of his pictures.

It is hardly necessary, in view of the treatment they received from Wither, to say much about the content of his emblems. Rollenhagen's material had been derived from Junius, Sambucus, Symeoni and others, and in subject, therefore, they resemble the emblems of Whitney and Peacham. Here, once more, are the familiar legends and fables, the choice of Hercules, the bear stealing honey, the personified figures of Occasion and Constancy, and diagrammatic emblems composed of a number of symbols such as the owl, skull and tomb for the melancholy *Memento mori*, or the helmet that has become a hive for bees to show that war is succeeded by the arts of peace. A few have been influenced by the conventions of profane love and represent the adventures of Cupid or some version of the emblematic heart: true love, for instance, is symbolised by hands clasped above a flaming heart with a death's head above them. Very few of the emblems are religious; the best of these is probably the engraving of the pelican in her piety, symbolising the sacrifice of Christ, which Blount reproduced as a typical emblem in his translation of Estienne's book (see Plate 24, p. 160). One of the most constantly repeated religious symbols in the seventeenth century,[1] it inevitably entered devotional poetry, sometimes quite directly

---

[1] It had, of course, long been current in mediaeval imagery; it formed the device of the Gild of Corpus Christi and had been used as a motif in religious decoration long before its incorporation into emblem books.

and explicitly, and sometimes as an underlying image as in
Crashaw's:

> Lo, how the streames of life, from that full nest
> Of loves, thy lord's too liberall brest,
> Flow in an amorous Floud
> Of WATER wedding BLOOD.[1]

The most extravagantly emblematic treatment of it is that of
Mildmay Fane, whose *Otia Sacra* published in 1648 contained a
number of patterned poems of this kind, and also poems
accompanied by emblematic engravings:

> A Pelican feeding her young with blood out of her
> own Brest, a type of our Saviour.

> C-ruores
> I-ndulgetq; A-lescant
> L-atus N-ati
> E-ximios V-ulneribusq;
> P-orrigit S-uis.

> Behold Here from the PELICANS Brest sprung
> A stream of precious blood to feed her young.[2]

Another of the emblems in Wither's *Collection* which has an
interest in relation to contemporary poetry is that of the compasses reproduced opposite. This design had been used by
the Plantin Press as its imprint, with the same motto, *Labore et
Constantia*.[3] Wither in his poem celebrates the virtues of constancy and perseverance: in order to draw a circle

> We cause the brazen *Compasses* to stand
> With one foot firmly fixed on the ground;
> And move the other in a *Constant-round*:

so in the same way man should stand firm and pursue without

[1] Crashaw, 'Vexilla Regis, The Hymn of the Holy Crosse'. Ed. cit. p. 277.
Cp. 'The Hymn to St. Thomas', where the image is also introduced.
[2] Op. cit. p. 31.
[3] Ben Jonson's Impresa was a 'Compass with one foot in Center, the other
Broken, the word: Deest quod duceret orbem' (Conversations with Drummond, 1619).

23

Good Hopes, *we beſt accompliſh may,*
By lab'ring *in a* conſtant-Way.

9

ILLVSTR. IX.   *Book.* 3

Ome Folkes there are, (and many men ſuppoſe,
That I my ſelfe, may paſſe for one of thoſe)
Who many likely Buſineſſes intend,
Yet, bring but very few, unto an end.
Which folly to prevent, this *Emblem*, here,
Did in a luckie houre, perhaps, appeare.
For, as to draw a *Circle*, with our hand,
We cauſe the brazen *Compaſſes* to ſtand
With one foot firmely fixed one the ground ;
And move the other in a *Conſtant-round :*
Right ſo, when we ſhall purpoſe to proceed
In any juſt, and profitable deed,
We firſt, ſhould by a *conſtant-reſolution,*
Stand firme, to what we put in execution:

From George Wither: *A Collection of Emblemes 1635*
[slightly reduced]

wavering the course to which he has put his hand. When, however, Donne used the same image in *A Valediction Forbidding Mourning* to symbolise the faith between lovers, he was criticised for its extravagance. Dr. Johnson, quoting the passage which ends:

> Thy firmness makes my circle just,
> And makes me end, where I begunne.

doubted whether 'absurdity or ingenuity had the better claim' in it. Yet the conceit is magnificently successful in its context, and when it is remembered that Donne was using an accepted emblem of constancy and was relying upon an association of ideas which every reader who had looked at the title-page of a book published by Plantin could have made for himself, its introduction into a poem upon the theme of constancy is less difficult to understand. For Donne, the pair of compasses embodies the whole relationship between the lovers, and his use of the image is justified by the wealth of meaning he gives it; but even in its origin it was not so remote from the ideas it conveys as has hitherto been supposed.

Wither's emblems belong in subject-matter to conventions that had been superseded, but the excellence of the engravings in which these conventions were represented must always have saved his book from neglect. It was included, together with Quarles's *Emblemes* and Farlie's *Lychnocausia*, in London's *Catalogue of the most Vendible Books in England* in 1657, and to its pictures the greater part of its merit, and probably its popularity, must be ascribed. The standard of morality is mediocre; the verse is tedious. Wither, it is true, thought that the rigid plan he had adopted of thirty lines and no more to each emblem 'much injured the liberty of my Muse', but it was not so much liberty that his Muse needed as restraint. The same indeed is true of the Muses of all the emblem writers discussed in this chapter, and it is only in the ordered and controlled treatment of George Herbert that the potentialities of the convention for the expression of devotional and psychological themes were fully realised.

Chapter 6

GEORGE HERBERT

IN the work of all the Metaphysical poets of the seventeenth century some consciousness of the emblem convention is shewn, and some use made of its themes and methods. By none was it entirely neglected, although the degree and value of its influence naturally varies widely with different writers. It is, of course, to be expected that a fashion so widespread would have its effect upon the minor poets of the period, and the consistently and consciously emblematic nature of the verse of even so mediocre a poet as Mildmay Fane, whose poem on the pelican was reproduced in the previous chapter, illustrates the extent of its support at such a level. His volume *Otia Sacra* contains poems arranged in patterns in the manner of that on the pelican; it contains others which are emblematic in a less extravagant way— 'To man on his frail Condition' for example, opens with:

> What permanence to Earth or Clay is due,
> Fond Man consider, for that Emblems you.
> This Day brings humane flesh under Death's yoke,
> And yesterday I saw a Pitcher broke.[1]

It also contains plates engraved by William Marshall which form an essential part of other poems. One, for instance, consists of a design of three interlaced hearts inscribed with the words 'In Obedientia Praestans', 'In Devotione Flagrans' and 'In Amore Abundans'; a motto above, *Cordium Concordia Vera*, and a short verse below explaining the significance of the device, complete the poem.[2] Mildmay Fane did not, indeed, make much of the convention for he was not a very good poet; the convention must rather be considered as having made him. But the more distinguished metaphysical poets also recognised its potentialities: even Donne, who relied least upon it, adopted one of its images

---

[1] Mildmay Fane, *Otia Sacra*. London. 1648. p. 47.   [2] Ibid. p. 45.

in *A Valediction forbidding mourning*, and his poem *The Primrose* is also clearly reminiscent of the form in its way of presenting and analysing a single image.[1] The two who made the most extensive use of it, however, were Vaughan and Herbert. Crashaw's religious interests naturally led him towards the themes of the Jesuit emblem books; and the imagery of his devotional poetry, with its bleeding and flaming hearts, its emphasis upon the sensations of the devout soul, and its emblematic pictures, perhaps engraved by himself, does in fact recall that aspect of the convention. But the relations of Vaughan and Herbert to it are less obvious and more interesting. Both owed a little and brought much to it, absorbing more than its merely superficial elements and yet succeeding, on occasion, in transforming it into great poetry.

The first appearance of its influence upon Vaughan is hardly promising. He introduced unmistakable emblems into his early love poetry, but the verse is poor and does its author little credit:

> ... And on each leafe by Heavens command,
> These Emblemes to the life shall stand:
> Two Hearts, the first a shaft withstood;
> ... The second, shot, and washt in bloud;
> And on this heart a dew shall stay,
> Which no heate can court away;
> But fixt for ever witnesse beares,
> That hearty sorrow feeds on teares.
> Thus Heaven can make it knowne, and true,
> That you kill'd me, 'cause I lov'd you.[2]

In the religious poetry of *Silex Scintillans*, however, the form is put to much better use. Here, it is true, the immediate sources of the images lie less in the emblem books than in the obscure symbolism of the Hermetic philosophy; *Regeneration*, for example, conveys its meaning through a series of symbols which have been traced to Thomas Vaughan's *Lumen de Lumine*.[3]

[1] 'The Primrose, being at Montgomery Castle, upon the hill, on which it is situate.' *The Poems of John Donne*. Ed. H. J. C. Grierson. 1912. p. 61.

[2] 'Les Amours'. ll. 25–34. *Poems*. 1646. Cp. also 'Upon the Priorie Grove' in the same volume. *The Works of Henry Vaughan*. Ed. L. C. Martin. Oxford, 1914. Vol I. pp. 5, 15. All quotations are made from this text.

[3] Ibid. Vol. II. p. 694.

Nothing is to be gained therefore by seeking parallels and origins in the books of emblems. Yet inevitably the two fields overlap, and although the main source of the symbols of this stanza is Thomas Vaughan's book, something is also due to the habitual representation in visual form in the emblem books of such concepts as that of weighing pleasure against pain or the world's joys against those of heaven:

> So sigh'd I upwards still, at last
> 'Twixt steps, and falls
> I reach'd the pinacle, where plac'd
> I found a paire of scales,
> I tooke them up and layd
> In th'one late paines,
> The other smoake, and pleasures weigh'd
> But prov'd the heavier graines; [1]

Sometimes Vaughan does base a poem upon the material of the emblem books. The central image of *The Palm-tree*, for instance, is one which occurs again and again in emblem literature, that of the palm-tree borne down by a heavy weight yet still flourishing. It was used to signify perseverance and patience in life, or love, or religion. Vaughan treats it much in the manner of the emblem books, first describing, and then drawing various lessons from it:

> . . . This Plant, you see
> So prest and bow'd, before sin did degrade
> Both you and it, had equall liberty
>
> With other trees: but now shut from the breath
> And air of *Eden*, like a male-content
> It thrives no where. This makes these weights (like death
> And sin) hang at him; for the more he's bent
>
> The more he grows. Celestial natures still
> Aspire for home . . . [2]

He gives the image, however, a fuller and richer meaning than it ever possessed in any emblem book by taking into account its

---

[1] 'Regeneration.' Vaughan, ed. cit. p. 397.
[2] 'The Palm-tree.' Ibid. p. 490.

other associations, connecting it as a tree with the Tree of Immortality, as a palm with the crown of victory, and so building up a complex idea of the nature of the religious life out of the original simple emblem. In the main, however, the interest of the emblem books in relation to Vaughan's poetry must be regarded as one of method rather than of content. Both in his habit of handling abstract ideas as if they were tangible and visible objects, and in his way of interpreting phenomena in the natural world which so powerfully impressed him, Vaughan writes in a manner that can be called emblematic. In *The World*, for instance, he chooses typical figures of worldlings and surrounds them with the emblems of their folly: the lover has near him

> his Lute, his fancy, and his flights,
> Wits sour delights,[1]

the statesman is 'hung round with weights and woe'. Except for the lute and the weights, these things cannot be visualised, but Vaughan treats them exactly as if they could and gives them equal prominence with what really is concrete in the emblematic picture he is creating. It is this mode of presentation which gives his poetry that simultaneous effect of precision and vagueness which is so peculiarly characteristic of it. His treatment of the natural world in some poems also closely resembles the technique of the emblem writer. In *The Water-fall*, he follows the structure of an emblem exactly. It is divided into three sharply distinguished sections, each marked by a change in form and rhythm. In the first the waterfall is described:

> With what deep murmurs through times silent stealth
> Doth thy transparent, cool and watry wealth
> Here flowing fall,
> And chide, and call,
> As if his liquid, loose Retinue staid
> Lingring, and were of this steep place afraid,
> The common pass
> Where, clear as glass,
> All must descend
> Not to an end:

[1] 'The World.' Ibid. p. 466.

But quickened by this deep and rocky grave,
Rise to a longer course more bright and brave.

Then it is interpreted, and the meaning, already implied in the
vocabulary of the second half of the description, is made explicit.
The waterfall is the emblem of the soul's progress to eternity:

Dear stream! dear bank, where often I
Have sate, and pleas'd my pensive eye,
Why, since each drop of thy quick store
Runs thither, whence it flow'd before,
Should poor souls fear a shade or night,
Who came (sure) from a sea of light?
Or since those drops are all sent back
So sure to thee, that none doth lack,
Why should frail flesh doubt any more
That what God takes, hee'l not restore?

The image itself is carried on in the language, the 'quick store'
and the 'sea of light', but the purpose of this passage is mainly
interpretative where that of the first had been mainly descriptive.
Finally, in the third section are set out a variety of morals or
applications, the 'sublime truths and wholesome themes' embodied in the waterfall and its meaning. It must be admitted that
there is a distinct falling-off in this part and that by the time
Vaughan has reached his 'Application' the influence of the emblem structure has ceased to be a happy one. But the fault lies
in his following the model too literally: while the significance
of the picture remained implicit as it did in the descriptive section,
and while its application remained implicit as it did in the interpretative section, all was well; but when the moral is expressed
directly, as it is in the third part, Vaughan's imagination fails and
he comes to the flat, dull exposition of:

O useful Element and clear!
My sacred wash and cleanser here . . . [1]

He can treat a moral idea only through symbols, never directly as
George Herbert could. He is at his best, therefore, in the two
earlier sections, and especially in the opening stanza, where

[1] 'The Water-fall.' Vaughan, ed. cit. p. 537.

the patterned shape first brings before the eye the image of the waterfall which is to be created so exquisitely in the alternating flows and hesitations of the rhythm and in the cool translucency of the vocabulary with its gliding alliterations and clear echoes of sound and rhyme. Yet even here Vaughan's method is not purely descriptive: the 'steep place', the 'common pass', the 'deep and rocky grave', all prepare the way for the interpretation which follows. It is not until the form he has adopted compels him to the necessity of moralising directly that it becomes a liability instead of an asset.

For Herbert the emblem convention had no liabilities. His poetry is, indeed, very different from that of Vaughan. Vaughan does not need an emblem book to reveal the merits of his work: it has that kind of brilliance and beauty which is recognised instantly and without qualification whenever it appears. Herbert's has not; its virtues are unobtrusive, its merits less striking. It is also much closer to the emblem convention. Vaughan never succeeded in vitalising the form as a whole; he was always unsuccessful when he began to moralise in the way it required if it were to be adopted in its entirety. Herbert, however, is a more reflective and philosophically-minded poet, and he could accept the technique in all its essential features. He was able to surmount the apparent limitations of the almost wholly visual nature of its imagery and the sententious forms of its moralisation, and to turn both to the fullest advantage. His poetry, in effect, achieves a richness of meaning and a subtlety of tone which is the more distinctive for the simplicity of the means it uses.

The Temple was published in 1633, before either Quarles or Harvey had made their renderings of the Jesuit emblems. Its poems are in many respects emblematic although, like Vaughan's, they have not necessarily any direct dependence upon particular sources for their content. In some later seventeenth-century editions engravings were attached to two of them,[1] but it is clear from the treatment of the imagery of a poem like *The Church-floore* that pictures could add nothing essential to Herbert's verse:

[1] To 'The Altar' and 'The Superliminarie' in the editions of 1674 and after.

Mark you the floore? that square & speckled stone,
    Which looks so firm and strong,
        Is *Patience*:

And th'other black and grave, wherewith each one
    Is checker'd all along,
        Humilitie:

The gentle rising, which on either hand
    Leads to the Quire above,
        Is *Confidence*:

But the sweet cement, which in one sure band
    Ties the whole frame, is *Love*
        And *Charitie*.

Hither sometimes Sinne steals, and stains
The marbles neat and curious veins:
But all is cleansed when the marble weeps.
Sometimes Death, puffing at the doore,
Blows all the dust about the floore:
But while he thinks to spoil the room, he sweeps.
Blest be the *Architect*, whose art
Could build so strong in a weak heart.[1]

Here visual images are certainly present—they form, in fact, the basis of the poem—but they are present in complete fusion with their moral significance. A plate such as the collections of emblems provided for each of its poems would have been superfluous; it would have acted only as an illustration, as a marginal note upon the poem's structure, and could have been no necessary part of the poem itself. For there can be no simple separation into 'picture' and 'word' where the floor 'so firme and strong', the 'gentle rising' of the chancel, and the 'dust' blown about by death, are concerned. They are what Vaughan later called 'bodied ideas', forms of expression in which the image and its significance are completely co-extensive with each other. In Quarles's *Emblemes* the poetry simply deduces ideas from a given image; it consequently requires the presence of an actual picture for the verse to

---

[1] *The Temple*, 1633. *The Works of George Herbert*. Ed. F. E. Hutchinson. Oxford. 1941. p. 66. All quotations are made from this text.

analyse in detail and build its argument upon. Herbert's poetry brings its pictures with it. It remains primarily visual, but the images presented have already been explored and when they enter the poem they enter it with their implications already worked out.

It is in this sense that Herbert's poetry is emblematic: it is at once visual and intellectual. Few of his poems actually conform with the stock emblem pattern—the strict sequence of picture, interpretation, application—and those which do are, moreover, the least successful among them. *Lovejoy*, for instance, does not represent his work at its best:

> As on a window late I cast mine eye,
> I saw a vine drop grapes with J and C
> Anneal'd on every bunch. One standing by
> Ask'd what it meant. I, who am never loth
> To spend my judgment, said, It seem'd to me
> To be the bodie and the letters both
> Of *Joy* and *Charitie*. Sir, you have not miss'd,
> The man reply'd; It figures JESUS CHRIST.[1]

The emblematic quality of the poetry is present in more general ways than this; it is apparent everywhere in the formulation of ideas, in lines like

> Thy root is ever in its grave,[2]

in the treatment of the images which are the foundation of such poems as *The Church-floore*, and in the consciously patterned shape of poems like *Easter Wings* and *The Altar*. It reflects, in fact, an habitual cast of mind, a constant readiness to see a relation between simple, concrete, visible things and moral ideas, and to establish that relation in as complete a way as possible without identifying the two or blurring the outlines of either. The connection between *The Temple* and the emblem books is not confined to single lines and scattered phrases, nor limited to a few isolated poems, but is expressed in Herbert's whole method of accumulating and interpreting images, and indeed in his whole

[1] 'Lovejoy.' Ibid. p. 116.   [2] 'Vertue.' Ibid. p. 87.

use of language. For this reason it is hard to define. The picture and the moral are so closely bound up with each other that although it is possible to see in the presentation and treatment of the images as images much that is comparable with the technique of the emblem writers, there is still much that escapes analysis. For the very nature of the images, their visual quality and precise outlines, the clarity and simplicity with which they express the ideas they embody, is deceptive; it suggests that the 'moral' is equally simple. In reality, they are the results of the concentration of ideas and their meaning is often profound. The moral of Herbert's poetry, unlike that of the emblem books, is a highly complex thing, but like that of the emblem books it is built up through images. Yet the function (and hence the quality) of these images is different: for Herbert they are the focus of ideas, for Quarles merely the source of ideas. Consequently, they are closely connected with other aspects of Herbert's poetry and it is necessary therefore before further discussing the emblematic nature of his imagery to take some of these into account.

The merits of Herbert's poetry are first noticed in its rhythm. It has not the spectacular qualities of the work of Vaughan or of Donne; its imagery is essential but rarely rich in itself, its language is austere. For these reasons it has been called simple. If, however, it is compared with the religious lyrics of the fourteenth century which possessed both the straightforwardness and the intensely personal note usually attributed to Herbert, some differences quickly become evident:

> Louerd, thu clepedest me
> an ich nagt ne ansuarede the
> Bute wordes scloe and sclepie:
> 'thole yet! thole a litel!'
> Bute 'yiet' and 'yiet' was endelis,
> And 'thole a litel' a long wey is.[1]

When Herbert treats such a theme he writes *The Collar*, a poem far more dramatic, far wider in its range of emotions, far more forceful in its rhythm and elaborate in its form—in fact a poem

[1] Carleton Brown, *Religious Lyrics of the Fourteenth Century.* 1924. p. 3.

altogether more complex than this. The truth is that behind Herbert's apparent simplicity there is a richness and a variety that is composed of many elements. In the first place, the preciseness of his imagery and the austerity of his language do not preclude intensity of feeling. Admittedly the intensity is rarely explicit, rarely to be found directly in the vocabulary. The anguish of *Perseverance* is not at all typical:

> Onely my soule hangs on thy promisses
> With face and hands clinging unto thy brest,
> Clinging and crying, crying without cease,
> Thou art my rock, thou art my rest.[1]

But the passion of the direct statement here is the measure of the strength of the emotion elsewhere. *Perseverance* is a poem which survives only in the Williams manuscript; it was not revised for publication. If it had been, its expression of feeling might have been more restrained. For emotion in Herbert's poetry is usually conveyed indirectly: it is implied in the rhythm rather than expressed in the language. This gives it a quietness which is often mistaken for weakness. Yet there is just as much strength of feeling in the calm assurance of:

> Whether I flie with angels, fall with dust,
> Thy hands made both, and I am there: [2]

or the sadness of:

> Lovely enchanting language, sugar cane,
> Hony of roses, whither wilt thou flie? [3]

as there is in *Perseverance*, though it is less obvious because it does not lie on the surface. *The Collar*, indeed, is a violent poem because its theme demands violence and demands that the rebellious feelings of the speaker should be expressed directly; but this is a dramatic device, and at the end these directly expressed feelings are controlled and brought to order in lines in which the emotion is only implicit, yet far stronger than any other in the poem:

[1] 'Perseverance.' Herbert, ed. cit. p. 204.
[2] 'The Temper.' Ibid. p. 55.   [3] 'The Forerunners.' Ibid. p. 176.

> But as I rav'd and grew more fierce and wilde
> At every word,
> Me thoughts I heard one calling, *Child*!
> And I reply'd, *My Lord*.[1]

Secondly, Herbert's apparent simplicity disguises a remarkable mastery of tone. Much is done dramatically and by implication:

> Then Money came, and chinking still,
> What tune is this, poore man? said he:
> I heard in Musick you had skill.[2]

There is the shrug of the shoulder suggested in:

> How canst thou brook his foolishnesse?
> Why, he'l not lose a cup of drink for thee:
> Bid him but temper his excesse;
> Not he: he knows where he can better be,
> As he will swear,
> Then to serve thee in fear.[3]

Or the reproach of:

> *What, Child, is the ballance thine,*
> *Thine the poise and measure?*
> *If I say, Thou shalt be mine;*
> *Finger not my treasure.*[4]

The dramatic nature of Herbert's poetry is no more conspicuous than its emotional force, but it is always present in the perfect appropriateness of the tone in which the ideas are expressed.

Finally, although the poems are lyrical and have the appearance of being direct statements of Herbert's personal religious experience, they are given an impersonality through their associations with the Liturgy. By its reference to particular parts of the divine service the meaning of Herbert's poetry is both enriched and widened, and what is individual in it is resolved into something universal. In *Peace*, for example, the poet after seeking vainly for peace first in the life of solitude and contemplation, and then in life of the court and the world, learns from a 'reverend good

---

[1] 'The Collar.' Herbert, ed. cit. p. 153.   [2] 'The Quip.' Ibid. p. 110.
[3] 'Miserie.' Ibid. p. 100.   [4] 'Dialogue.' Ibid. p. 114.

old man' that his desire can be satisfied only through Christ. The
old man tells him a parable about Christ's life, and how after His
death twelve stalks of wheat sprang up out of His grave:

> It prosper'd strangely, and did soon disperse
> Through all the earth:
> For they that taste it do rehearse,
> That vertue lies therein,
> A secret vertue bringing peace and mirth
> By flight of sinne.

> Take of this grain, which in my garden grows,
> And grows for you;
> Make bread of it: and that repose
> And peace, which ev'ry where
> With so much earnestnesse you do pursue,
> Is onely there.

The poem is an allegory of human experience, and the economy
with which it is written is a sign not of poverty of content but
of compression. In the last verse the references to the garden and
to the bread indicate how rich and full the meaning of the whole
really is. The garden is the Garden of Paradise, the bread, the
Bread of Life: through them the redemption of man by Christ
is defined not only as an historical fact in the past—the ostensible
theme of the allegory—but also as a reality in the present. The
cadence of the lines

> Take of this grain, which in my garden grows,
> And grows for you; [1]

echoes the words of administration in the Holy Communion
Service, and links the old man's parable of the death of Christ
with the Sacrament in which it is daily celebrated. The old man
has become the officiating priest, the event of the past the experience of the moment: the whole point of the allegory is
established through the unstated, but none the less unmistakable,
reference to the Liturgy.

Many other poems make use of the Liturgy in this way.

[1] 'Peace.' Ibid. p. 125.

Repentance has a general background of psalms and intercessions behind it, *Even-song* recalls the service for the burial of the dead in the finality of the terms in which the coming on of night is expressed:

> Yet still thou goest on,
> And now with darknesse closest wearie eyes,
> Saying to man, *It doth suffice*:
> *Henceforth repose; your work is done.*[1]

and the reference to the 'ebonie box' in the next line suggests the same undercurrent of ideas. In the titles of the poems—*Trinitie Sunday, Easter, Good Friday, H. Baptisme, The H. Communion, Mattens*—the connections with the feasts of the Church and its services are acknowledged; indeed, names like these much better represent the scope of Herbert's poetry than does *Affliction* or *Longing*. Yet the poems remain lyrical in form and in the way their themes are treated; the Liturgy provides a setting for them, it is the means by which personal and individual religious experience is united to the experience of all Christians at all times, but it is rarely used directly. The only poem which is liturgical in a strict sense is *The Sacrifice*; for there the form itself of the poem is determined by the form of a religious rite. The poem is a monologue, the lament of Christ to sinful man. It is written entirely in the first person, its refrain, repeated at the end of every stanza, is cast in personal terms:

> *Oh all ye, who passe by,* whose eyes and minde
> To worldly things are sharp, but to me blinde;
> To me, who took eyes that I might you finde:
> Was ever grief like mine?

Yet the effect of the whole is not primarily that of a personal appeal. The figure of Christ which it creates is the Christ of mediaeval painting—an embodiment of doctrinal truth. The

---

[1] 'Even-song.' Herbert, ed. cit. p. 63. Cp. 'Write, From henceforth blessed are the dead which die in the Lord; even so saith the Spirit; for they rest from their labours' (*Rev.* xiv. 13). *The Book of Common Prayer*: 'The Order for the Burial of the Dead.

24

Our Pelican, *by bleeding, thus,*
Fulfill'd the Law, *and cured* Vs.

ILLVSTR. XX.   *Book.3*

Ooke here, and marke (her fickly birds to feed)
How freely this kinde *Pelican* doth bleed.
  See, how (when other *Salves* could not be found)
To cure their forrowes, fhe, her felfe doth wound;
And, when this holy *Emblem,* thou fhalt fee,
Lift up thy foule to him, who dy'd for thee.
  For, this our *Hieroglyphick* would expreffe
That *Pelican,* which in the *Wilderneffe*
Of this vaft *World,* was left (as all alone)
Our miferable *Nature* to bemone;
And, in whofe eyes, the teares of pitty ftood,
When he beheld his owne unthankfull *Brood*
His *Favours,* and his *Mercies,* then, contemne,
When with his wings he would have brooded them:

From George Wither: *A Collection of Emblemes 1635*
[slightly reduced]

words which are put into His mouth express a complex set of
ideas, the ideas involved in the doctrines of the Fall, the Atonement
and the Incarnation:

> Then on my head a crown of thorns I wear:
> For these are all the grapes *Sion* doth bear,
> Though I my vine planted and watred there:
> >   Was ever grief like mine?

> So sits the earths great curse in *Adams* fall
> Upon my head: so I remove it all
> From th'earth unto my brows, and bear the thrall:
> >   Was ever grief like mine? [1]

They have only to be compared with lines from *Paradise Lost*,
where the emphasis is upon the human as well as upon the cosmo-
logical aspects of the Fall for their character to be made clear.
In the plucking of the apple in Milton's poem it is the personal
factors in the situation which are stressed:

> Earth felt the wound, and Nature from her seat
> Sighing through all her Works, gave signs of woe,
> That all was lost. [2]

The incidence of the loss is on the two human beings who have
caused it. But in *The Sacrifice* the personal is submerged in the
doctrinal: individual action and its consequences in the 'earth's
great curse'. This impersonal quality is given to Herbert's poem
by the close connection it retains with its liturgical source: it
derives from the Improperia or Reproaches of Christ which in the
Roman Use are recited on Good Friday. [3] In adopting this rite
for his framework Herbert preserved much of the general character of the original. The form and the content of *The Sacrifice*
depend upon it, and so, to a large extent, does the style. The
language is deeply moving, and yet has all the formality which
belongs to ritual. The effect it creates is that of the flat monotone
of a chant: it is bare and abstract, but at the same time the slightest

---

[1] 'The Sacrifice.' Ibid. p. 26.   [2] Milton, *Paradise Lost*. IX. 782–4.
[3] These were omitted from the first Prayer Book of Edward VI and did not
ever form part of the liturgy of the Church of England.

alteration of the emotional pitch becomes exceedingly emphatic. The whole poem, in fact, is rooted in ritualistic practice. But here Herbert has departed from his usual custom, and *The Sacrifice* is unique in the canon of his work for the closeness with which it relies on religious ceremony.[1]

These are some of the qualities of the poetry of *The Temple*, and it is to the building up of so rich a simplicity that the emblem

[1] It is difficult to do justice to *The Sacrifice* in a short space because it is a very complex poem in which the ideas are built up by a series of cross references so that the effect of every line is deepened emotionally and intellectually by other lines. The original Reproaches emphasise the irony involved in the Atonement; each sentence contains an ironic contrast: 'Ego dedi tibi sceptrum regale: et tu dedisti capiti meo spineam coronam'. Herbert develops this structure so that the irony does not lie only in the direct reversals of Ego-tu but in every aspect of the situation. The refrain with its apparent stress on personal grief is the focusing point for all the complexities of meaning implied in the theme. The quality of Herbert's treatment of the theme is best estimated by contrasting his poem with one of the mediaeval vernacular versions of the Reproaches. Two are printed in Carleton Brown: *Religious Lyrics of the Fourteenth Century*. 1924. pp. 17 and 88. It may perhaps be added that the lament of Charles I printed in some texts of *Eikon Basilike* seems to have been composed with *The Sacrifice* in mind. The implications of regicide for believers in the Divine Right of Kings are fully recognised. These verses may be compared with Herbert's:

3. Nature and Law by thy Divine Decree,
   The only Root of Righteous Royaltie,
   With this dim diadem invested me.

5. The fiercest furies that doe daily tred,
   Upon my Grief, my gray Discrowned Head,
   Are those that owe my Bounty, for their Bread.

6. They raise a War, and Christen it, *The cause*,
   Whilst Sacrilegious hands have best applause,
   Plunder and Murder are the Kingdoms Lawes.

16. With my own Power my Majesty they wound,
    In the King's name the King himself's uncrowned
    So doth the dust destroy the Diamond.

18. They promise to erect my Royal Stem,
    To make me Great, t'advance my Diadem,
    If I will first fall down and worship them.

(*Eikon Basilike*. The Hague. 1648).

162

method makes a contribution. It cannot be too strongly emphasised that Herbert's images remain emblems and at no time encroach upon the wider provinces of the symbol. There is no necessary and essential resemblance between the church floor and the human heart, between stained glass windows and preachers, or between two cabinets filled with treasure and the Trinity and the Incarnation. His method is always to create meaning by creating likenesses: the likenesses are rarely inherent in the imagery chosen nor can they often be seen from the outset. But by the end of the poem the reader always understands and accepts them, for the emblematic image is made wholly convincing as a symbol through the completeness with which the relation is established between it and the ideas it embodies. Each of the epithets in *The Church-floore* adds simultaneously to the image and to the generality behind it, creating the picture in the moral and the moral in the picture, and at the same time preserving the sharp outlines of both. Out of these is built up the central parallel, which is directly expressed only in the last couplet:

> Blest be the *Architect*, whose art
> Could build so strong in a weak heart.

Herbert himself sums up his method in the poem called *The Rose*:

> But I will not much oppose
> Unto what you now advise:
> Onely take this gentle rose,
> And therein my answer lies.[1]

It is to infuse the image chosen with as rich a meaning as possible.

It is chiefly in the principles underlying his treatment of imagery that Herbert's affinities with emblems are most clearly to be seen, but there are, here and there, references to the familiar themes of the emblem books themselves. In *The Church-porch*, for instance, Isis and her ass appear:

> The shrine is that which thou dost venerate,
> And not the beast, that bears it on his back.[2]

---

[1] Herbert, ed. cit. p. 177.   [2] 'The Church-porch.' Ibid. p. 6

In *The Size* he makes use of an emblem to clinch the argument
of the poem:

> . . . Call to minde thy dream,
> An earthly globe,
> On whose meridian was engraven,
> *These seas are tears, and heav'n the haven.*[1]

Apart from one noteworthy exception, however, Herbert cannot
be said to have confined himself in any poem to the material of
the emblematists. Memories of Amor and Anima are perhaps
behind the *Dialogue* and the better known 'Love bade me welcome
but my soul drew back . . .' and lines like:

> Wit fancies beautie, beautie raiseth wit:
> The world is theirs; they two play out the game
> Thou standing by: [2]

are reminiscent of similar episodes in Quarles's *Emblemes*. *Good
Friday* must have been written with the pictures of the emblems
of the heart in mind:

> Since bloud is fittest, Lord, to write
> Thy sorrows in, and bloudie fight;
> My heart hath store, write there, where in
> One box doth lie both ink and sinne:

> That when sinne spies so many foes,
> Thy whips, thy nails, thy wounds, thy woes,
> All come to lodge there, sinne may say,
> *No room for me,* and flie away.[3]

In all these, however, the influence of the emblem books is reflected in only a general way. The sole exception is *Love unknown*.
It was quoted by Coleridge in support of his contention that the
characteristic fault of the earlier poets was to convey 'the most
fantastic thoughts in the most correct and natural language', and,
without its context in the tradition to which it belongs, it certainly
reads obscurely and presents, as Coleridge says, 'an enigma of
thoughts'.[4]

The pursuit of the unintelligible was never one of Herbert's
interests and there is no suggestion of it in the tone of the poem.

[1] Herbert, ed. cit. p. 137.   [2] 'Love.' Ibid. p. 54.
[3] 'Good Friday.' Ibid. p. 38.
[4] *Biographia Literaria.* Ed. J. Shawcross. 1907. Vol. II. p. 73.

He is merely attempting to do briefly what had already been done at greater length on the Continent and what was afterwards to find its way to England in Christopher Harvey's *Schola Cordis*. The poem is an allegory of religious experience made up of three incidents. It is centred in the human heart:

> A Lord I had,
> And have, of whom some grounds, which may improve,
> I hold for two lives, and both lives in me.
> To him I brought a dish of fruit one day,
> And in the middle plac'd my heart . . .

The Lord, however, rejects the offering and summons instead a servant to wash and wring the heart in a font. Then

> After my heart was well,
> And clean and fair, as I one even-tide
> (I sigh to tell)
> Walkt by my self abroad, I saw a large
> And spacious fornace flaming, and thereon
> A boyling caldron, round about whose verge
> Was in great letters set AFFLICTION.

The heart is made subject to further purification, and the poet hastens home:

> But when I thought to sleep out all these faults
> (I sigh to speak)
> I found that some had stuff'd the bed with thoughts,
> I would say *thorns.*

Finally the images are explained and the moral enforced by the listener who has heard Herbert's story:

> *Truly, Friend,*
> *For ought I heare, your Master shows to you*
> *More favour then you wot of. Mark the end.*
> *The Font did onely, what was old, renew:*
> *The Caldron suppled, what was grown too hard:*
> *The Thorns did quicken, what was grown too dull:*
> *All did but strive to mend, what you had marr'd.*
> *Wherefore be cheer'd, and praise him to the full*
> *Each day, each houre, each moment of the week,*
> *Who fain would have you be new, tender, quick.*[1]

[1] 'Love unknown.' Herbert, ed. cit. p. 129.

The picture reproduced opposite from *Schola Cordis* will provide enough evidence to show that it was from this convention that the poem derives. Harvey's translation was not published till 1647 but there were already a number of foreign books of the kind available to Herbert and he may well have seen one. A possible source for the material of the poem was the concordance made by the ladies of Little Gidding which was given to him by Nicholas Ferrar; it has not survived but another from the same source, preserved in the British Museum, shows the type of book it was. This is the Book of Revelation, illustrated with a number of engravings of the type of the school of the heart, which Nicholas Ferrar had probably collected among the books and engravings which we know he brought back from his travels abroad. The plates include pictures of Christ entering a heart crowded with salamanders and poisonous creatures, Christ enthroned in the heart, Christ knocking at its door; another represents a font full of hearts into which the blood of Christ is streaming. Herbert's concordance, 'wch he sayd, he prized most highly, as a rich jewel worthy to be worn in ye heart of all Xtians & . . . most humbly blessed God, y^t he had lived now to see womens scizzers brought to so rare an use as to serve at Gods altar', was presumably illustrated in the same fashion,[1] and perhaps it was upon some of its plates that *Love unknown* was based. The structure of the poem certainly suggests that three such pictures were actually before him. Herbert draws upon the same tradition in the poem *Grace*:

> Sinne is still hammering my heart
> Unto a hardnesse, void of love:
> Let suppling grace, to crosse his art,
>   Drop from above.[2]

but *Love unknown* is the only poem which versifies the material of that particular group of emblem books so consistently and ob-

---

[1] See F. E. Hutchinson's commentary on the letters of George Herbert, op. cit. p. 577. for the evidence of Herbert's being given a Gidding Concordance, and p. 567 for Nicholas Ferrar's collection of books on his travels.

[2] 'Grace.' Ibid. p. 60.

From Christopher Harvey: *Schola Cordis 1647*

viously. It is the *Schola Cordis* in little. The poem is not one
of Herbert's best; it is too much an experiment, too much lacking
in emotional power to rank with those in which the emblem
tradition is used more obliquely. One of his editors, Mr. G. H.
Palmer, suggested that it was largely autobiographical, the dish
of fruit being an allusion to Herbert's poetry and to his scholarship
at Cambridge, and the cauldron an echo of the state of mind out
of which the five poems called *Affliction* were written. It seems
injudicious, however, to attribute such interests to any of Herbert's poems, certainly in this the conventional elements so far
outweigh the personal as to suggest a formal exercise.

These connections with specific emblem books are only occasional and while they do establish incontrovertibly Herbert's
closeness to the form, scattered parallels are never a very fruitful
method of comment. And the emblem mode had for Herbert a
wider application in that in all the poems ideas are constantly formulated through images, each of which is brief and completed,
yet fully investigated. Poems like *Prayer*, which consist wholly in
images, are only one manifestation of a process which takes
place everywhere. In the last two stanzas of *Faith*, for example,

> That which before was darkned clean
> With bushie groves, pricking the lookers eie,
> Vanisht away, when Faith did change the scene:
>   And then appear'd a glorious skie.
>
> What though my bodie runne to dust?
> Faith cleaves unto it, counting ev'ry grain
> With an exact and most particular trust,
>   Reserving all for flesh again.[1]

the close particularisation of the phrase 'pricking the lookers eie'
shows how fully the image has been explored. In *A Priest to the
Temple* Herbert had advocated the 'diligent collation of Scripture
with Scripture',[2] and this habit of collation and exploration lies
behind all his poetry and gives it its weight. True renunciation is
shown in *The Pearl* to exist only when the value of what is re-

---

[1] 'Faith.' Ibid. p. 49.
[2] Chapter IV, 'The Parsons Knowledge'. Ibid. p. 229.

nounced is fully understood: in the last stanza, the ways of Learning, of Honour, and of Pleasure which have been rejected are still present in the mind:

> I know all these, and have them in my hand:
> Therefore not sealed, but with open eyes
> I flie to thee . . .[1]

This, as Walton's account of Herbert makes clear, was the principle on which his religious life was built up. It is also the principle behind his poetry, for from this habitual completeness of knowledge the simplicity of its style springs. The experience of a mind which has travelled far in thought and felt intensely is contracted into a single image; and each poem offers a picture that is deceptively precise and clear-cut. In some the stanza form supplies in itself an unacknowledged central image. *Easter-wings* and *The Altar*, for instance, are written in those actual shapes, *Sunday* has stanzas of seven lines, and in *Sinnes round* his 'offences course it in a ring', each verse beginning with the last line of the preceding one; in *A Wreath* the same method is repeated, and Herbert achieves a remarkable *tour de force* in building up a poem of overlapping lines:

> A Wreathed garland of deserved praise,
> Of praise deserved, unto thee I give,
> I give to thee, who knowest all my wayes,
> My crooked winding wayes, wherein I live. . . .[2]

In all these the title describes what has been done by the stanza form, demonstrates the picture which the actual appearance of the poem on the page would offer to the eye. In others the same method is used more subtly. In *The Pulley* the image of a pulley is nowhere present in the substance of the poem; yet the title makes its whole point:

> When God at first made man,
> Having a glasse of blessings standing by;
> Let us (said he) poure on him all we can:
> Let the worlds riches, which dispersed lie,
> Contract into a span.

[1] Herbert, ed. cit. p. 88.   [2] 'A Wreath.' Ibid. p. 185.

So strength first made a way;
Then beautie flow'd, then wisdome, honour, pleasure:
When almost all was out, God made a stay,
Perceiving that alone of all his treasure
Rest in the bottome lay.

For if I should (said he)
Bestow this jewell also on my creature,
He would adore my gifts in stead of me,
And rest in Nature, not the God of Nature:
So both should losers be.

Yet let him keep the rest,
But keep them with repining restlesnesse:
Let him be rich and wearie, that at least,
If goodnesse leade him not, yet wearinesse
May tosse him to my breast.[1]

In the same way in *The Collar* one image informs the whole, though again it is not explicit. All through the poem an active profession of violence and confusion has been made, and yet, collarwise, all is controlled at the end by the single word *Child*. Herbert named his poems with care, and sometimes renamed them upon revision. A number of alterations in their titles were made between the Williams manuscript and the text that was intended for publication, sometimes to make the meaning clearer, sometimes in adjustment to revisions in the phrasing or content of the poems themselves. *The Passion*, for example, has become *Redemption* because that better expresses the point of the poem. *Perfection* became *The Elixir* after the last stanza which had begun 'But these are high *perfections*' was replaced by one introducing the image of the philosopher's stone or elixir:

This is the famous stone
That turneth all to gold:
For that which God doth touch and own
Cannot for lesse be told.[2]

The new stanza gives point also to a reference to the 'tincture' earlier in the poem so that the changed title underlines the

[1] 'The Pulley.' Ibid. p. 159.　　　　[2] 'The Elixir.' Ibid. p. 184.

alchemical imagery through which the theme is now expressed. In the same way *Prayer* in the Williams manuscript becomes *Church-lock and Key* after the word 'locks' had been introduced in place of the original 'stops' of the first line:

> I know it is my sinne which locks thine eares.

In making these alterations Herbert seems always to have been concerned with specifying his meaning more closely and directing the attention towards what was of central importance in the poem. The titles are changed to something more concrete in order to make the point of the whole sharper. The poem which begins 'When first my lines of heav'nly joys made mention' was originally called *Invention*: Herbert afterwards changed the title to *Jordan*, thus connecting his poem with another he had written upon the same theme and also emphasising its moral. The two poems are about his own art; in both he concludes that religion is better served in verse in which the beauty lies only in the truth expressed. In the one he had first named *Invention* he repudiates all ornament and decoration:

> . . . I sought out quaint words, and trim invention;
> My thoughts began to burnish, sprout, and swell,
> Curling with metaphors a plain intention,
> Decking the sense, as if it were to sell.

They could not convey what he wished, for

> This was not quick enough, and that was dead.
> Nothing could seem too rich to clothe the sunne,
> Much lesse those joyes which trample on his head.

The answer comes finally:

> *There is in love a sweetnesse readie penn'd:*
> *Copie out onely that, and save expense.*[1]

Plainness and simplicity of language are worth more than all the adornments that rhetoric could give. And so the original *Invention*, with its technical associations with the Art of Rhetoric, was re-

---

[1] 'Jordan (II).' Herbert, ed. cit. p. 102.

placed by *Jordan*, the symbol of purification.[1] Such changes are not very numerous but when they do occur they are always illuminating because they indicate the precision of thought which extends even to the titles of the poems in *The Temple*.

His use of personification also reflects Herbert's modification of the ways of the emblematists. It was not a device that he employed often, and his figures were entirely his own. They carry no bit, bridle, anchor, or other recognisable paraphernalia, nor is any single one of them described directly. Any attributes they may have are shown by implication. Glorie comes

> puffing by.
> In silks that whistled.[2]

Religion and sin are contrasted:

> Religion, like a pilgrime, westward bent,
> Knocking at all doores, ever as she went,

and sin:

> travell'd westward also: journeying on
> He chid the Church away, where e're he came,
> Breaking her peace, and tainting her good name.[3]

Yet figures like these are much more fully realised than those which are described at such length by the emblem writers. Their attributes are not hung upon them from outside like the clothes of a cardboard doll, but are intrinsic. They appear only briefly but their function is always completed. In *The Quip* a series of figures is introduced each of which has his characteristic speech and gesture:

> First, Beautie crept into a rose,
> Which when I pluckt not, Sir, said she,
> Tell me, I pray, Whose hands are those?
> *But thou shalt answer, Lord, for me.*

[1] For the interpretation of the meaning of the title see F. E. Hutchinson's notes to 'Jordan (I)'. Op. cit. p. 495.
[2] 'The Quip.' Ibid. p. 110.
[3] 'The Church Militant.' Ibid. p. 190. ll. 29, 30; 104–6.

The poem describes a trial of faith. It is also a definition of faith. The strength of the resisting virtue is measured by the plausibility of the figures which confront it; and there emerges at the same time a clear conviction of the nature of that virtue. For each figure is the single embodiment of both tempter and temptation. Once again the image has been explored to its farthest limits.

The ability to express complex thoughts and sensations in poetry was typical of the metaphysical poets as a whole, but the precision and simplicity which Herbert achieved in his expression of them could perhaps be attained only when the emblem convention flourished. Certainly no other poet has been able to concentrate so rich a meaning within so simple a framework.

26

landſt ſecurely at the part; and ſhalt find in thy ſelf,
how worthily it was ſayd: *the Virgins name was Marie.*

THE EMBLEME.

THE POESIE.

The
Pauſe.

He glorious *Sunne* withdrew his beames of light;
My ſinne was cauſe: So I in diſmal night
Am ſayling in a ſtormie dangerous Maine;
And ere the Sunne (I feare) returne againe,
Shal ſuffer ſhipwrack, where the fraite's my Soule.
My onlie Hope's a Starre, fixt neere the Pole,
But that my Needle now hath loſt its force,
Once touchd with grace , and ſaile out of courſe.
Starre of the Sea, thy Sun hath giuen thee light;
Til he brings day, guide me in ſinnes dark night.
I ſeeke, what Sages heertofore haue donne,
Guided by thee a Starre, to find the Sunne.

From Henry Hawkins: *Partheneia Sacra 1633*

Chapter 7

CATHOLIC EMBLEM BOOKS IN PROSE

ALTHOUGH it was in a Protestant form, in the work of Quarles and Harvey, that the methods of the Jesuit writers were best known in England, there was still scope for the production of similar books for English Catholics. Such books were naturally few. The demand was limited and could be supplied only under difficult and dangerous conditions: recusant books had to be printed secretly by one of the illicit presses or else smuggled in from abroad. In either event they might be seized and suppressed.[1] For many Catholic readers, too, the Latin and French of the already numerous foreign religious emblem books would not have presented any obstacle: Quarles's and Harvey's translations of Hugo and van Haeften were so successful because they were made not for those for whom they had originally been written but for those to whom they would otherwise have been inaccessible.

It is perhaps for these reasons that the three Catholic emblem books in English which do exist are of some literary merit. They are more explicitly devotional than those which reached England through Protestant channels, for they were intended not for ephemeral reading but for continual use. Accordingly, their contents are not confined to the picture and poem of the stock emblematic conventions. Their main purpose is the practice of meditation, and to this purpose the emblems are no more than contributory factors. Henry Hawkins's translation of Fr. Luzvic's *Le Cœur Devot*, for instance, which is a recusant counterpart of Harvey's *School of the Heart*, was not put into the hands of its readers merely for their pleasure and entertainment. It is based on the usual theme of the preparation of the heart for its heavenly

---

[1] There is a record of such a seizure in 1626 when a consignment of 'Popish books' was discovered on a Dutch ship at Newcastle. Vide Helen White, *English Devotional Literature, 1600–1640*. Univ. of Wisconsin Studies, 1931. p. 136.

guest, but by far the greater part of it is taken up with prose meditations for which the emblematic pictures and poems are a focusing point. Its object is to combine the functions of an emblem book with those of a devotional manual. Devotion is the first essential, and Hawkins, moreover, thought it necessary to excuse the means which fostered it on the grounds that 'though the instruments I use, may seeme prophane, so prophanely used nowadays, as *Devises* consisting of *Impreses*, and *Mottoes*, *Characters*, *Essayes*, *Emblemes* and *Poesies*; yet they may be like that *Panthaeon* once sacred to the feigned Deities, and piously since sanctified, converted, and consecrated to the honour of the glorious *Queene*, and al the blessed *Saints of Heaven*'. In all three Catholic emblem books the authors are governed by the same purpose: the emblems are 'piously sanctified' and are used as the basis of a religious meditation.

The books which constitute this group are Henry Hawkins's *Partheneia Sacra*,[1] his translation of *Le Cœur Devot*, and thirdly *Ashrea or the Grove of Beatitudes* by an unidentified writer whose initials were E.M. Of the three, *Partheneia Sacra* is by far the most remarkable. Apart from its unusually well designed plates and at least passable verse, it contains passages of prose which are memorable in both substance and style. Hawkins had a mind which found in the emblem method a particularly satisfactory form of expression. He looked upon his world with an almost Elizabethan freshness of insight, finding in it always a beauty that was *tam antiqua et tam nova*. Ideas to him were fascinating in and for themselves; yet it is a fascination which never loses sight of the phenomena of the visible world. The whole book is rooted in a desire 'to learne of each creature how to serve the common Creator of us all', and the objects which are to him the means of teaching this lesson are described with all the powers of sensuous evocation that he had at his disposal. The Tulip for example

[1] The authorship of *Partheneia Sacra* has been disputed on the grounds that the initials H.A. under which it appears are not those of Henry Hawkins, who is known to have published a number of other books initialled H.H. It has also been suggested that it is a translation. Both these points are discussed in Appendix 3.

is a singular ornament to this Garden; looke and observe it wel. How were it possible, one would think, so thin a leaf, bred and nourished in the same ayre, and proceeding from the same stem, should be golden in the bottome, violet without, saffron within, bordered on the edge with fine gold, and the prickle of the point blew as a goodlie Saphir? [1]

'How were it possible?' is a philosopher's question, and philosophy for Hawkins was more than the intellectual pursuit of abstract ideas: it was a passion which sprang from his sharpest awareness of colour and texture. 'How were it possible . . .' follows naturally from the vivid experience he had of the world round him; the question is never very far removed from the concrete realisation of created things. *Partheneia Sacra* is the devotional outcome of such a mode of experience: it rests upon the same principles as have been exemplified in the emblem books discussed in the previous chapters, that is, upon the establishment of a relationship between particular images and general ideas; but all is done with a new purpose. The aim is to use these means to promote and direct religious meditation.

All three emblem books share this aim but neither of the others is comparable with *Partheneia Sacra* in literary merit. It is, therefore, with it that the greater part of this chapter will be concerned.[2]

Of Hawkins himself all too little is known. The records of his life are few and brief, and his works, however expressive of his personality, add almost nothing to the meagre collection of facts. He was one of the thirteen children, seven boys and six girls, of Sir Thomas Hawkins of Nash Court in Kent.[3] The family was

---

[1] *Partheneia Sacra.* 1633. p. 10.

[2] I should add that as *Partheneia Sacra* has never been reprinted and is difficult of access, a rather more detailed account of it has seemed necessary than the proportions of this book would otherwise require; I have illustrated what I have to say of it at length for that reason.

[3] They were Thomas, Henry, Daniel, Richard (to whom the estates finally came, as Henry and Daniel left no children and Sir Thomas's two sons died young), Ciriac, John, Charles, and Susan, Anne, Benedicta, Anne, Francis and

actively and openly Catholic and remained so through the seven-teenth century: one of the reasons why so little is known of Henry is that Nash Court was plundered by a Protestant mob in 1715 and all its contents, furniture, deeds, portraits, family papers and even the library, were destroyed.[1] Henry's elder brother, Sir Thomas, who inherited the estates, was known to be 'a great papist and a harbourer of priests'. He was also a translator of Catholic books and something of a poet.[2] The family seems indeed to have possessed considerable literary ability, for another brother, John, who was a doctor in London, wrote a book on grammar and published a few minor translations.

Henry himself was born in 1571 or 1575 and entered the English College at Rome in 1609. Little is known about his life before that date. Apart from one translation,[3] he published nothing until he was over fifty and though *Partheneia Sacra* seems to be the work of a man who had lived much in the world, it gives no indication of the manner in which its author had spent his time. A record at the English College made in 1613 says that he was as 'a son of a cavalier, lord of a castle, a man of mature age, intelligent in affairs of government, very learned in the English laws, and that he had left a wife, office, and many other commod-ities and expectations to become a priest in the Seminaries'.[4]

[1] Joseph Gillow. *A Bibliographical Dictionary of English Catholics.* 1885. 'Sir Thomas Hawkins.'

[2] He published an English version of Fr. Binet's *La Vie de S. Elzear*, and undertook the arduous task of translating Nicholas Caussin's *The Holy Court*. This last, which was designed to show by precept and example that piety could flourish as well in Courts as in monasteries and places of retreat, was so long that others were called in to assist, notably Sir Basil Brook to whom Henry Hawkins dedicated his translation of Maffaeus, but the main burden of the work was borne by Sir Thomas. He also published a few original verses and a translation of Horace.

[3] Fr. John Floyd. *Synopsis Apostasiae Marcii Antonii de Dominis.* St. Omer. 1617.

[4] Stonyhurst MS. Angl. Vol. IV. n. 41. printed in H. Foley: *Records of the English Province of the Society of Jesus.* 1877. Vol. III, p. 491.

Katherine. A copy of *Partheneia Sacra* belonged to Benedicta, and was inscribed 'For Dame Benedicta Hawkines, w(r)itten By her borther Henery Hawkines of the Societie of Jesus'. E. Hasted, *The History of Kent.* 1778–99. Vol. III. p. 4.

He did not, however, cut himself off from his former associations, and the dedications of his books suggest that after his return to England friendships of the past were renewed and fresh ones formed.[1] He entered the Society of Jesus in 1615 and, after a period spent in Belgium, came to England where he was captured and imprisoned. The position of Catholics in England was not, however, so insecure as it had been in the years immediately following the gunpowder plot, and no worse fate befell Hawkins than that of condemnation to perpetual exile from which he promptly returned to labour, mostly in London, for the next twenty-five years. The marriage of Charles I with Henrietta Maria resulted in some measure of toleration for Catholics, and Hawkins's work in England must have been carried on under conditions of comparative quiet. His name was on a list of Jesuits found among some papers seized at Clerkenwell in 1628 but no action seems to have been taken against him, and he was finally able to withdraw from his work—probably at the outbreak of the Civil War—and to spend the remainder of his life in the house of the English Tertian Fathers at Ghent. He died there in 1646.

Hawkins's books consist mainly of translations of saints' lives from the French and Italian, and, apart from the one early work already mentioned, their publication was confined to a brief period of his life between 1630 and 1636 when he was presumably still working among the Jesuits in London. All were printed abroad.[2] The two books of immediate interest in relation to the

---

[1] *The History of S. Elizabeth*, translated by Hawkins in 1632, is dedicated 'To the right honourable the Lady Mary Tenham'. Lord Teynham, one of the recusant peers, was a near neighbour of the Hawkins family in Kent as he lived at Linsted Lodge, some seven miles from Nash Court. The two families later intermarried. He married Lady Mary Petre in 1616; she died in 1640, and it was to her that the Life of St. Elizabeth is dedicated.

[2] For a list of Hawkins's books see Appendix 3. p. 243. The date of publication was not of course necessarily the date of composition, and it seems more likely that the long gap in his literary career between 1617 and 1630 was caused by the difficulties in publishing for a Catholic priest in England than that he should have written nothing during those years. A reference in the preface of his *History of S. Elizabeth* to the translation he made of Fr. Binet's *Vie de St*

emblem literature, his translation of Father Luzvic's *Le Cœur Devot* and his own *Partheneia Sacra*, were published in 1634 and 1633 respectively. So far as is known, *Partheneia Sacra* has no foreign source and is the only one of all Hawkins's books in which he was free to appoint both the matter and the style. *Le Cœur Devot* was of Jesuit origin, composed first in French in 1627, and translated into Latin in the same year. The two books have much in common. Both were written for societies dedicated to the service of the Virgin Mary, and both follow the same general plan of meditation and worship. Although they contain different types of emblems, it is likely that the theme of those in *Partheneia Sacra* was suggested to Hawkins by one of the chapters of Fr. Luzvic's book; for that reason *The Devout Hart* may be considered first and treated as an introduction to *Partheneia Sacra*, even though Hawkins did not publish his translation until the year after his own emblem book had appeared.

The Devout Hart belongs to the convention already described in Chapter 5—that exemplified in Christopher Harvey's *Schola Cordis*. The engravings in Fr. Luzvic's book were copied from Wiericx's *Cor Iesu amanti sacrum*, a series of pictures representing the preparation of the heart for its heavenly guest. Christ is represented knocking at the door of the heart, then entering it, sweeping out the dust and devils from within, and purging and purifying it until he is able to rest within it. Then he sings in its choir while attendant angels accompany him on musical instruments: the heart 'enflamed with the love of Jesus shines al with light and flames', it is crowned with palms and laurels, and finally Christ 'manifestes himself and the most holy Trinity in the mirrour of the heart'. These plates provided Fr. Luzvic with subjects for his devotional exercises. He attached to each four passages of prose an *Incentive*, in which the mind is directed towards the theme of the picture, a *Preamble to the Meditation*, in which the parallels between the image and the religious ideas it

Aldegonde suggests that he had work ready for printing when the opportunity should present itself, for the translation was not published till 1636, four years after the reference to it.

27

18

THE III. SYMBOL,
THE LILLIE.
THE DEVISE,

Niueo candore nitescens

THE CHARACTER.

The Impresa   HE Lillie is the Scepter of the chaſt *Diana*; whoſe Flower-deluce, the crowne; and ſtemme, the handle; which ſhe chaſtly wealds amidſt the Nimphs of flowers. It is a Siluer-Bel, without ſound to the eare, but ful of ſweets to the brim; and where it can not draw the eares, the eyes it wil; and inebriats the curious with its ouer-ſweets. It is a Box of Ciuets, which opens to the *Zephirs*, and pro-digally powers forth its ſpices to the ſtanders round-about, though they come not very nigh it. *Flora* it ſeemes

From Henry Hawkins: *Partheneia Sacra 1633*

represents are drawn in detail, the *Meditation* itself, and finally a brief *Colloquy*. All these Hawkins translated, adding also a contribution of his own in the form of a short lyrical poem on each emblem. Only the pictures were omitted from his version, and it is clear from what he says in the Preface that he had intended to include them also.

In the section in which 'The Hart consecrated to the love of Jesus is a flourishing garden', a symbolical garden is described in some detail, and various flowers are introduced as emblems of the heart which is fit to receive its lord. The lily, for instance, is one of them:

Here the lilly rising somewhat higher, from the ground, amidst the whitest leaves, in forme of a silver cup, shewes forth her golden threads of saffron in her open bosome; a noble Hierogrifike of a snowy mind, a candid purity, and a cleane hart, which now long since have been thy loves.[1]

Partheneia Sacra is an expansion of this theme of the garden: in it Hawkins develops further the general structure of the meditations in *The Devout Hart*. The subtitle of the book is 'The Mysterious and Delicious Garden of the sacred Parthenes', the garden thus providing a framework for the whole scheme of devotion. It symbolises the Mother of God, and in it are placed flowers, birds, trees emblematic of her. It was a 'Garden shut up indeed from the beginning', unlike that in which man was first placed, 'for that the Garden of *Eden*, or Terrestrial Paradice was not so exempt from Sinne, but the place where Sinne began; and was not so free from the Serpent, but that he could get-in and work the mischief'. Its flowers included the four named in *The Devout Hart*, the Rose, Lily, Violet and Sunflower, and many others: there were also formally trimmed bushes, trees, a fountain, a mount, pools and walks; and from all these are chosen twenty-four to be elaborated as emblems in the sections which follow and made the basis of twenty-four acts of devotion.

In evolving this scheme for his book, Hawkins was following

[1] Op. cit. pp. 163-4.

the example of a number of others written to encourage the worship of Mary. In the sixteenth and seventeenth centuries the cult of the Virgin was given new impetus by the foundation of Sodalities or Congregations whose members chose her for their patroness and pledged themselves to her service. These Sodalities first sprang up in the Colleges of the Society of Jesus, and although they were not afterwards confined to members of the Society they remained under Jesuit control. The movement spread with extraordinary rapidity, for the Jesuits were quick to see that they had in their hands a powerful weapon against heresy, and they used the Sodalities as a means of propagating the faith. In function the Sodalities resembled the social and religious gilds of the Middle Ages. The members bound themselves together in the practice of piety, and were noted everywhere for the virtue and sanctity of their lives. Furthermore, the original foundation at the College of Rome had set before itself a literary as well as a devotional aim. An academy had been founded within the Sodality to encourage the production of religious dramas and to foster literary work generally, and this example was in due course followed by other Sodalities. The result was the widespread publication of books in honour of the Virgin. In 1576 Francis Coster, the director of the Sodalities in France, published his *Libellus Sodalitatis Beatissimae Virginis Mariae*, which was intended especially for their use, and countless manuals of every kind devoted to the same purpose were issued afterwards in rapid succession. They included anthologies of the hymns written in honour of the Virgin, meditations appropriate to the various feasts celebrated by the Church in her memory, books of emblems in her praise, and pictures of her images with accounts of the different miracles they had performed. Dictionaries of the names of the Virgin and bibliographies of Marian books were compiled for the use of worshippers and writers.[1] In England two Jesuits, Sabin Chambers

---

[1] The two chief bibliographies are Ippolyto Marracci's *Bibliotheca Mariana*. 1648. and the subject index of P. Alegambe's *Bibliotheca Scriptorum Societatis Jesu*. 1643. Theophilus Raynaudus's *Nomenclator Marianum*. Lyons. 1639. gives an annotated list of names and a glossary.

and Thomas Worthington, published books of instructions for saying her Rosary,[1] and Catholic controversalists supported her cult as part of their general apology for the Church of Rome. Antony Stafford, for example, wrote *The Female Glory* in 1635 as a reproach to those Puritans and heretics who 'as in their coarse oratory they called Queene Elizabeth, *Queene Bess*, so they give this Holy Virgin no higher a stile, than that of *Mal*, Gods Maide'. In England, too, Sodalities were formed, and it was for the use of one of them, the Parthenian Sodality of the Immaculate Conception that *Partheneia Sacra* was written.[2]

These organisations and the books they inspired naturally gave wide currency to the symbols that had been associated with the Virgin Mary since the very beginning of her cult. Devotion to the Mother of God had been universally practised in the Church from the eighth century onwards and, as it developed, a number of images drawn partly from the Song of Solomon and partly from other passages in the Old Testament came to be connected with her name. She was the Hortus Conclusus—Hawkins's 'Garden shut up from the beginning'—the Lily among thorns, the Tower of Ivory, the Ark of the Covenant, the Rod of Jesse, the Burning Bush. These images occur repeatedly in the Latin hymns written in her honour, and from them filtered into the mediaeval English lyric. Some were enshrined in the Litany of Loretto which was recited by those devoted to her service. They were represented pictorially in the stained glass windows and

[1] *The Garden of our Blessed Lady* by Sabin Chambers. 1619. *The Rosarie of Our Ladie* by Thomas Worthington. Antwerp. 1600.

[2] There is no evidence in the book to show where the Sodality to which it is dedicated was established. At the end of the seventeenth century there was a Sodality of the Immaculate Conception attached to the newly opened Jesuit College in the Savoy, and its director, Fr. Edward Scarisbrick, published a book (*Rules and Instructions for the Sodality of the Immaculate Conception of the most Glorious and ever Virgin Mary Mother of God.* London. 1703). In this he summarises the history of the movement, but says little of foundations in England. If the estimate of Brian Magee in *The English Recusants*. 1938. that about an eighth of the population of England in the seventeenth century was Catholic can be accepted, it would be reasonable to suppose that several such organisations were in being at the time when Hawkins wrote *Partheneia Sacra*.

sculpture of churches;[1] Antoine Vérard's *Heures à l'Usage de Rouen*, 1503, for instance, which was the source of countless sixteenth century paintings of the Virgin, shows her surrounded by fifteen emblems each labelled: *Electa ut sol, pulchra ut luna, porta coeli, plantatio rosae, exaltata cedrus, virga Jesse floruit, puteus aquarum viventium, hortus conclusus, stella maris, lilium inter spinas, oliva speciosa, turris David, speculum sine macula, fons hortorum, civitas Dei.*[2] The same epithets were preserved in the Catholic literature of the seventeenth century and particularly in that associated with the Sodalities. Antony Stafford's *The Female Glory*, which was published two years after *Partheneia Sacra*, is preceded by a poem in which a list very similar to that from Verard's picture is given:

> Put off thy shooe, tis holy ground,
> For here the flaming Bush is found,
> The mystic Rose, the Iv'ry Tower,
> The morning Star and *Davids* bower,
> The rod of *Moses*, and of *Jesse*,
> The fountain sealed, *Gideons* fleece,
> The woman clothed with the Sunne,
> The beauteous throne of *Solomon*,
> The Garden shut, the living Spring,
> The Tabernacle of the King,
> The Altar breathing sacred fume
> The Heaven distilling honie-combe,
> The untouch'd Lilly, full of dew,
> A Mother, yet a Virgin true. . . .[3]

[1] For example, the window in the easternmost chapel on the south side of King's College Chapel contains Flemish glass, *c.* 1530, on which Christ, represented as a unicorn, is driven from heaven by Gabriel and finds shelter in the lap of the Virgin who is surrounded by her symbols.

[2] E. Mâle, *L'Art Religieux de la fin du moyen âge.* 1922. p. 214.

[3] Op. cit. 'A Panegyrick on the Blessed Virgin Mary.' The meanings of the symbols are usually self-evident. Gideon's fleece is probably the least intelligible: it was one of the many which signified the Virgin Birth and the alternating dryness and damp of the fleece are explained as: 'The fleece wet with dew is the holy Virgin having conceived. The dry threshing floor is her inviolate Virginity. The floor was on the second occasion wet with dew, because the church was pregnant with the gifts of the Holy Spirit.' F. J. E. Raby, *A History of Christian-Latin Poetry.* 1927. p. 363.

These symbols could be taken separately to form the basis of an act of devotion to the Virgin and many Jesuit writers made use of them for this purpose. Books were published in which each act was accompanied by an emblematic engraving of its theme, a means often being found through the pictures of co-ordinating the different images into a unified whole. In Hawkins's book this is done by the adoption of a central symbol, that of the Hortus Conclusus, into which all the rest are fitted. Another Jesuit author, Maximilian Sandaeus, whose methods have much in common with those of Hawkins, grouped together sets of images of the same type, and between 1627 and 1639 published a whole series of books for the use of Sodalities in which the Virgin was symbolised by birds, flowers, jewels, etc. In *Maria Gemma Mystica* the six central events of her life are expressed in six jewels, the jasper, carbuncle, emerald, agate, sapphire and pearl. In *Maria Flos Mysticus* and *Aviarum Marianum* flowers and birds provide the symbols; in *Maria Sol Mysticus* and *Maria Luna Mystica* the different positions of the sun in the heavens and the different phases of the moon are used; and finally there is *Maria Mundus Mysticus*, where ingenuity is stretched to its farthest limits and the Virgin compared with Earth, Heaven, Hell and the four elements. Sandaeus's books offer a representative collection of images within the classes he has chosen, and many of those used by Hawkins can be found among them. The Dove, Hen, Swan, Nightingale, and Phoenix of the Virgin's Garden are among his birds, the Rose, Lily, Violet, and Sunflower among his flowers. Such books as Sandaeus's illustrate the literary and religious background of *Partheneia Sacra*, and it was from them or from books like them that its 'symbolical theologie' is derived.

The plan of *Partheneia Sacra* is a somewhat complicated one. The twenty-four symbols associated with the Virgin are all gathered together in the plate which formed the frontispiece to the book: it is reproduced on the following page. This plate provides a kind of pictorial index to the whole and is accompanied by an explanation entitled 'The Platform of the Garden', in which the symbols are all identified. The four flowers, the *Lily*, *Rose*,

Violet and *Heliotropion* (Sunflower or Marigold) can be seen standing up in their beds; there are two trees, the *Palm* and the *Olive*, in the foreground. The *Bee* (at the back near the Rose) is gathering *Dew* as it falls from the air. Perched on the top of the *House* is the *Dove*; another bird, the *Nightingale*, is sitting on the highest bough of the Olive tree, while the *Hen* is picking up *Pearls* near the *Fountain*. Above are the *Heavens*, with the *Moon*, the *Stars* and the *Rainbow*. The *Mount*, the *Sea*, and the *Ship* make up the number, with two other birds, the *Phoenix* and the *Swan*, who are placed outside the Garden because, as Hawkins explains, he had no leisure to finish them and they are accordingly treated less fully in the accompanying text than are the others. The main part of the book is then divided into twenty-four sections, one for each of these symbols and one for the Garden itself which is also a symbol. All the sections follow the same plan but each is quite self-contained and constitutes a separate act of devotion in itself.

The structure of this act of devotion is more elaborate than that of *The Devout Hart*. It is divided into nine distinct parts based on the study of two pictures entitled '*The Device*' and '*The Embleme*', a poem, and six passages of prose. With the psychological acuteness of a man who had been trained as a Jesuit, Hawkins handled the process of meditation in such a way that the mystical significance of each symbol could be discovered only slowly and gradually. It was to be contemplated at length and in detail: for the Garden, he maintains, 'being so mysterious and delicious an Object, requires not to be rashly lookt upon, or perfunctoriously to be slighted over, but, as the manner is of such as enter into a Garden, to glance at first thereon with a light regard, then to reflect upon it with a better heed, to find some gentle mysterie or conceipt upon it, to some use or other: and then liking it better, to review the same againe' . . . and so on, until all is understood. Accordingly the nine parts of the section on any one symbol have each their own special place in the scheme and their own contribution to make to the progress of the meditation. The six passages of prose are severally designated *The Character*, *The Morals*, *The*

28

From Henry Hawkins: *Partheneia Sacra* 1633
[slightly reduced]

Essay, *The Discourse*, *The Theories* and *The Apostrophe*, and together with *The Devise*, *The Embleme* and *The Poesie* they form
the steps by which the act of devotion comprehended in the whole
section is accomplished. The form and content of each are very
different, for not only the matter but also the style of the various
parts is governed by the purpose they serve in the complete
scheme.

It may be asked at this point, in what sense *Partheneia Sacra* is
an emblem book at all. Admittedly it contains emblems: one of
the two pictures in each section is labelled *The Embleme*, and is
accompanied by its explanatory poem, *The Poesie*. Strictly, therefore, emblems occupy two-ninths of the book only. In a broader
sense, however, the whole structure of *Partheneia Sacra* is emblematic. The twenty-four symbols[1] which are chosen to represent the
Virgin provide its framework and its main themes. Each section
opens with an engraving of the one which is to form the centre
of this particular act of devotion, so that a picture of it may be
constantly before the worshipper's eye; and the whole of the text
which follows is then built up round this symbol. The various
passages of prose which make up the section are all different ways
of using and interpreting the central image, as a brief account of
the content and function of each will show. The structure of
Hawkins's book, in fact, is in itself an extension of the emblem
method; and *Partheneia Sacra* is emblematic both in general outline and in detail.

The Devise

Each section of the book begins with a picture of the symbol
which provides its subject. This is called *The Devise* and consists
of an engraved plate with a motto. The engravings for these
and for *The Emblemes* which appear later were made by Jacob van
Langeren and are beautifully designed and executed. The plate
on page 179 shows *The Devise* for the Lily; a picture of the flower
itself enclosed in an ornamental border. All the other *Devises*

---

[1] I am using the word 'symbol' as a generic term for the images associated
with the Virgin. It is not intended to suggest any idea of value; see the discussion of the senses of the term, above, pp. 23. ff.

follow this pattern: in them the symbol is first presented to the reader so that he may have a concrete image of it fixed in his mind.

The Character

Its properties are then briefly outlined in the prose *Character* which follows. This is intended only as 'a first entertainment of the Reader', to introduce him to the subject of his meditation. Its whole content is usually made up of a number of conceits, all of them the results of the play of fancy rather than of imagination, and none of them developed to any great length. This, for example, is the opening of *The Character* of the Starre:

> The *Starres* are the glittering lamps of Heaven, set up as so manie lights, in the close or upper seeling of the ample Theater of the world. They are as sparckling Diamants strewed in the Firmament, to entertaine the World with, as a goodlie maister-piece of the great CREATOUR. They are the silver Oes, al powdred heer and there, or spangles sprinckled over the purple Mantle or night-gowne of the heavens: the seede of pearle, sowne in the spacious fields of the Heavens, to bring forth light. Have you seen a statelie Mask in Court, al set round, and taken up with a world of beautiful Ladies, to behold the sports and revels there? Imagin the *Starres* then, as sitting in the Firmament, to behold some spectacle on Earth, with no other light than their owne beauties.[1]

The stars here are represented successively as lamps, diamonds, Oes and spangles on costume, seeds, spectators at a masque—and Hawkins goes on in the rest of *The Character* to transform them into the flocks of the Gods and the nymphs of Diana. All is done not so much for purposes of information about the nature of the symbol—that comes later—but to awaken an interest in it in the reader's mind so that he will be induced to examine it further. *The Character* is, in short, Hawkins's 'glance at first with a light regard' into his garden.

The Morals

After *The Character* comes *The Morals* which is based upon the

[1] *Partheneia Sacra.* pp. 114–15.

motto of the *Devise*, and, as its name suggests, is the place for the application of the moral sentiments there contained. It is intended to stimulate the mind by its discussion of general ethical questions arising from the motto. The device of the Olive, for example, has for its word *Speciosa et Fructifera*; and the theme of its *Morals* is 'fruitfulness'. The lion which whelps only once in five years is contrasted with the wren which 'wil bring forth a 16 or 20 yong in a neast, that besides a litle skin and bone is litle more then a tuft of feathers'; the barrenness of the magnificent Sycamore is set beside the fertility of the bitter sloe, Rachel beside Leah. Finally, all are contrasted with the Blessed Virgin who was both beautiful and fruitful at the same time. *The Morals*, though admirably consistent with the traditions of the emblem books, forms one of the duller parts of each section, and it is with pleasure that the reader moves on to *The Essay* or Review where the original symbol is explored in much greater detail than it was in the preceding *Character* and where Hawkins's powers as a prose writer find their best expression.

The Essay

From the literary point of view *The Essays* constitute the most interesting part of *Partheneia Sacra*. They are largely descriptive, and although the Virgin is not forgotten she is not mentioned at all in this part. Hawkins's object is to create an imaginative idea of the symbol upon which the reader may dwell *con amore*, and from which he may afterwards be led to contemplate the virtues of the Virgin of which this is only a shadow. In *The Essays*, accordingly, the world of appearances is freely investigated, in a manner that sometimes suggests close and accurate observation of nature. This is Hawkins's account of the Lily:

When they are come forth, Nature solicitous of these treasures so odoriferous, seekes to guard them carefully, and adorne them curiously; arming some with thorns, others with prickles; covering these with rough, and others with large and shadie leaves, to conserve their luster. Among the which the *Lillie* carries hers very long, and green; the stem, high and round, streight, united, fat, and firme, al clothed with leaves. On the top whereof, grow out as it were certain wyers, with heads thereon, or buttons somewhat long, of the coulour of the hearb, which in time grow white, and fashion themselves in forme of a bel of satin or silver. From the bottome and hart thereof, grow upright, some litle wyers of gold, with heads like hammers of the same. The leaves wherof, of an exquisit whitnes, al streaked and striped without, goe enlarging themselves, like a bel, as before is sayd. The seed remaines in these hammers of gold. The stemme to carrie the head the better, is knotted and strengthned throughout; for that the *Lillie* is ever with the head hanging downwards, and languishing, as not able to beare up itself. There are some of them red, some of them azure. These are al so delicious, that even to behold them were a great delight.[1]

Temporarily, the symbolical meaning of the flower is set aside; but only so that the nature of the symbol may be apprehended more fully, and in the passage which follows, *The Discourse*, it becomes clear that Hawkins's purpose in treating the Lily in so much detail is primarily emblematical, and that each part of the description is now to be applied to the Virgin. The straight stalk symbolises her mind, that 'like a staf was always streight, and tending to God', the pendant leaves, her humility; the fragrance, her divinity; the whiteness, her purity; the root, her charity. The material of *The Essays*, however minutely particularised, is never more than a preparation for the acts of worship that are to follow.

Yet Hawkins's notion of what constitutes preparation is a generous one. It takes into account the susceptibility of the human mind to the influence of experience gained through the senses, and is characteristic of the Jesuits in its thorough grasp of psychology. Accuracy of fact does not appear to be essential: what mattered was the force and vividness of the impression made upon the senses by the description. Since, however, this vividness of impression was attained largely through attention to detail—to colour, shape, texture, scent and sound—Hawkins's descriptions do, in effect, achieve a considerable measure of accuracy. His picture of the Lily is a mixture of virtuosity and

[1] *Partheneia Sacra.* pp. 31–2.

botanical truth:[1] truth, on the whole, here predominates. The other descriptions reflect in varying proportions the same qualities of faithful observation and evocative embroidery. In *The Essay* on the Mount, for instance, Hawkins describes a landscape seen from the mountain-top:

MOUNTAINS are one of the gallantst things in Nature, especially if we regard the Prospect they afford, to deliciat the eyes with; when taking a stand upon some good advantage, you behold from thence a goodlie river underneath; which, in token of homage, as it were, runnes kissing the foot thereof, along as it goes. But then most delicious it is, when you see on the other side, a vaste playne suspended before you, and diversified with little risings, hils, and mountains, heer and there, which bounding not the view too short, suffers the eyes with freedome to extend themselves into the immensitie of Heaven, while the River, creeping along the meadows with *Meander*-windings encloses the Hil about, in forme of an Iland, whence manie vessels of al sorts riding there at ancker may be discryed, the neerest questionles very easilie discerned, & the rest farther off through interposition of bancks between, not perceaved, the tops of the masts only appearing, like a Grove or wood in winter without leaves; the little closes or fields thereabout, with the hedge-rowes environing the same, seeming as Garden-plots hedged in with prim, and the lanes and highwayes as dressed into allyes. The verdures give forth themselves delicious to behold, like a Landskap in a table, with all the greenes to be found in the neck of a mallard, heer a bright, there a dark, and then a bright and a dark againe, & al by reason of the levels, with the risings, and fallings togeather, with the lights & reflections caused through the dawning of the day in the morning or twylight of the evening, the rayes of the sunne being an open enemie to such neer prospects, offending the view with too much simplicitie and sinceritie of dealing.

[1] In its main parts, the white petals, the golden stamens, with their pollen (the 'seed') and the way in which the flower droops from the stem, the description fits the *lilium candidum* while the streaks and stripes on the outer side of the petals are compatible with the variety *striatum* which was known in Hawkins's time. Red lilies such as the martagon are described in Gerard but there was no blue lily then existing unless Hawkins is thinking of the Iris. Parkinson explicitly rejects the classification of the Iris with the Lily (*Paradisi in Sole, Paradisus terrestris*. 1629. p. 176) but outside botany it was often made.

It is a great curiositie in Nature, to enquire how these *Mountains* first came up, so to surmount the lesser *Hils* and lower vallyes.[1]

In one sentence the river is personified, kissing the feet of the mountain, in the next the way in which only the tops of the masts of the more distant ships can be seen is carefully noted. At one time the whole view is compared to a painted landscape, at another the different effects of the changing light are commented upon; and the reference to the varied greens of the Mallard's neck suggests some individual observation, though its appropriateness as an image in this context is doubtful.[2] It is, in fact, difficult to tell how far Hawkins really had his eye on his object. But his main purpose was not to be photographic. He wished only to make the symbol strike powerfully upon the senses so that the mind might then be fully receptive to the contemplative ideas which are to follow. As he brought exceptional literary abilities to this task, and an unusual sensitiveness to visual impressions, *The Essays* have this peculiar intensity of observation and expression which makes them remarkable in their context and, indeed, in the prose of their time.

The Discourse

The three passages which succeeded *The Essay* were for Hawkins the most serious part of his book, for in them the symbol is interpreted and applied to the object of his devotion. *The Discourse* or Survey follows first, and it is generally introduced by some such phrase as, 'But now come we to our mystical *Ship*. . . .' or 'Now what may this *Moon* denote and signify to us, but the glorious *Queene* of *Heaven*? . . .' In it the symbol is explained in detail, and the descriptions of *The Essays* together with the general ethical issues raised in *The Morals* are made the means of extolling

[1] *Partheneia Sacra.* pp. 226–7.

[2] The neck of the dove was almost a commonplace of description in the seventeenth century. Hawkins mentions its varying colours twice (The Sea, Essay. p. 237. and The Dove, Essay. p. 201). The mallard appears less often but it does appear, and Hawkins may therefore be using a conventional comparison. Blount in his additions to Peacham's *The Compleat Gentleman* refers to 'Gangren colour i.e. divers colours together, as in a Mallards, or Pigeons neck' (edition of 1661, p. 155).

the virtues of Mary. *The Discourse*, which is about twice as long as either of these, is the place for theological and doctrinal discussions of the nature of grace or the Virgin's part in the Incarnation. In the discourse on the Moon, for example, various points of resemblance between the Virgin and the Moon are developed. The moon is sometimes obscured, sometimes bright, and sometimes obscured and bright at the same moment. In its obscurity it resembles the Virgin who was darkened first through her excessive humility, 'which was a kind of obscure clowd that overshadowed her brightnes or splendour in the eyes of the world', then through the bitterness of her sorrow, and, finally, through her corporal death. In its brightness it signifies the Assumption, and when it is partly bright and partly obscure, the Passion.

The Theories and The Apostrophe

The two concluding passages are *The Theories*[1] or Contemplation and *The Apostrophe*. The first is recapitulatory: in it a short contemplation of three points raised in the preceding sections is undertaken, and its sole object is to recall some of the ideas with which the mind has been stored by the other exercises, not to suggest new ones. *The Apostrophe* or Colloquy is a brief review of the virtues of Mary. It constitutes for Hawkins 'the utmost scope and fruition of the whole' and through it the whole devotional act is directed towards the problems of personal life.

The Embleme

There remain *The Embleme* and its *Poësie*. These are placed between *The Discourse* and *The Theories* to provide an interval of rest and entertainment for the worshipper. *The Discourse* had contained much learned reference and scriptural allusion and had required considerable mental effort to follow; *The Theories* would also demand concentration, so *The Embleme* or, as Hawkins also termed it, the Pause was included as a means by which strength and refreshment could be gained before the final meditation and prayer. It consists of an engraved plate, a motto and a poem. The

[1] In the sense of contemplation or mental view from the Greek θεωρία, a contemplation.

differences between emblems and devices were discussed in Chapter I of this book, and it was pointed out there that these were negligible in the Elizabethan type of emblem book, but became more important later on. In *Partheneia Sacra* there is a clear distinction between the two. *The Devise* represents the thing-in-itself: it was intended for general application, and all the points raised in the ensuing passages were referred to it. *The Embleme*, in contrast, was more limited in its scope. It represents some event or single incident; as in Quarles, it is the place for narrative. *The Embleme* of the Violet, for instance, reproduced opposite, presents not a typical violet such as formed *The Devise*, but the eye of the Lord searching out His particular violet on a particular occasion. In the same way, *The Embleme* of the Dove, which is made up of two parts, shows the descent of a white dove to symbolise the Annunciation, and a black dove to symbolise the Virgin mourning for the death of her Son; and in *The Embleme* of the Moone, reproduced on page 198, Diana controls the sea just as the Virgin can control the wayward human heart and draw it back to God. 'Devices' in *Partheneia Sacra* are single in form and are capable of taking on a number of different significations, while 'emblems' are more complicated in appearance, their content is narrative, and they are incomplete without the explanatory poem which was written to accompany them. Hawkins keeps the two types entirely separate, *The Devise* being used as the focus for the ideas contained in the whole section, and *The Embleme* providing merely one element in the constitution of the whole.

Hawkins is more interesting as a writer of prose than of poetry, but the poems of *Partheneia Sacra* are not without merit. They have more technical assurance than Hawkins shows in any of the poems in his other books, and they do their work of explanation adequately. At best, whenever the verse shakes itself free of straightforward exposition, it reveals an unexpected rhythmical strength. The last four lines of the poem on *The Starre*, for instance, rise with considerable emotional force out of the flat statements which lead up to them:

29

THE EMBLEME.

THE POESIE.

 N Heauen the humble Angels GOD beheld;   *The*
And on the earth, with Angels paralel'd,   *Pause.*
The lowlie Virgin viewd; Her modest eye,
Submißiue count'nance, thoughts that did relye
On him, that would exalt an humble wight,
And make his Mother. Alma, ne're in fight,
With vertues, fragrant odours, round beset,
Close to the earth lay like the Violet;
Which shrowded with its leaues, in couert lyes,
Found sooner by the sent, then by the eyes.
Such was the Virgin rays'd to be Heauens Queene,
Who on the earth neglected, was not seene.

THE

From Henry Hawkins: *Partheneia Sacra 1633*

The glorious Sunne withdrew his beames of light;
My sinne was cause: So I in dismal night
Am sayling in a stormie dangerous Maine;
And ere the Sunne (I feare) returne again,
Shal suffer shipwrack, where the fraite's my Soule.
My onlie Hope's a *Starre*, fixt neere the Pole,
But that my Needle now hath lost its force,
Once touchd with grace, and saile out of course.
Starre of the *Sea*, thy Sun hath given thee light;
Til he brings day, guide me in sinnes dark night.
I seeke, what Sages heertofore have donne,
Guided by thee a *Starre*, to find the Sunne.

In the poem on the Heavens, too, some strength of feeling is
conveyed in single lines:

Then more to glorify
This Heaven, from his, the *Sunne of Justice* came,
Light of the world, with his eternal flame . . .

and in its conclusion:

For in her makes abode
The first blest Soule, that had the sight of GOD.

The success or failure of the poem as a whole, indeed, depends
upon the success or failure of its last lines; sometimes it drifts in-
distinctly to its end, sometimes, as in those on the star and the
heavens, it has sufficient rhythmical power to give the whole a
quiet distinction. The poems need, however, the support of their
devotional setting; they were not intended to stand alone but
were written to be read with the surrounding passages of prose
in mind, and their unobtrusiveness and lack of any kind of
ornament gains in effectiveness in contrast with style of these,
whereas it loses when the poems are isolated from their context.

Such then, is the general design of *Partheneia Sacra*. The author's
devotional purpose is accomplished through a structure which is,
in effect, an elaborate development of the emblematic method.
Distinctive as Hawkins's work is in many respects, it remains faithful to the principles out of which other emblem books had grown,

and were to grow. All he has done is to separate the various elements in their constitution—description, interpretation, moralisation, application—and make these serve the particular end he had in view. They were, moreover, principles peculiarly well suited to his own interests and abilities. It was part of his natural habit of mind to learn, and part of his training to teach, from the world of appearances; concrete things were the visible manifestations of the hand of the Creator in the universe. With them began a train of speculative thought, back to them speculative thought constantly returned. It is not that Hawkins lacked interest in abstract ideas as such. He was well informed and widely read.[1] He had entered the English College as a man of mature years and much experience, and he spent the rest of his life actively serving his Order. His topics are gathered from many parts of the world and from many fields of human activity, and he frequently refers to, or makes use of, philosophical and practical ideas which interested his contemporaries. The Ptolemaic system, the music of the spheres, the locality of the earthly Paradise, the theory that every land beast has its ectype in the sea, all find a place in his book. He comments on the power of gunpowder and the speed of the cannon ball; he has clear and decided opinions on building and a ready scorn for those architects who know their art only by theory and are 'good for nothing but to build a house for *Plato*, of *Ideas*, al suspending in the ayre'. Ideas of all kinds, indeed, fascinated him, but his interest in them always finds expression in concrete examples. When he writes of the stars he finds a source of profound astonishment in the idea of the speed at which they can travel:

[1] Hawkins quotes or alludes to classical legend and literature with the unpremeditated ease of complete familiarity. A knowledge of English literature is also apparent from a number of references which he makes to Elizabethan poetry and drama. He quotes from Southwell's *Retired thoughts enjoy their own delights*, and borrows the epitaph on Argalus and Parthenia from Sidney's *Arcadia* to celebrate 'those amorous palmes' Christ and his mother. He refers to the coloured cloths which Tamberlaine hung out to signify peace or war, and an occasional phrase suggests that he knew Shakespeare; e.g. there is probably an echo of *Macbeth* in 'For birds, we know, breed where they harvest most, and delight to harbour and carouse in all the day.'

For the swiftnes of their motions, it is a thing almost incredible, what they write, that one *Starre* in the firmament, should goe 200000. Italian miles in a minute of an hower; so as neither the flight of a bird, nor force of an arrow, nor the furious shot of a Canon nor anie thing of the world, can approach or come neere the imaginable swiftnes of these *Starres*; but yet most true.[1]

and this astonishment is expressed through a series of comparisons with the speed of earthly things. Even when he is discussing metaphysical theories he cannot for long conceive ideas apart from their concrete realisation. In a passage on cosmology, for instance, the notion of a single heaven is put forward in such terms as these : 'they beleeved, there was but one onlie, wherin the starres did sweetlie glide heer and there, and glance along as in a liquid crystal floud'.

Given a cast of mind of this type, it was inevitable that Hawkins should be attracted to the emblem form. In it he could satisfy both his desire to put forward and discuss general ideas and his constant inclination to formulate them in terms of particular images; and it gave ample scope to that remarkable susceptibility to sense impressions in which his chief strength as a prose writer lay. The literary interest of *Partheneia Sacra* rests largely upon the responsiveness of its author to the beauty of the natural world round him and the qualities of the prose in which this appreciation was expressed. The strongest imaginative appeal was made to him by things associated with what was light and shining—stars, water, jewels, brightly coloured flowers. The rainbow is 'the chamaeleon of the ayre' and reflects 'the sparkle of the Diamant, the flames of the Carbuncle, the twinkle of the Sapphire'. The primrose and the violet in the woods together make 'an excellent enamel of blue and yellow' and even the Dew, notwithstanding the 'poorness of this little creature in itself' is jewelled and magnificent in the sunlight:

A little drop of *Deaw* falling from the heavens, for example, on the Flowerdeluce, would seeme perhaps to you but a little round point of

---

[1] *Partheneia Sacra.* pp. 117–18.

water, and a meer graine of Cristal, but if the Sun do but shine upon it, Ah! what a miracle of beautie it is? while of the one side it wil looke like an Orient-pearl, and being turnd some other way, becomes a glowing Carbuncle, then a Saphir, and after an Emerald, and so an Amethist, and al enclosed in a nothing, or a litle glasse of al the greatest beauties of the world, that seem to be engraved therin.[1]

The style becomes more conscious and more lyrical whenever any topic of this kind comes within its range. For Hawkins, light was a quality in objects, not merely a transparent medium through which they are to be seen. It is there in the brilliance of the mallard, in the nameless colours that shift and change in the neck of the dove, in the glittering surface of the sea, in the endless metamorphoses of the dew; and in all its manifestations it could evoke a strong emotional response from him. A desire to decorate, a certain fancifulness of mind, is never very far distant in Hawkins's prose; but at its best his description does reflect faithfully a genuine delight in what he has seen. At all times it is characterised by the curious blend of exactness and virtuosity noticed in *The Essays* on the Lily and the Mount; a single sentence is as elusive as the longer passages. The sunflower, for instance, when night falls and the sun disappears 'wincks and shrowds herself the while, in the thin eyelids of her leaves, to meditate upon him'. The phrase is a conceit about eyes and winking, but embedded in it is a glimpse of the closing petals of an actual flower.

This mixture of observation and fancifulness in the content of Hawkins's descriptions is borne out in his style. The prose is highly ornate, conspicuously rhetorical and self-conscious, and at the same time oddly natural and sometimes even colloquial in tone. A constant use of imagery and personification is to be expected from his general preoccupation with the appearances of things; and devices are at times accumulated for a purely rhetorical effect. In this passage, for instance, the Virgin is compared to the Doves who build 'their little pavilions' high up in the sides of the rocks and so make themselves safe from all attack:

[1] *Partheneia Sacra.* pp. 65-6.

And then consider, how this *Dove of Doves*, this same most prudent *Virgin*, being higher then the rest, and more profound, had placed her nest or chamber in *Christ* her Rock; where being always safe and kept inviolable, the slights of the Divels and the subtleties of Hereticks could doe nothing against her; but what they did, was against the Rock itself, rebounding back upon the impious themselves, like the waves against the cliffes, the ships against the shelfs, the rusling of the winds against the towers, the fomie froth against the beach, the edge of the sword against the Adamant, the reed against a target, drifts of snow against a helmet, fire against gold, & lastly a slender cloud against the Sun.[1]

The artifice of this passage is deliberate— '& lastly' indicates how consciously the images have been piled up—and even if it may be regarded as having some justification, in that these comparisons are the means by which the insubstantiality of the heresies so vainly hurled against the Church is emphasised and so help to further the author's meaning, it leaves no doubt as to the rhetorical nature of his style. Such artifice is used at times to achieve an exquisitely lyrical effect, as when, for instance, he adopts the old emblematic image of the sunflower and describes its pursuit of the sun:

For in the morning it beholds his rising; in his journey, attends upon him; and eyeth him stil, wheresoever he goes; nor ever leaves following him, til he sink downe over head and eares in *Tethis's* bed, when not being able to behold him anie longer she droops and languishes, til he arise; and then followes him againe to his old lodging, as constantly as ever; with him it riseth, with him it falles, and with him riseth againe.[2]

Yet, however conscious of effect Hawkins appears to be in individual passages, his prose as a whole preserves an appearance of naturalness and spontaneity. This is due largely to his vocabulary which is extremely individual and which contributes much to the freshness of his prose. The individuality of his language consists largely in his habit of using words, the normal associations of which, even in his own day when they may be presumed to

[1] Ibid. pp. 208–9.　　　　[2] Ibid. p. 51.

have been less rigidly fixed, were far from the context in which he places them. The Virgin is 'a bush, and burning too, yet incombustible', mountains 'a Rendezvous and haunt of our Lord'. Colloquial phrases occur frequently: maidens are warned not to loiter in the streets 'or to hold unprofitable chats in public', St. John 'did very well to dresse up God all in gold', and 'had not Mount Ararat stood so a tipt-toe as it were, the Ark had been forced to have made a longer navigation'. The vocabulary for this devotional work is drawn from science, from religion, from the traffic of daily life; and the context never dictates the kind of associations a word introduced into it ought to have. Single words have in consequence often the power to offset a fanciful image or a too carefully considered rhythmical effect. A passage like this is given spontaneity by the cavalier air of the single phrase 'the whirle about', so unexpectedly informal in its context:

This great Bowle of the *Heavens*, roules and turnes about an Axeltree, fixt in a certain place, and flyes with the winged swiftness it hath; the Angel gives it the whirle about, and makes it turne round according to the Divine providence, crowning the world with its vaulted Arch enameled al with stars.

The qualities of Hawkins's prose are consistent with the other qualities of his book. All through, in its matter and its style, naturalness is combined with artifice, simplicity with sophistication. He made something new out of the emblem convention, and, while remaining within the limits of the form he chose, gave it a variety and a charm which it had not possessed before.

Ashrea, the remaining emblem book of the type of *The Devout Hart* and *Partheneia Sacra*, was not published until after the Restoration when the impulses behind the emblematic mode of expression had already begun to lose their force. There is no definite evidence as to its origins. It is Catholic rather than Protestant in interest all through and both the terminology used and the whole treatment of the subject suggest a Roman background and Roman readers, though they are never quite explicit enough

30

THE EMBLEME.

QUO TE CVNQVE SEQVOR

THE POESIE.

He *Empreſſe of the Sea,* Latona *bright,*
Drawes like a load-ſtone by attractiue might
The *Oceans ſtreames, which hauing forward runne*
Calles back againe, to end where they begunne.
The Prince *of darknes had ecclipſed* Eues *light,*
And Mortals, clowded in Cymmerian night,
Were backwards drawne by Eue, *as is the* Maine;
'Twas *only* Marie *drew to* GOD *againe:*
O *chaſt* Diana, *with thy ſiluer beames,*
Flux & reflux (as in the Oceans ſtreames)
'*Tis thou canſt cauſe.* O *draw! and draw me ſo,*
That I in vice may ebbe, in Vertue *flow.*

THE

From Henry Hawkins: *Partheneia Sacra 1633*
[slightly reduced]

for certainty. The author signs himself at the end of the dedication with the initials E.M. which have sometimes been accepted as those of Edward Manning, a somewhat disreputable pamphleteer, but a more probable author is Edward Mico, an English Jesuit who in 1669 published a volume of meditations which resemble *Ashrea* in substance and style.[1] As an emblem book it is inferior to *Partheneia Sacra*: it is simpler in structure, its emblems are fewer, and its prose has not the interest or distinction of Hawkins's. It has, however, one unusual feature and illustrates an aspect of the convention which had not previously been seen in English emblem literature. On that account, therefore, besides whatever literary merit it may have of its own, it is not to be neglected.

The word 'Ashrea', according to the author, signifies in Hebrew 'a wood or grove' and is derived from Ashar 'to beatify or make blessed'. In the book the eight Beatitudes are represented by emblems of trees, each accompanied by a prose essay in which the parallel between the tree and one of the Beatitudes is elaborated. The Cornel Tree, for instance, symbolises the poor in spirit:

The *Cornelia*, or *Cornel-tree*, in *February* begins to bloom, and bears blossoms long before there is any appearance of Leaves, to secure and shrowd them from the injuries of Wind and Weather. This is the true Embleme of Man, who is born naked, and springs forth like a tender Blossome; as *Job* saith, *Naked came I from the womb of my Mother, and naked shall I return.*

From which we may learn this Lesson, That as man is born *poor* and naked in *Body*, so should he be in *Spirit*; that is, in *Will* and *Desire*; seeing that as he *brought nothing into this World, so shall he not carry anything out of it.*[2]

Similarly, the Meek are symbolised by the Indian Fig Tree which inherits the earth because its branches bend so low to the ground that they take root and become new trees; Those which are Persecuted for Righteousness' sake, by the Vine which has to be

[1] For a discussion of the authorship see Appendix 4. p. 249.
[2] *Ashrea*. p. 4.

pruned in the cold and unfriendly month of February; Those
that Mourn, by the Myrtle because it 'naturally distills, and, as it
were, sheds tears; but more abundantly when it is prick'd and
wounded. Behold the Embleme and Type of Man, who is born
weeping, as being (to use St *Austin's* expression) a Prophet pre-
saging his own future calamities.' [1] The trees chosen are very
different from those in Alciati's emblem book, and E.M. seems
to have been drawn to them more by the strangeness of their
properties than by any traditional moral or religious associations
they may have possessed. He offers much curious information
about curious plants: the Adam's Apple Tree, the Indian Fig Tree,
the Clove, combine with the more familiar Vine and Honeysuckle
to point the way to salvation. And the kind of analogy which he
prefers is always one that is ingenious rather than illuminating.
The Adam's Apple Tree, for example, which proves to be the
banana,[2] is the emblem of the Merciful. Its large leaves supply
materials for quilts and mattresses, and in the same way the man
who is merciful 'parts with his leafy substance to cloath the naked'.
It is tall, 'above the reach of an Elephant', but it 'would continue a
low shrub, and the leaves would bend down-wards to the ground,
if they were not cut off from time to time; by which means, the
Tree grows up higher and the Leaves become larger'; in the same
way the merciful man voluntarily abandons the things of the
world and reaches up to Heaven. It shoots out new stalks when
the old ones decay; and the merciful man 'leaves the young shoots
of his posterity to succeed him in his good works'. It is difficult
to imagine a set of comparisons more inappropriate to the true
nature of the virtue symbolised; but E.M. was a writer of emblems, and like all his fellows he had no hesitation in finding out
resemblances where none should be.

The emblematic representation of the eight Beatitudes in a

[1] *Ashrea.* p. 27.
[2] There was considerable difference of opinion about the identity of the tree
of good and evil. The apple was the favourite because its Latin name, malum,
also signified evil. Sir Thomas Browne cites several alternatives, the orange,
the lemon, the melon. (*Pseudodoxia Epidemica.* 1646. Bk. VII. Ch. 1.) E.M.
derives most of his information from *Gerard's Herbal*.

series of trees was not, however, the only concern of *Ashrea*; they are also to be recalled through the contemplation of the crucified Christ. E.M.'s book is arranged in eight sections, one for every tree. Each has its engraving and motto, followed by a prose essay in which the properties of the trees are described in relation to the Beatitude they symbolise, and finally there are *Some Considerations upon the Beatitudes* in which both the tree and the beatitude are brought to mind together through the contemplation of the Crucifixion. Thus 'the Eyes of our Blessed Saviour weeping' recall simultaneously the myrtle tree and those that mourn; his wounded heart recalls the fig tree and the pure in heart. This act of recollection is made in accordance with certain regular principles which E.M. lays down in his preface—the principles of the *Ars Memorativa*—and it is the combination of these with the ordinary methods of the emblem writers that gives *Ashrea* its distinctiveness and sets it apart from the others in the convention.

The *Ars Memorativa* to which E.M. refers was a highly elaborate system with a long history. The principles underlying it remained essentially the same but there was room for any number of individual variations in their application. It is based upon the use of a repository, that is, the substitution of a single image, of a kind that could be divided into almost unlimited parts, for the set of ideas to be remembered. A common device among the Greeks and Romans, for instance, was to substitute a house with all its contents for the different things to be called to mind. In this single repository all the ideas, however diverse, could be placed, and the necessary association was then effected by various means: the things to be remembered could be visualised as actually appearing in the rooms of the house, or certain objects in the house which in some way resembled them could be substituted for them, or objects which did not resemble them in the least could be substituted, the connection then being quite arbitrary and, one would suppose, quite unreliable; there was also a *scriptile* association where the things could be visualised as written on a tablet hanging on the walls of the room—a particularly valuable device when exact words were to be remembered.[1] The possible variations of the method were, in fact, very numerous and very complicated— and in practice very extravagant. John Buno's Bilderbibel, in which the whole Gospel of St. Mark [2] was localised by means of pictures and words in the figure of a lion, and E.M.'s illustration in his preface of the various uses that can be made of the reposi- tory of Jonah's Whale show the lengths to which the scheme could be carried; and although the choice of both the repository and the means of association used was governed partly by the nature of the things to be remembered, the mere business of learning by heart would appear to make far lighter demands upon the memory than the ingenuity of the system which was designed to relieve it.

Fortunately E.M.'s application of the Art of Memory in *Ashrea* is simpler than the treatment of Jonah's Whale which he outlines in the preface. It is, he says, a method which God himself has taught us in putting the Rainbow in the sky by which He would remember His covenant with man. Man may therefore by the same method remember the eight Beatitudes in the Crucifixion:

Behold heer the eight places for the exercise of this pious Art of Memory, wherein the devout Reader may find, as it were written, the *Eight Beatitudes*, in a Book, which lies always open, to be read, with such large Characters, as the shortest sight must needs reach, and the weakest memory retain; so lively set forth, that *Beatitude*, as in a Crystal-Mirrour shall still present it self unto us:

1. For, how can I behold Christ *naked*, and not remember how *poor* he was *in Spirit*, Will and Desire, who, living and dying, had no place whereon to rest his Head?

2. How can I view his dying *Head* humbly bowing down, with infinite patience, and not call to mind that, *Blessed are the meek*, who of this meekest Lamb, may learn patience and humility.

[1] An account of the different types of association and examples of repositories can be found in John Willis's *The Art of Memory*. 1621.
[2] Reproduced by L. Volkmann, 'Ars Memorativa', *Jahrbuch der Kunsthis- torischen Sammlungen in Wien*. 1929. pp. 111–200.

31

The Seventh
BEATITUDE.

*Bleſſed are the Peace-makers, for they
ſhall be called the Children
of God.*

EMBLEME VII.
The Wood-Bind.

Pacis conjunctio firma. 7.

*Thus, while two foſter deadly hate,
A third ſteps in to end debate;   (Hands,
Makes Peace, unites both Hearts and
How bleſt is he who makes ſuch bands!*
                                        To

From E. M.: *Ashrea 1665*

The other Beatitudes and the emblematical trees with which they had been associated are recalled in the same manner, and so by the Art of Memory the themes of the whole book are bound together.

The prose of *Ashrea* is not remarkable but it has a certain distinction in its use of imagery. Metaphors and similes are introduced for the purpose of illustration and they are always appropriate and to the point. The comparisons are not laboured, though E.M, as in his handling of the emblems themselves, is quick to see where they can illuminate at more points than one. The image of the silkworm, for instance, here follows naturally upon 'the spirit that swells and puffs up the heart', therefore its primary object is to make concrete the notion of the darkness and oblivion into which such spirits finally come.

Contrariwise, How rich were he in Spirit (in Will and Desire) whose Soul should be wholly addicted to Self-love, and proper Interest? That breathes nothing wherein Christ is concerned, but pursues only Ambition, (a Spirit that swells and puffs up the heart)? That moves not but by the agitation of a coveting Spirit: Like a silk-worme: in fine, to involve it self in a web of darkness and oblivion.[1]

Ashrea establishes a useful link between the emblem books and the science of mnemonics to which they were in some ways akin. John Willis in his *Art of Memory* refers to the emblems of Alciati and Peacham as a means by which ideas that combine pictures and writing can be remembered. He also derives some of his examples of repositories from the emblem books. Melancholy, for instance, is to be remembered by 'a man very sad, who having his armes wreathed up, and his hatt pulled downe in his eyes, goeth up and downe in a discontented manner'.[2] The other personifications, stock symbols of the emblem books, find a place among his illustrations, as it is to be expected that they should. But *Ashrea* is the only emblem book in which the connection in method is openly expressed.

[1] *Ashrea*. p. 11.   [2] Op. cit. pp. 47–8, 27.

Chapter 8

JOHN BUNYAN: THE END OF
THE TRADITION

THE Restoration of 1660 is generally accepted as the turning
point in seventeenth-century thought. There took place a
radical change in all spheres of life, and the emblem book was one
of the many productions of the past which did not survive it. The
best work in the convention had been done before the Civil War,
in the *Emblemes* and *Hieroglyphikes* of Quarles and in *Partheneia
Sacra*, but the fashion itself still remained an important one for
some time to come. Based primarily upon the taste for allegory,
it had life so long as that had life; but when the interests, first
of the learned, and then of the ordinary reader, shifted away
from all that had encouraged and strengthened a liking for the
allegorical aspect of things, the emblem book became what it
had always been in danger of becoming, a trivial and rather
childish mode of expression instead of a serious literary form. By
1687 Prior and Halifax could satirise Dryden for having inspired
an emblem upon a subject which in itself shows what status the
convention now had:

Bayes I must needs say at a *Fable* or an *Emblem* I think no Man comes
near me, indeed I have studied it more than any Man. Did you
ever take notice *Mr Johnson*, of a little thing that has taken mightily
about Town, a *Cat with a Top-Knot*?
Johnson Faith, Sir, 'tis mighty pretty, I saw it at the Coffee-House.
Bayes 'Tis a Trifle hardly worth owning; I was t'other Day at
Will's throwing out something of that Nature; and I'gad, the
hint was taken, and out came that Picture; indeed the poor Fellow
was so civil to present me with a dozen of 'em for my Friends, I
think I have one here in my Pocket; would you please to accept
it, Mr *Johnson*?
Johnson Really, 'tis very ingenious.

Bayes Oh Lord! Nothing at all, I could design twenty of 'em in an Hour, if I had but witty Fellows about me to draw 'em. I was proffered a pension to go into *Holland* and contrive their Emblems. But hang 'em they are dull Rogues and would spoil my Invention.[1]

Even then the emblem form was not entirely extinct. A year earlier, Arwaker had attempted to restore to Hugo the recognition owed to him by Quarles, and the fresh translation he made was republished twice within the next twenty years. Quarles's own work, and that of Christopher Harvey, continued to be reprinted, and a few new books were written. But the main interests of literature had moved elsewhere and there was no poetry outside the convention to testify to the strength of that within, as there had been previously. The Elizabethan emblems had found their way into the drama and had formed an important element in the work of the greatest non-dramatic poet of the period; the emblems of the early part of the seventeenth century were transformed into poetry in the work of such men as Herbert and Vaughan; but, with the exception of *The Pilgrim's Progress*, there is nothing of importance in Restoration literature which owes anything to the emblematic convention. Hobbes's mockery of poems shaped like wings and eggs was indicative of the new trends of taste; beside the modern elegance and lucidity, the work of the emblematists seemed merely obscure and confused.

Such emblem books as were produced after 1660 show how meaningless the convention had now become. Although they did not vanish as quickly as they had appeared, their survival was due to other reasons than to an interest in emblems as such. The dialogue about the fictitious *Cat with a Top-Knot* suggests that the form still possessed a certain fanciful charm, and this charm is exploited in an emblem book published at almost the same time, Philip Ayres's *Emblemata Amatoria*, 1683.[2] It is a successful

---

[1] Halifax and Prior. *The Hind and the Panther Transversed to the Story of the Country-Mouse and the City-Mouse.* 1687. p. 11.

[2] For an account of Ayres's book see H. Thomas, *The Emblemata Amatoria of Philip Ayres.* 1910.

attempt to make something of the triviality to which a convention that had lost its connection with contemporary thought was all too easily reduced. The engravings in Ayres's book were copied from the Dutch, its graceful four-lined poems in copper-plate hand required no intellectual effort to follow, the subject was love— the book was, in fact, admirably suited to the drawing-room and the ladies for whom it was destined. Other emblem books after the Restoration owed their existence to equally fortuitous causes. Quarles's *Emblemes* continued to be published for their pictures, and also perhaps because Quarles was admired as a poet; Arwaker's translation of Hugo was an afterthought, probably stimulated by the popularity of Quarles; *Ashrea*, published in 1665, still had the support of the Catholic tradition behind it; and Bunyan published a set of emblems intended not for adult readers but for the amusement and the moral and religious instruction of the young. There was, in fact, still scope for devotional emblems, for nursery emblems, and for emblems as the lightest of entertainments; but there was no longer any place for emblems in the main course of literature.

As the first emblem book written expressly for children, Bunyan's collection has a certain historical importance, for it directed the convention into the channel in which it was ultimately to survive. Had the rest of Bunyan's work been confined to sermons and religious tracts there would be little more to say about it than this, and its historical interest would remain its chief merit; but the success of *The Pilgrim's Progress* and, in a lesser degree, of *The Holy War* proves that for him the convention was more than a dead letter: it still had literary possibilities, was still capable of transformation into something greater than itself. *The Pilgrim's Progress* and *The Holy War* were indeed the only books published after the Restoration in which allegory kept its old vitality, and part of their power to convince is derived from the naturalness with which their dual meaning is presented. In adopting this form rather than that of direct exposition Bunyan knew he could rely upon the emblematic habits of thought fostered in the

Puritan mind by Quarles and Wither. It is noticeable that when he makes his apology for the use of similitudes he makes it upon moral grounds alone, never doubting his audience's capacity or inclination to penetrate to the truths that lay beneath the surface, and the course of the book itself shows this assumption in practice—a single word in the margin suffices to elucidate some of the symbols used, others are expounded at length in the text because such explanations were still expected and enjoyed. Yet, for all its reliance upon such mental habits in the reader, *The Pilgrim's Progress* is outside the main trend of contemporary literature in a way that *The Faerie Queene* is not; and Bunyan's unpretentious little emblem book reflects the altered status of allegory quite distinctly. It had become the property of a lower social class and an inferior type of intellect. Simplification is, of course, the basic principle of all allegory; but Spenser simplified as a philosopher, Bunyan as a preacher. For Spenser, the emblem books of his time provided concrete images in which his ethical and philosophical ideas could conveniently be formulated: his function as a poet was to convey the general in terms of the particular, and among the various possible ways of particularisation open to him the accepted emblematic imagery lay ready to hand. Through it he could, as Sidney said, yield 'to the powers of the mind an image of that whereof the Philosopher bestoweth but a wordish description: which doth neither strike, pierce, nor possess the sight of the soul so much as that other doth'.[1] Bunyan's simplification is prompted by a different motive, by the perennial need of the preacher to express himself in a manner that can be 'understanded of the people'. He therefore translated his ideas into the idiom of the people, borrowing from the emblematists their technique of reducing abstract notions to elementary terms. The value of the emblem convention was for him not so much imaginative as practical: the people whom he wished to instruct had read Quarles and had amused themselves with Wither's lottery: to the methods of Quarles and Wither then would he turn. Men of letters already despised such devices, but Bunyan's purpose was

[1] Philip Sidney. *An Apologie for Poetrie.* 1595.

not 'literary' as Spenser's had been, nor were the tastes of his readers cultured or informed. His own emblem book, in fact, illustrates the level of the appeal that the convention now made, and in the contrast between its scope and that of Whitney's *Choice*, published precisely a hundred years earlier, can be seen one of the changes which separates *The Pilgrim's Progress* from its great allegorical predecessor.

Difference of status is not the only factor that divides the allegories of *The Pilgrim's Progress* and *The Faerie Queene*. The altered content and methods of the emblem books of Quarles and his imitators are matched in the altered technique Bunyan uses; and just as the work of Whitney helps to illuminate the material and manner of *The Faerie Queene*, so something may be learnt from these Puritan emblem books about the art of *The Pilgrim's Progress*. They cannot, of course, account for it. *The Pilgrim's Progress* springs from a tragic vision of life which is Bunyan's own. It is a vision engendered by his piercing insight into the depths and subtleties of spiritual wickedness, and at the same time, for it is tragic not satiric, by his profoundly imaginative apprehension of the goodness as well as the power of God. 'Man crumbles to dust at the presence of God; yea though he shows himself to us in his robes of salvation'[1]—the sternness of the first part of the book, the compassion of the second, are the dual expression of that sad certainty. With this, and with the art that comes from an uncompromising consistency to it, the mere external forms of presentation have nothing to do. But they provide the necessary framework, and if the greatness of Bunyan's art derives from the intensity and integrity of his vision alone, the structure into which it is built was partly the work of others. In the composition of the allegory, the devices of the emblem writers have their place: they assist in its general outline, they contribute to its details. Even Bunyan's own emblem book has something in common with it, far removed from the real themes of *The Pilgrim's Progress* though the experiences of childhood with which it deals may at first appear to be.

[1] Bunyan. *A Treatise of the Fear of God.* 1679.

THE END OF THE TRADITION

A Book for Boys and Girls: or Country Rhymes for Children was published in 1686, and in a much altered form it became very popular in the early years of the eighteenth century.[1] The original editions contained seventy-two emblems of varying length, but no cuts. In 1701, however, it was republished as *A Book for Boys and Girls or Temporal Things Spiritualised* and in this edition, made after Bunyan's death, the text was fully revised. Some of the educational material at the beginning of the book and twenty-five of the original emblems were omitted altogether; among what remained there was a general dilution and toning down of the more vigorous elements of Bunyan's style. The principle upon which the editing was done is difficult to determine: poems upon subjects which might have offended the susceptibilities of the eighteenth-century child such as 'Fly Blowes' and 'a stinking Breath' were omitted, and a few of the doctrinal or propagandist poems were excluded at the same time, but even so there seems to be no clear and consistent basis for the revisions. In subsequent editions very crude woodcuts were added, and the title was later changed again to *Divine Emblems*.[2]

Since it was intended primarily for children, the book contains certain material to further their general education. Bunyan explains his object in the Preface:

> I bow
> My Pen to teach them what the Letters be,
> And how they may improve their A, B, C.
> Nor let my pretty Children them despise;
> All needs must there begin, that would be wise.

Three alphabets are therefore given, Blackletter, Roman and Italic, and with them general instructions in spelling and word-making. There are also lists of boys' and girls' names and a scale of Roman and Arabic figures. Some specific religious education

---

[1] It was republished eight times between 1701 and 1724. For its bibliographical history see F. M. Harrison, *A Bibliography of the Works of John Bunyan.* Supplement to *Bibliog. Soc. Trans.* No. 6. 1932.

[2] No copy of the first edition was known until that formerly belonging to Narcissus Luttrell was brought to light at the end of the nineteenth century. It has been published in facsimile and edited by John Browne. Eliot Stock. 1889.

was also thought necessary, and among the 'emblems' are metrical versions of the Lord's Prayer, the Creed and the Ten Command-ments. A poem on the Sacraments ensures that the child shall not be led into any popish idolatry:

> Two Sacraments I do believe there be,
> Baptism and the Supper of the Lord:
> Both Mysteries divine, which do to me,
> By Gods appointment, benefit afford:
> But shall they be my God? or shall I have
> Of them so foul and impious a Thought,
> To think that from the Curse they can me save?
> Bread, Wine, nor Water me no ransom bought.[1]

There are also a few poems on Biblical subjects, upon 'Moses and his Wife', or 'The Barren Fig Tree in God's Vineyard', and one or two on theological matters such as the four brief lines which explain to the simple the distinction between Time and Eternity:

> Eternity is like unto a Ring
> Time, like to Measure, doth it self extend;
> Measure commences, is a finite thing,
> The Ring has no beginning, middle, end.[2]

Doctrinal topics, however, occupy only a small part of the book; the main bulk of the emblems is secular in content and ethical in application. The subjects are chiefly of the kind believed to in-terest youthful minds. Many of them, 'the mole in the ground', the spider, the cuckoo, the swallow, the frog, are taken from nature; for the book was, as its title indicates, a collection of *country* rhymes. Others are drawn from the everyday occupations of childhood, or from familiar objects of household use like a lantern or a pair of spectacles; even 'the sight of a pound of candles falling to the ground' is capable of inspiring a meditation upon 'God's elect in their lapst state'. Once the child's attention has been attracted by a brief description of the subject chosen, the moral lesson can be brought home without further ado. This, for instance, is Bunyan's emblem of the frog in full:

[1] *A Book for Boys and Girls.* 1686. XIV. p. 17.   [2] Ibid. LXXII. pp. 75–6.

The Frog by Nature, is both damp and cold,
Her Mouth is large, her Belly much will hold:
She sits somewhat ascending, loves to be
Croaking in Gardens, tho unpleasantly.

Comparison

The Hyppocrite is like unto this Frog;
As like as is the Puppy to the Dog.
He is of nature cold, his Mouth is wide,
To prate, and at true Goodness to deride.
He mounts his Head, as if he was above
The World, when yet 'tis that which has his Love.
And though he seeks in Churches for to croak,
He neither loveth Jesus, nor his Yoak.[1]

All the applications are as simple in treatment as the objects upon which they are based.

Bunyan's view of the child's world is characteristically Puritan and exactly what might be expected from a man who was converted during a game of cat. The Boy on his Hobby Horse and the Boy and the Butterfly both symbolise those who wilfully run after the fading, empty joys of this world. The paper of plums in the possession of another child is equally sinister:

What hast thou there, my Pretty Boy?
Plumbs? How? Yes, Sir, a Paper full.
I thought 'twas so, because with Joy
Thou didst them out thy Paper pull . . .

Comparison

This Boy an Emblem is of such
Whose Lot in worldly things doth lie:
Glory they in them ne'er so much,
Their pleasant Springs will soon be dry,
   Their Wealth, their Health, Honours and Life,
Will quickly to a period come;
If for these, is their only Strife,
They soon will not be worth a Plumb.[2]

No infant pastime was wholly innocent; the industrious observance of religious duties, together with a perpetual awareness of

[1] Ibid. XXXVI. p. 46. [2] Ibid. XLVII. pp. 55–6.

the vanity of all else, is the least that can save a child from Hell.
Bunyan's emblem book is, however, notably less lurid than most
of the literature published for children by the Puritans of his time.
If it lacks the kindliness and humanity of Dr. Watts, it lacks also
the ferocity of James Janeway.[1] The Puritan ethic is ever present
to quench the child's natural high spirits, but it is an ethic freed
from its grimmer aspects. The vision of Hell is absent altogether,
and at a time when the exemplary lives and early deaths of their
fellows were considered the most fitting subjects for children's
books, Bunyan was offering them rhymes about frogs and hobby
horses and papers of plums. Even if the ideals of utility and profit
are too constantly reiterated:

> A comely sight indeed it is to see,
> A World of Blossoms on an Apple-tree.
> Yet far more comely would this tree appear
> If all its dainty blooms young Apples were.[2]

and the child urged to remember that 'Death's a cold comforter
to Girls and Boys', the lively nature of the subjects must nevertheless have done much to compensate for the damping effects
of the morality.

As an emblem book, Bunyan's collection differs in some respects from those of his predecessors. The term is used vaguely
to cover a number of different types of poems, some of which
could not be called emblematic in any sense; the 'Awakened
Child's Lamentation', for instance, a mournful hymn of repentance twenty-nine verses long, is quite without the characteristics
of the formal emblem. Nor are the poems provided with cuts or
mottoes, although the presence of a picture is implicit in most of
them. Bunyan no doubt knew the work of Quarles and Wither,
but his book does not suggest that he allowed himself to be
influenced directly by either. Most of the subjects are his own, and
those which can be found elsewhere are treated with complete
independence; the snail, for instance, had been used previously

---

[1] For an account of Puritan children's books, and Bunyan's among them,
see Harvey Darton, *Children's Books in England*. 1932. pp. 53–69.

[2] *A Book for Boys and Girls*. XXVI. p. 33.

by Wither but there is no resemblance between the two presentations of the subject. Indeed, Bunyan's total lack of any rhetorical
or poetic interests and his natural sense of allegory combine to
make his treatment of the fashion unlike anything that had been
achieved by previous writers. Partly because his themes were
more elementary, and partly because he had a remarkable gift of
making his symbols completely co-extensive with their significance, the comparisons in *A Book for Boys and Girls* are always
both direct and effective: like Quarles, he is concerned to multiply
likenesses, but unlike those in the *Emblemes*, his are never laboured
and drawn out at length. His 'Meditations upon an Egg' may offer
no less than fourteen different points of resemblance between man
and that unpromising symbol, but each is set out in the briefest
and most businesslike fashion. In structure the poems are usually
divided into two parts, the first to take the place of the picture
and describe the subject directly, the second, labelled the *Comparison*, to point the moral. The two parts are kept sharply distinct
from each other, for it was Bunyan's great strength as an allegorist
that he knew how to endow his images with solid literal sense.
In 'The Child with the Bird at the Bush', the first part is complete
in itself without the comparison which follows. It represents the
child trying unsuccessfully to entice the bird from its life of
freedom, in words which show that Bunyan knew the 'Passionate
Shepherd to his Love', or one of its many imitations:

> 'My little Bird, how canst thou sit;
> And sing amidst so many Thorns!
> Let me but hold upon thee get;
> My Love with Honour thee adorns . . .

> 'I'll feed thee with white Bread and Milk,
> And Sugar-plums, if them thou crave;
> I'll cover thee with finest Silk,
> That from the cold I may thee save.

> 'My Father's Palace shall be thine,
> Yea in it thou shalt sit and sing;
> My little Bird, if thoul't be mine,
> The whole year round shall be thy Spring.

'I'll teach thee all the Notes at Court
Unthought of Musick thou shalt play . . .'

But lo, behold, the Bird is gone;
These Charmings would not make her yield:
The Child's left at the Bush alone,
The Bird flies yonder o'er the Field.

The subject of this poem is not to be found in earlier emblem
books: it belongs to no accepted tradition but is emblematic
because Bunyan makes it so. Once the 'Comparison' begins, the
details of the child's appeal take on a new significance:

This Child, of Christ an Emblem is,
The Bird to Sinners I compare . . .[1]

Bunyan's handling of the convention is, in fact, much freer than
that of any of his predecessors: he has not collected his material
from familiar literary sources nor is he tied to a particular mode
of representation. The 'emblematic' quality of his images depends
not upon their content but only upon their application.

Bunyan's verse, in contrast to his prose, was always unpro-
fessional: its language is the language of everyday speech, and
its rhythm at times breaks down completely. In *A Book for Boys
and Girls* such technical naïveté is not necessarily a defect, for it
often gives the poems the spontaneity of a nursery rhyme. The
verse has at least the virtues of vigour and economy. This passage
from the poem on the snail is a fair indication of its merits and
weaknesses:

She goes but softly, but she goeth sure,
She stumbles not, as stronger Creatures do:
Her Journeys shorter, so she may endure,
Better than they which do much further go.
She makes no noise, but stilly seizeth on
The Flow'r or Herb, appointed for her food
The which she quietly doth feed upon,
While others range, and gare, but find no good.

[1] *A Book for Boys and Girls.* XXXI. pp. 40–2.

And tho she doth but very softly go,
How ever 'tis not fast, nor slow but sure;
And certainly they that do travel so,
The prize they do aim at, they do procure.[1]

Bunyan certainly wanted art; the clumsiness of some of the syntax here and the sudden change-over to dactyls at the end cannot be defended. Yet the vocabulary is not undistinguished, despite its simplicity, and the style is eminently suitable for the purpose: it is, in fact, amateurish rather than positively bad, bearing some of the marks of genius working in a wrong medium. What, consequently, should be the merest doggerel is never altogether inconsiderable. The dolorous lament of the Awakened Child, for example, has nothing to recommend it from the technical point of view; but in its twenty-nine verses the total desolation of the child's state of mind is conveyed. Although its effect is cumulative, a few verses will give an indication of its gloomy pathos:

When *Adam* was deceived,
I was of Life bereaved;
Of late (too) I perceived,
I was in sin conceived.

And as I was born naked,
I was with filth bespaked,
At which when I awaked,
My Soul and Spirit shaked . . .

Had I in God delighted,
And my wrong doings righted;
I had not thus been frighted,
Nor as I am benighted . . .

But God has condescended,
And pardon has extended,
To such as have offended,
Before their lives were ended.

Oh Lord! do not disdain me,
But kindly entertain me;
Yea in thy Faith maintain me,
And let thy Love constrain me!

[1] Ibid. LVII. pp. 63–4.

In both parts of *The Pilgrim's Progress* there is much that can be related in general terms to the emblem convention. It was part of Bunyan's design to make use of emblems in the course of the story and he introduces them in groups from time to time. The various scenes, for example, which Christian and, afterwards, Christiana witness in the house of the Interpreter are nothing less than a series of emblems; in fact, the Interpreter in expounding one of them calls it 'an emblem, very apt to set forth some Professors by'. Another set of a similar nature occurs when the Shepherds reveal to the pilgrims a number of visions from the top of the Delectable Mountains. Among others they show Christiana and Mercy 'one *Fool* and one *Want-wit* washing of an *Ethiopian* with the intention to make him white, but the more they washed him, the blacker he was', and explain their meaning as follows:

Thus shall it be with the vile Person; all means used to get such an one a good Name, shall in conclusion tend but to make him more abominable. Thus it was with the *Pharisees*, and so shall it be with all Hypocrites.[1]

The scenes described on such occasions as these belong quite explicitly to the genre to which Bunyan was later to make his own contribution, and they can be treated entirely independently of the main story. The development of the action is held up while the moral lessons are expounded, and the attention of the pilgrims and the reader is focused wholly upon them.

For the content of these emblems Bunyan owes little to his predecessors. As is to be expected from his fertile power of image-making, the majority of them are original, though there may be behind others a memory of emblematic pictures he had seen. The blackamoor no doubt he derived from one of its previous appearances in emblem books, and some of the pictures set before Christian by the Interpreter are reminiscent of other aspects of the convention; Patience and Passion perhaps descend from Amor

[1] *The Pilgrim's Progress.* Ed. E. Venables. 1925. p. 266. An emblem of the Ethiopian occurs in Whitney, *A Choice of Emblemes*.

and Anima; and the emblem of the dusty parlour symbolising the unsanctified heart of man which can be swept clean only by the Gospel is in the tradition of the *Schola Cordis*. In Part II some parallels may be drawn with the poems in *A Book for Boys and Girls*. The dialogue in the emblem book between the Sinner and the Spider, for example, in which the Sinner's first repugnance of the 'venomed thing' is gradually replaced by the conviction that he himself is the more repugnant of the two, is comparable with one of the experiences of Christiana and Mercy in the Significant Rooms of the Interpreter. The poem begins with an encounter between the two figures:

Sinner

What black? What ugly crawling thing art thou?

Spider

I am a Spider——

Sinner

A Spider, Ay, also a filthy Creature.

Spider

Not filthy as thyself, in Name or Feature:
My Name intailed is to my Creation;
My Feature's from the God of thy Salvation.

Sinner

I am a Man, and in God's Image made,
I have a Soul shall neither dye or fade. . . .

The Spider then begins a spirited comparison between itself and the Sinner with the object of bringing home to him the extent of his wickedness:

Thy Soul, thy Reasons, yea thy spotless State
Sin has subjected to th'most dreadful fate.
But I retain my primitive condition
I've all, but what I lost by thy Ambition.[1]

It admits that in so far as it is ugly and venomous it bears some resemblance to man: man can in consequence learn his destiny

[1] *A Book for Boys and Girls*. XVII. pp. 18-25.

from it. Its web, symbolising the empty pleasures he enjoys and the flimsy hopes of salvation he cherishes, will point out for him the path to Hell; but the persistence and determination of character by which it can find its way into the palaces of kings, may equally be a model to him in his search for Heaven. In the second part of *The Pilgrim's Progress*, the same lesson is taught in a more dramatic form. Mercy and Christiana are led into an apparently empty room, where Mercy can see nothing but 'an *Ugly Spider* who hangs by her Hands upon the Wall'. Their guide, however, asks them: 'Is there but one *Spider* in all this spacious Room?'

Then the water stood in *Christiana's* Eyes, for she was a Woman quick of apprehension: and she said, Yes, Lord, there is more here than one. Yea, and *Spiders* whose Venom is far more destructive than that which is in her. The *Interpreter* then looked pleasantly upon her, and said, Thou hast said the Truth. This made *Mercy* blush, and the Boys to cover their Faces: For they all began now to understand the Riddle.[1]

The Interpreter begins to explain to them how man, sinful and venomous though he be, is enabled by faith and grace to reach the best room in the King's Palace. Among the other things shown to Christiana are a hen with her chickens, a robin with a spider in its mouth, a rotten tree, a butcher killing a sheep, all of which are symbols of the same type as those which make up the subjects of *A Book for Boys and Girls*, though none are actually repeated there. The Interpreter was consciously looking for what best suited the intellect of his audience: 'I chose, my Darlings, to lead you into the Room where such things are, because you are Women and they are easie for you,' and he accordingly sets images before them which would be within the range of their experience and which contain lessons obvious to the slowest wits. For the same reason Mercy and Christiana are shown many more emblems in the course of the book than were considered necessary for Christian's masculine intelligence. The real interest of Bunyan's use of emblems, however, lies less in their possible sources than

[1] *The Pilgrim's Progress.* Ed cit. p. 185.

in his treatment of them as literary devices and in their contribution to the allegory as a whole.[1]

Bunyan's method of presenting his meaning varies considerably from emblem to emblem. The most elementary, some of those chosen as especially suitable for the women, for instance, are handled in an entirely straightforward manner. 'The Hen and her Chickens' offers a series of parallels with Christ and his flock each of which is demonstrated point by point in the same fashion as those in 'Meditations upon an Egg':

So one of the Chickens went to the Trough to drink, and every time she drank she lift up her head and her eyes towards Heaven. See, said he, what this little Chick doth, and learn of her to acknowledge whence your Mercies come, by receiving them with looking up. Yet again, said he, observe and look: So they gave heed, and perceived that the Hen did walk in a fourfold Method towards her Chickens. 1. She had a *common call*, and that she hath all day long. 2. She had a *special call*, and that she had but sometimes. 3. She had a *brooding note*. And 4. she had an *out-cry*.

Now, said he, compare this *Hen* to your King, and these Chickens to his obedient ones. For answerable to her, himself has his Methods, which he walketh in towards his People. By his common call, *he gives nothing;* by his special call, he always *has something to give;* he has also a brooding voice, *for them that are under his Wing.* And he has an out-cry, to give *the Alarm when he seeth the Enemy come.*[2]

The advantage of this technique lies in its compactness; the comparisons are made as shortly as possible yet at the same time as comprehensively. Many of the Interpreter's emblems are manipulated in this way; the pilgrims look at the man with the muck-rake, the harvested field, the garden, the burning fire, or the woman sweeping the room and the meaning is then fully expounded to them with economical directness. When Patience and Passion are shown, Patience 'very quiet' and Passion 'much

[1] In an article in *The Review of English Studies*. April 1945. on 'Bunyan and the English Emblem Writers', which appeared after I had written this chapter, Mr. Roger Sharrock traces the sources of the Interpreter's emblems with much greater thoroughness and attention to detail than I have done.

[2] Ed. cit. p. 186.

discontent', the Interpreter begins his explanation of their behaviour in the businesslike fashion of the professional emblem
writer: 'These two lads are Figures; *Passion* of the Men of *this*
World; and *Patience* of the Men of *that* which is to come. . . .'
The treatment of other emblems, however, is more complicated,
and it would be misleading to suggest that all the scenes in the
Interpreter's house and with the Shepherds conform exactly to
the emblematic pattern. A dramatic element is introduced which
sometimes disposes of the need for any direct exposition of a
symbol. Christian watches the valiant man hacking his way to
the palace and forestalls the Interpreter with a smile: 'I think
verily I know the meaning of this.' This dramatic element in
the treatment is combined with material which resembles that used
by Bunyan in his preaching; the lesson taught by the sweeping of
the parlour is precisely that under a different image of Jenner's
'Impediments to a Christian Conversation' (see Plate 14.
p. 87) which had illustrated a sermon earlier in the seventeenth
century. When, therefore, the man in the iron cage, who symbolises despair, is made to be so articulate that he himself becomes
the expositor of his own significance, it is impossible to determine
whether he is the author or the object of the moral lesson he
instils. One cannot, in fact, in *The Pilgrim's Progress* work out the
point at which emblem writing stops and parable, illustration,
and the other adjuncts of the sermon begin: clearly so much else
besides the technique of this particular convention has gone into
the making and application of Bunyan's similitudes that the
emblems he uses, while preserving their own completeness and
remaining instantly recognizable *as* emblems, at the same time
provide a framework for other elements of popular appeal. The
passion which his readers had for riddles and the secret meanings
hidden in images is exemplified in other forms elsewhere in the
book. In the Palace Beautiful a kind of religious guessing game
takes place between Matthew and Prudence:

M.   *Where have the Clouds their Water?*
P.   Out of the Sea.
M.   *What may we learn from that?*

P.   That Ministers should fetch their Doctrine from God.

M.   *Why do they empty themselves upon the Earth?*

P.   To show that Ministers should give out what they know of God to the World.

Other questions, such as 'Why doth the Fire Fasten upon the Candle-wick?'; 'Why doth the Pelican pierce her own Breast with her Bill?', or 'What may one learn by hearing the Cock to Crow?', are countered with answers of the same sort.[1] All, presented slightly differently, could constitute emblems. The intellectual stimulus that such riddles, and the emblems among them, could provide is evident from the frequency and length with which they are employed in *The Pilgrim's Progress*; and the pleasure the solutions gave may be measured in the fervour with which Emanuel's own explanation of some of his darker sayings is received in *The Holy War*:

> *Emanuel* also expounded unto them some of these Riddles himself; but Oh how they were lightned! they saw what they never saw, they could not have thought such rarities could have been couched in so few and such ordinary words. I told you before whom these *Riddles* did concern; and as they were opened, the people did evidently *see* 'twas so. Yea, they did gather that the things themselves were a kind of a *Pourtraicture*, and that of *Emanuel* himself; for when they read the *Scheme* where the Riddles were writ, and looked in the face of the Prince, things looked so like the *one* to the *other*, that *Mansoul* could not forbear but say, This is the *Lamb*, this is the *Sacrifice*, this is the *Rock*, this is the *Red-Cow*, this is the *Door*, and this is the *Way*; with a great many other things more.[2]

Bunyan's use of similitudes of all kinds was that of an experienced preacher. The emblems and riddles are like, and sometimes identical in substance with, those which he used to diversify his sermons and draw in the illiterate.

As a minister Bunyan devoted much of his time to the literal exposition of texts, and this bore fruit in *The Pilgrim's Progress*. His cast of mind, moreover, seems to have been such as to make

---

[1] *The Pilgrim's Progress.* Ed. cit. pp. 214-15.
[2] *The Holy War.* Ed. John Brown. 1905. p. 298.

him peculiarly well fitted to do so. Figurative speech in which the metaphor had only a general incidence is always reduced to a concrete and single application. The prophecy *He that wandereth out of the way of understanding shall remain in the congregation of the Dead* is fulfilled in the wanderings of the men made blind by Giant Despair among the Tombs; [1] and the Valley of the Shadow of Death is edged on one side by a very deep Ditch, 'that Ditch is it into which the blind have led the blind in all Ages; and have both there miserably perished'.[2] The emblems and the riddles spring naturally from such image-making as this and are part of Bunyan's habitual method of allegory. Consequently there is much that is generally emblematic scattered all through the book, although, unlike the emblems just discussed, it is completely involved in the story. Christiana, for instance, was given the Golden Anchor that hung on the wall of the Palace Beautiful before she began to go through the Valley of the Shadow of Death: 'for, said they, you shall have it with you, for 'tis of absolute necessity that you should, that you may hold of that within the vail, and stand stedfast, in case you should meet with turbulent weather'.[3] The moral significance of this type of incident may be accepted or ignored as the reader is disposed: the anchor can be interpreted as the magic talisman of the fairy tale or as an emblem of hope; in the story it does the duty of both. In the same way, when the boys retreat behind Greatheart at the place of the Lions, Bunyan notes in the margin, 'An Emblem of those that go on bravely when there is no danger; but shrink when troubles come'; [4] and the candle which the Interpreter brings with him to light the pilgrims as they enter the Significant Rooms has an emblematic meaning which is indicated by the marginal note 'Illumination'. All this is consistent with the method employed in the presentation of the scenes in the Interpreter's House or with the shepherds; but the action is not, as it is there, temporarily suspended while the moral lessons are drawn. The significance is completely absorbed in the story.

[1] *The Pilgrim's Progress.* Ed. cit. p. 112. [2] Ibid. p. 59.
[3] Ibid. p. 216. [4] Ibid. p. 202.

In discussing the methods and aims of the early emblem writers it was possible to make some comment on the nature of the allegory as a whole in *The Faerie Queene*; similarly it is possible, though more difficult, to discuss the allegory of *The Pilgrim's Progress* in connection with the methods of the later emblematists. The difficulties are caused chiefly by the fact that the later emblem books of the seventeenth century, as contrasted with those of the earlier type, are much more elastic in their form and content. They do not draw primarily upon traditional material and they allow of much greater freedom in interpretation and handling. The Art of Memory, the Cult of the Virgin, the honest and pleasant recreations of Puritan tradesmen are all equally their province. Where old themes are used they are adapted to new purposes and are never considered sufficient in themselves. Action has a more important status. Links as close as those between the content of *The Faerie Queene* and the early emblem books are, therefore, hardly to be expected; for the chief characteristic of these later works is their individualism, and of that Bunyan had his full share. Nevertheless, the changes within the convention that were effected by Quarles and the later emblematists have their counterpart outside it in the different way in which Bunyan handles his allegory, and something may usefully be said about it in the light of the changed standards of the emblem writers.

The feature of *The Pilgrim's Progress* which makes it so unusual, and so successful, as an allegory is its realism. The story concerns a number of figures who are designated as types, and the typical, although by definition it cannot be entirely individual, is not necessarily unreal or lifeless. Bunyan has various means by which his type figures move and act credibly in a setting which is naturalistic in comparison with that of *The Faerie Queene*. Sometimes the characters are made alive by the isolation of a single physical or moral feature which becomes symbolic of the whole personality. This gives an illusory individuality to what is still, in fact, a type. Mrs. Batseyes, and the cook, Taste-that-which-is-good, in the house of Gaius are examples, as are also the kindred of By-Ends:

223

Mr *Smooth-man*, Mr *Facing-both ways*, Mr *Anything*, and the Parson of our Parish, Mr *Two-tongues*, was my Mother's own Brother by Father's side: And to tell you the truth, I am become a Gentleman of good Quality, yet my Great-Grandfather was but a Water-man, looking one way, and rowing another: and I got most of my Estate by the same occupation.[1]

In the same way, the members of the jury in *The Pilgrim's Progress* and in *The Holy War*, each with his single comment character-istic of his nature, remain types although the total effect of their presence is realistic.

When the figures are treated at any length, realism is achieved through the addition of a number of distinguishing character-istics of behaviour or tricks of speech, which give an element of individuality while at the same time underlining the allegorical meaning. Talkative, who in appearance was 'a tall Man, and some-thing more comely at a distance than at hand', speaks in a way that bears out this description—fluently, impressively, but super-ficially. Hold-the-world's case for serving God and Mammon is made through a series of clichés and proverbial expressions which distinguish his style of speech from that of the others taking part in the discussion, and Madame Bubble is identified by her manner: 'Did she not speak very smoothly and give you a Smile at the end of a Sentence?' These people come to life through the details given, which thus expand the literal meaning. Yet it is seldom that Bunyan adds a detail which is not at the same time allegorically significant. Perhaps Discretion's strange emotion at Christian's request for a night's lodging at the palace Beautiful is a piece of simple naturalism:

She smiled, but the water stood in her eyes: And after a little pause, she said, I will call forth two or three more of the family.[2]

But such occasions are rare. They occur more often in Part II where the allegorical and literal meanings of the story are less successfully blended. Mercy's insistence that her unmarried state is the result of choice not necessity can scarcely be taken allegori-

[1] See above, p. 92–3. [2] *The Pilgrim's Progress*. Ed. cit. p. 45.

cally; conversely, the episode of Matthew's sickness and its cure has more force on the symbolic than on the naturalistic plane. In Part I the two aspects of the story go hand in hand and neither in character nor in incident is one sacrificed to the other.

Such realism creates figures which are very different from the old personifications of *The Faerie Queene*, *Minerva Britanna* or Ripa's *Iconologia*. Bunyan's types are to be interpreted not through their outward appearance, their garments embroidered with eyes and ears, their double faces, long locks of hair, and the like, but through their behaviour and speech. Their allegorical significance is made part of their personalities and is no longer objectified and external. Their names derive from their natures: the Doubters and the Bloodmen in *The Holy War* are unbelieving and murderous, Mr. Money-Love and Mr. Save-all, in *The Pilgrim's Progress*, avaricious and worldly. They spring in fact from direct observation, to a degree that makes it impossible to separate the moral quality conveyed from the person who conveys it; and the names Bunyan gives them are as much a criticism as an indication of their characters. The phrases which define the various figures who form the jury in Vanity Fair are themselves the result of a close study of human nature: each is typical of the vice personified, but it is also typical of a certain kind of person, and Bunyan by labelling the vice exposes the person. ' "Hanging is too good for him," said Mr Cruelty'—the name is the comment upon the sentiment and its commonplace wording. In the more developed characters the name acts as a constant reminder of the evil presented, and enables Bunyan to make his points by implication and to avoid too much didacticism. The study of By-Ends, for example, is peculiarly subtle: the insidiousness, the hypocrisy, the intellectual and moral dishonesty of a time-server are suggested by everything he says and does, by his reticence about his name, by the evasive tone of his conversation, by the account he gives the pilgrims of his religious practice, and by the line he takes in the argument with his friends about principles; but nowhere are they expressed directly. That is the function of the name, *By-Ends*. It sums them all up and recurs as a continual pointer for the

reader to the lack of singlemindedness that lies at the root of
them. The virtues and vices of *The Pilgrim's Progress* are no longer
Platonic absolutes, but human beings, and Mr. Covetousness can
masquerade as Mr. Good-husbandry, Mr. Pride can call himself
Mr. Neat or Mr. Handsome if necessary, where Spenser's Avarice
and Pride would be unrecognisable if they changed their outward
appearance. In *The Faerie Queene* the seven deadly sins have not
sinful natures: they *are* sin. The distinction is plainly made by
Honest in *The Pilgrim's Progress* when he insists on the proper
form of his name:

> The Old Gentleman blushed, and said, Not Honesty in the *abstract*
> but *Honest* is my Name, and I wish that my *Nature* shall agree to
> what I am called.[1]

In the Malbecco incident Spenser moves from the particular to
the general and absolute; Malbecco begins as a jealous man and
ends as Jealousy. For Bunyan such an abstraction was meaningless.

These aspects of Bunyan's characterisation may be partly the
result of his introduction of contemporary figures into the story.
His enemy Edward Fowler was probably a model for By-Ends,
and the attacks made on the various sects in the persons of Form-
alist, Hold-the-World, Love-gain and Ignorance may also have
been directed against particular members of them whom Bunyan
knew. There is much that is topical in *The Pilgrim's Progress*, and
both the subjects and the protagonists of the controversies in
which he took part are there reflected.[2] The exact nature and
extent of the allusions are not here important, for with the sole
exception of Ignorance whose presentation is distorted by some
unresolved personal animosity in Bunyan's mind, the characters
are perfectly objectified and treated with complete detachment.
Like Chaucer's pilgrims, about whom the same question has been
raised, they have their *raison d'être* in their author's art alone. In

---

[1] *The Pilgrim's Progress.* Ed. cit. p. 229.
[2] For the allusions and topical elements in *The Pilgrim's Progress* see W. Y.
Tindall, *John Bunyan Mechanick Preacher*, 1934. Chapter III. and J. W. Draper,
'Bunyan's Mr Ignorance'. *Modern Language Review*. Vol. 22. 1927. pp. 15–26.

the book they bear the stamp of living people, and whether taken from life or not, are illustrations as well as personifications of the moral qualities they represent.

Bunyan's characterisation, with its psychological realism and its emphasis upon the significance of conduct, assists the allegory in a way that Spenser's more abstract methods cannot. It gives force to every point, and at the same time it is the means by which the story is developed. Each step, each gesture of the characters has its meaning, and consequently makes its contribution not only to the progress of the narrative but also to its import. Like the later emblem writers, Bunyan is concerned with action; and he adopts the old symbolical material only to turn it to his own purposes. Just as the earlier forms of personification are completely transformed in the figures he draws, so the other devices of the emblematists are absorbed into the narrative. The candle which symbolised for Farlie and Quarles the light of life is carried by the Interpreter into the rooms which reveal to the pilgrims the mysteries of salvation; the bodiless hand from the clouds of Peacham and Paradin brings to Christian the leaves of the tree of life by which his wounds are miraculously healed after his fight with Apollyon; even the heraldry of the past is given a place. The four captains in *The Holy War* have their 'badges of honour conceitedly emblazoned', but they are badges which have lost their original characteristics of formality and regimentation and are chosen to reflect an inward state: Captain Charity's scutcheon is 'three naked orphans embraced in a bosom'. Everything, in short, is focused on the story; action, so prominent in the emblems of Quarles, becomes the strength of the allegory of *The Pilgrim's Progress*. It was this power of welding narrative with symbolism which made Bunyan, in truth, 'Salvation's first Defoe'.

The Pilgrim's Progress is the last link of the emblem convention with greatness. After Bunyan it virtually ceased to exist. Educationalists in the eighteenth and nineteenth centuries published a series of emblems for children in which the old themes were sometimes repeated, but the old methods had disappeared. In *Emblems for the Improvement and Entertainment of Youth,* an edition of which was published in 1788, there were no less than nine hundred and thirty pictures arranged in sets of fifteen on a page. They consist of animals, trees, birds or objects of everyday experience likely to appeal to children, and they include also a surprising number of the subjects of the original emblem books: there are the familiar palm trees, the sunflower, the hen defending her chickens, the ivy twining round the pillar, with the motto *Te stante virebo*. The 'improvement' was cramped into a few notes at the bottom of each page. One of the author's objects was presumably to enlarge the child's vocabulary, and each picture is accordingly identified in the notes—a motto, translation and brief moral comment being added:

7. A Tuberose. *Diarii Omnes*. All short-lived. So is Beauty.

A last flicker of the emblem tradition can perhaps be caught in this laconic and rational preservation of its external features, but it is plain that its essentials, what the emblematists themselves had called 'the soule', have vanished. In Neale's *Emblems for the Young* not even the externals remain, and the book is simply a collection of parables illustrated with engravings.[1] Allegory became, as the reception of Blake's poetry was to show, no more than 'a continuance of extraordinary Dreams, such as excellent Poets and Painters, by being over studious, may have in the beginning of Feavers'.[2]

[1] Published by the Religious Tract Society. 4th Edition, 1838.
[2] Sir William Davenant on the allegory of Spenser; *Preface to Gondibert*. 1650.

Appendix 1

BIBLIOGRAPHY OF ENGLISH EMBLEM
BOOKS TO 1700

A. Printed Books

The order is alphabetical. Translations are classed under the translator's and not the author's name.

A. H. (HENRY HAWKINS)

> *Partheneia Sacra* or the Mysterious and Delicious Garden of the Sacred Parthenes. Symbolically set forth and enriched with Pious Devises and Emblemes for the entertainement of Devout Soules. By H. A.
> Rouen. John Cousturier. 1633. 8vo.
> Engravings throughout by J. van Langeren. Engraved title-page by P. van Langeren.

> *The Devout Hart* or Royal Throne of the Pacifical Salomon. Composed by F. St Luzvic. S.J. Translated out of Latin into English.
> Rouen. John Cousturier. 1634. 12mo.
> No plates.
> (Translated from the Latin edition 1627 of Etienne Luzvic's *Le Cœur Devot* . . . Douai. 1627.)

ARWAKER. Edmund, (The younger)

> *Pia Desideria:* or Divine Addresses, in three books. Illustrated with XLVII Copper-Plates. Written in Latine by Herm. Hugo. Englished by Edm. Arwaker. M.A.
> London. Printed for Henry Bonwicke. 1686. 8vo.
> 2nd edition, 1690. 3rd edition, 1702.
> (Translated from Herman Hugo's *Pia Desideria Emblematis, Elegiis et affectibus S.S. Patrum illustrata.* Antwerp. 1624. from which the plates were copied.)

ASTRY. Sir James,

> *The Royal Politician* represented in One Hundred Emblems. Written in Spanish by Don Diego Saavedra Faxardo . . . Done into English from the Original. By Sir Ja. Astry.

London. Printed for Matt. Gylliflower at the Spread Eagle in Westminster-Hall. And Luke Meredith at the Star in St. Paul's Church Yard. 1700. 2 vols. 8vo.
With plates.
(Translated from Don Diego Saavedra Fajardo's *Idea de un Principe politico cristiano*. Munich. 1640. etc.)

AYRES. Philip,

Cupids Addresse to the Ladies. Emblemata Amatoria. Emblems of Love. Embleme d'Amore. Emblemes d'Amour. In four Languages. Dedicated to the Ladys. By Ph. Ayres Esq.
London. 1683. 8vo.
Plates throughout. Title-page engraved by Francis Barlow. French edition published same year. 3 undated editions *c*. 1700. Another 1714. (Most of the plates derive directly, or indirectly through the medium of *Thronus Cupidinis*, an anonymous collection published at Amsterdam ?1618, from the emblems of Otho Vaenius and Daniel Heinsius.)

B. J. (JOHN BUNYAN)

A Book for Boys and Girls: or Country Rhimes for Children. By J. B.
London. Printed for N.P. 1686. 8vo.
No plates.
2nd edition 1701 entitled *A Book for Boys and Girls; or, Temporal Things Spiritualised*. In the 9th edition 1724 and subsequently it was issued as *Divine Emblems; or Temporal Things Spiritualised*, with cuts.
(The first edition contains 74 emblems: in the second and later editions these were reduced to 49 and many alterations made in the text.)

B. R. (ROBERT or RICHARD BURTON; pseudonym)

Delights for the Ingenious, In above Fifty Select and Choice Emblems, Divine and Moral, Ancient and Modern. Curiously Ingraven upon Copper Plates. With Fifty Delightful Poems and Lots for the more Lively Illustration of each Emblem, whereby Instruction and Good Counsel may be promoted and furthered by an honest and pleasant Recreation . . . Collected by R. B. . . .
London. Printed for Nath. Crouch. 1684. 8vo.
With plates.
6th edition, London. For Edmund Parker. 1732.

BIBLIOGRAPHY

(A selection of 50 Emblems from Wither's *A Collection of Emblemes*
1635; the pictures are copied and poems reprinted without
acknowledgement.)

COMBE. Thomas,

The Theatre of Fine Devices translated by Thomas Combe.
London, R. Field. 1614. (Entered in S.R. 1593.) 8vo.
With plates.
(Translated from Guillaume de la Perrière's *Le Theatre des Bons
Engins* 1539.)

DE MONTENAY. Georgette,

A Booke of armes, or remembrance, wherein ar one Hundered
Godly Emblemata, in peeces of brasse very fine graven, and
adorned pleasant to be seen. . . .
Frankfort. 1619. 8vo.
With plates.
(Polyglot edition in Latin, Spanish, Italian, High Dutch, English,
Low Dutch translated from the French *Emblemes, ou Devises
Chrestiennes* 1571. Another edition in the same languages was
published also in 1619 entitled *Monumenta emblematum Christian-
orum virtutum*.)

FARLIE. Robert,

Lychnocausia sive Moralia Facum Emblemata. Lights Moral
Emblems. Authore Roberto Farlaeo Scoto-Britanno.
London. Tho. Cotes for Michael Sparke. 1638. 8vo.
With plates.
(In Latin and English.)

G. H. (Sir HENRY GODYERE)

The Mirrour of Maiestie: or, The Badges of Honour conceitedly
emblazoned; with Emblemes annexed, poetically unfolded.
London. Printed by W. I. 1618. 4to.
With plates.

H. J. (JOHN HALL)

Emblems with Elegant Figures, newly published. By J. H. Esquire.
London. R. Daniel. 1648. 12mo.
With plates.

APPENDIX I

(HARVEY. Christopher,)

Schola Cordis or The Heart of it Selfe, gone away from God; brought back again to him; and instructed by him in 47 Emblems. London. For H. Blunden. 1647. 12mo.

Plates engraved by William Marshall and Michel van Lochem. 2nd edition, 1664. 3rd edition, 1674.

(Published anonymously. Described on the titlepage of 3rd edition as 'By the *Author* of the *Synagoge* anex'd to Herberts poems.' Reprints of 1808, 1812, 1823 and 1866 ascribe it to Quarles. Adapted from B. van Haeften's *Schola Cordis*. Antwerp. 1629. from which the plates were copied.)

HEYWOOD. Thomas,

Pleasant Dialogues and Drammas . . . With sundry Emblems extracted from the most elegant Iacobus Catsius.

London. By R. O. for R. H. Sold by T. Slater. 1637. 12mo.

(Not an emblem book proper but contains translations of Cats's emblems.)

(JENNER. Thomas,)

The Soules Solace or Thirtie and one Spiritual Emblems.

London. Sold by Thomas Jenner. 1626. 4to.

With plates.

Other editions 1631 and 1639. Reprinted as *Divine Mysteries that cannot be seene, made plain by that which may be seene.* 1651.

M. E.

Ashrea: or, The Grove of Beatitudes, Represented in Emblemes: And, by the Art of Memory, to be read on our Blessed Saviour Crucifi'd.

London. For W. P. 1665. 12mo.

With plates.

PEACHAM. Henry,

Minerva Britanna or A Garden of Heroical Devises, furnished, and adorned with *Emblemes* and *Impresa's* of sundry natures, Newly devised, *moralised, and published*, by Henry Peacham.

London. Wa. Dight. 1612. 4to.

Woodcuts by the author.

BIBLIOGRAPHY

QUARLES. Francis,
  Emblemes.
  London. 1635. 8vo.
  Engravings by William Marshall, William Simpson and one by John Payne.
  Reprinted 1639 (with the *Hieroglyphikes*), 1643, 1658, 1660, 1663, 1676, 1684, 1696, 1717, 1736, 1777 (with Harvey's *Schola Cordis* etc.
  (Plates of Books I and II derived from *Typus Mundi*, an emblem book published by the College of Rhetoric of the Jesuits at Antwerp 1627; Books III, IV and V from Hugo's *Pia Desideria*. Vide Arwaker above.)

  Hieroglyphikes of the Life of Man. Fra. Quarles.
  London. Printed by M. Flesher for Iohn Marriot. 1638. 8vo.
  Engravings by William Marshall.
  Reprinted 1639 and thereafter with the *Emblemes.*

S. P.
  The Heroicall Devises of M. Claudius Paradin Canon of Beau[l]ieu.
  Whereunto are added the Lord Gabriel Symeons and others.
  Translated out of Latin into English by P. S.
  London. William Kearney. 1591. 16mo.
  With plates.
  (Translated from Paradin's *Devises Heroiques.* Lyons. 1551.)

VAENIUS. Otho,
  Amorum Emblemata . . . Emblemes of Love. With verses in Latin, English, and Italian.
  Antwerp. 1608. 4to.
  Engravings by Cornelius Boel.
  (Polyglot edition of which three versions were published in 1608, the others being in Latin, Dutch and French, and Latin, Italian and French.)

WHITNEY. Geoffrey,
  A Choice of Emblemes and other Devises, for the most parte gathered out of sundrie writers, Englished and Moralized. And divers newly devised, by Geoffrey Whitney.
  Leyden. 1586. 4to.
  With plates.

WILLET. Andrew,

Sacrorum emblematum centuria una, . . . a purissimis Scripturae fontibus derivata, et Anglolatinis versibus reddita.
Cambridge. John Legate. n.d. 4to.
No plates.
(Published between February 1591 and August 1592. Verses in Latin and English.)

WITHER. George,

A Collection of Emblemes, Ancient and Moderne: Quickened with Metrical Illustrations, both *Morall* and *Divine*: and disposed into Lotteries, That *Instruction*, and *Good Counsell*, may bee furthered by an Honest and Pleasant *Recreation*. By George Wither.
London. Printed by A.M. for Richard Royston. 1635. Folio.
Frontispiece by William Marshall. Engravings by Crispin van de Passe.
(The plates had already been used in Rollenhagen's *Nucleus Emblematum selectissimorum*. 1611–13.)

B. *Manuscripts*

[ALCIATI. Andrea,

The Emblems of Alciati in English verse. n.d.
This manuscript, belonging to the reign of James I, was incomplete and contained 92 emblems of which 79 were coloured. Each was accompanied by the Latin text and English verses. For a description of it see H. G. *The Mirrour of Maiestie* ed. Henry Green. 1870. p. 88, and J. B. Yates. *Transactions of the Liverpool Literary and Philosophical Society*. Nov. 5. 1849, in whose possession it then was. I have been unable to trace it.]

BROWNE. William, of Tavistock.

Bod. Ashmole MS 767.
See below under Thomas Palmer.

FRAUNCE. Abraham,

Bod. Rawlinson MS D. 345.
Emblemata varia, ad principes Europae et rem historicam spectantia, calamo bene depicta, et versibus Latinis illustrata. n.d.

BIBLIOGRAPHY

This manuscript consists of two works, both by Abraham Fraunce:

1. *Tractatus de usu dialecticis* dedicated to Sir Philip Sidney.

2. *Emblemata varia* ff. 17 ad fin. There are 40 emblems each consisting of an oval pen-and-ink drawing, very finely executed, a motto and Latin verses. Notes are provided on the page opposite each emblem.

PALMER. Thomas,

    I. Bod. Ashmole MS 767.

This manuscript contains two books of emblems. The subjects of both are trees, flowers, and herbs, the pictures being done in watercolour, with poems and mottoes attached. No title, author, or date is given, but the manuscript belonged formerly to William Browne of Tavistock, whose autograph, together with the crest of Lord Burleigh, appears in both books.

The author of the first collection has been identified by Percy Simpson (*The Bodleian Quarterly Record*, Vol. VI. pp. 172–3) as Thomas Palmer, who composed it for a new year gift to Lord Burleigh. From evidence in a revised copy in the British Museum Mr. Simpson shows that this new year was 1598. The emblems include such familiar devices as the palm-tree which triumphs in spite of oppression, the ivy wound round the pillar, the rose with a scarabee in it, the camomile trodden under foot, besides a large number of more obscurely emblematic plants and fruits.

The author of the second collection has been identified by Geoffrey Tillotson ('A Manuscript of William Browne.' *Review of English Studies*, Vol 6. pp. 187–91) as William Browne himself. Browne began to copy Palmer's plates and mottoes and to write new and longer verses for them. The book is unfinished, and the majority of the pictures have been left without poems.

Mr. Simpson in his note on the MS gives a description of two other emblem books made by Thomas Palmer. These are now in the British Museum, but I have been unable to see them owing to the evacuation of books from the library. I therefore quote Mr. Simpson's note on each:

    2. B.M. Sloane MS 3794.

' "Two hundred poosees devysed by Thomas Palmer", dedicated to Robert Dudley, Earl of Leicester, who died in 1588. . . . A few of the emblems have pen-and-ink drawings, but most of them have woodcuts taken from Aneau's *Picta Poesis*, 1552, and the Paris edition of Alciati, 1534.'

APPENDIX 1

3. B.M. Additional MS 18040.

' "The Sprite of Trees and Herbes", originally had two hundred and twenty-three emblems, and is a revised and amplified version of the Ashmole MS with similar pictures. It has been badly mutilated: sometimes whole pages have gone; sometimes the picture at the top of the page has been torn out. The mutilated pages could be restored from the Ashmole MS if they had a scrap of literary interest, which unfortunately they have not.'

PEACHAM. Henry,

1. Bod. Rawlinson MS Poetry 146.

ΒΑΣΙΛΙΚΟΝ ΔΩΡΟΝ. In Heroica Emblemata Resolutum, ac digestum per Henricum Peachamum Anglum. Scripta in gratiam serenissimi Principis Henrici Frederici Regis Jacobi, Angliae, Scotiae, Franciae, et Hiberniae filii Cui optima jure debentur.

This consists of 56 emblems based on the *Basilikon Doron* of James I and is divided into three books containing respectively 16, 26 and 14 emblems. The pictures are in pen and ink and each is accompanied by a Latin quatrain and, with nine exceptions, by a motto in Latin and a quotation from the original text. The title-page is without decoration and there is no preface or introduction. Miss Pitman dates it 1603-6.

2. B.M. Harleian MS 6855 art. 13.

ΒΑΣΙΛΙΚΟΝ ΔΩΡΟΝ ΕΙΣ ΤΑ ΕΜΒΛΗΜΑΤΑ ΒΑΣΙΛΙΚΑ totum versum, et in tres libros (Regia methodo observata) divisum. Authore Henrico Pechamo.

Huic operi, in calce adiecta est, ad Regem in quatuor partibus, cantio votiva, seu congratulatoria, ab alumnis Quatuor Regnorum, Anglo sc: Scoto, Gallo et Hiberno concinenda. Ab ipso authore composita.

In general plan like the above but the emblems have been increased to 67, 17 in Book I, 36 in Book II and 14 in Book III. The drawings are in pen and ink and there is a prose dedication in Latin to King James. At the end is a madrigal for four voices in autograph signed Henry Pecham called *King James his Quier*. Miss Pitman dates it 1603-8.

3. B.M. Royal MS 12. A. lxvi.

ΒΑΣΙΛΙΚΟΝ ΔΩΡΟΝ. In Basilica Emblemata totum versum, singula suis iconibus et tetrastichis Latinis donata. Authore Henrico Peachamo.

This contains 78 emblems, 19 in Book I, 53 in Book II and 16 in

236

Book III. The pictures are in watercolour, each about 3 × 3½ inches in size and there is a two-page Latin dedication to Prince Henry. Prince Henry's arms are prefixed to Book II. The date can be fixed as 1610 by the dedication to Prince Henry in *Minerva Britanna* 1612 in which Peacham says:

> 'It is now two years since I presented unto Your Highness some of them ('mine emblems') with their pictures drawn and limned by mine own hand in their lively colours.'

There has seemed no point in cataloguing the differences between the three manuscripts. They range from slight modifications of the quatrains to entirely new pictures for the same text and verse. Most of the 56 emblems in (1) appear in some form in (2) and/or (3), but a few are omitted altogether; an increase in personified figures is noticeable; (1) has 4, (2) has 7, and there are 10 in (3). Only 5 of these were transferred to *Minerva Britanna*. Of the three manuscripts (2) and (3) are much more like each other in style and content than either is to (1).

King James's book was first published in Edinburgh in 1599 when Prince Henry was five years old. It was reprinted in 1603 when the King sent a copy to his son with a letter. In the same year it was turned into Latin and English verses by William Willymat as *A Princes Looking Glasse*.

THYNNE. Francis,
  Emblemes and Epigrames. Presented to Sir Thomas Egerton. 1600.
Edited by F. J. Furnivall. E.E.T.S. 1876.

WHITNEY. Geoffrey,
  Bod. Rawlinson MS Poetry 56.
This manuscript is anonymous and is undated. It has no pictures but contains 126 mottoes and poems. These mottoes and poems all occur in Whitney's *A Choice of Emblemes* where they are arranged in approximately the same order but are interspersed with others to make up the total of 248. The manuscript may, therefore, be an early draft for the *Choice* made by Whitney himself, or it may be a selection from the published book made afterwards either by Whitney or by one of his readers.

In his Address to the Reader in the *Choice* Whitney explains the origin of his book: he had made a collection of emblems and 'presented the same in writing unto my Lorde' (i.e. the Earl of Leicester) before

APPENDIX 1

Leicester went to the Low Countries. Being pressed by friends to have this collection published he was now offering it 'in the same sort as I presented it before. Onelie this excepte: That I have now in diverse places, quoted in the margent some sentences in Latin & such verses as I thought did beste fit the severall matters I wratte of. And also have written somme of the Emblemes, to certaine of my frendes, to whome either in dutie or frendship I am divers waies bounde, which both weare wanting in my first edition, and now added hereunto.' In a note in the *Bodleian Quarterly Record*. Vol VI. pp. 173–4, Mr. H. H. E. Craster points out that the manuscript fulfils the requirements of the 'first edition' in being without the Latin marginal notes and in having no emblems dedicated to friends; and as no mention is made in it of the Earl of Leicester, but on the contrary the two poems which in the printed book are dedicated to him appear here addressed to 'the right vertuous Gentlewoman Mris Elyzabeth Parrott', he suggests that it was a version of the same manuscript which Whitney gave to Leicester, made before he found 'a better patron'. Whitney does not, however, make clear in his Address to the Reader whether he enlarged the volume he gave to Leicester, or not. He may have made more emblems to dedicate to his friends, or he may merely have added dedications to emblems already there; certainly a number of the poems which are without dedications in the Bodleian manuscript appear with them in the *Choice*. We cannot therefore be sure that the Leicester manuscript did not contain as many emblems as the printed book. Furthermore, the poems in the Bodleian manuscript are drawn from sources as varied as those in the *Choice* so that there is nothing to suggest that Whitney enlarged his collection because he obtained more emblem books from abroad. It is possible that this manuscript represents a selection made from the *Choice* after it had been published either by Whitney himself or by some other friend of Mistress Parrott.

NOTE

Only those works which have the distinctive features of an emblem book have been included in this bibliography. I have taken for my criterion four characteristics commonly agreed to be essential by the emblem writers themselves. These are:

1. An emblem book should be a collection of moral symbols.
2. It should have pictures, or, as in such emblem books as those by Willet and Bunyan, should postulate the existence of pictures.
3. Attached to each picture should be a motto or brief *sententia* interpreting and completing it.

4. There should be an explanatory poem or passage of prose in which the picture and motto are interpreted and a moral or religious lesson is drawn.

Certain books which have in them emblematic elements have been rejected as not fulfilling these conditions. Colman's *La Danse Machabre or Death's Duell* 1632, for example, contains an emblematic title page of Death and Time engraved by T. Cecil, interpreted in an accompanying *Mind of the Front*, and another plate of Death, but the text consists of one long poem on the theme *Mors omnibus communis*.[1] It cannot therefore be described as a collection of moral symbols. John Vicars' *A Sight of yᵉ Trans-actions of these latter yeares, Emblemized with engraven plats which men may read without spectacles.* n.d. is an account, from the Parliamentarian side, of the history of the period from the first Parliament of Charles I to 1646 and is illustrated with very poor pictures of incidents such as the execution of Strafford, the burning of images, etc. Its only claim to inclusion lies in the use of the word 'emblemized' in connection with the pictures, but these are in no sense symbolical, and the book is simply an illustrated history book. Van der Noot's *A Theatre for Worldlings* has been discussed in the text of Chapter 2 above. Something much closer to an emblem book proper is John Saltmarsh's *Holy Discoveries and Flames*, 1640, a collection of meditations engraved by William Faithorne: the engravings consist of an eye, which is repeated above each 'Discovery', and a burning heart above each 'Flame'. The meditations are each made up of two Discoveries, close examinations of short biblical texts, and one Flame, an apostrophe of praise or intercession. The lack of variety in the engravings and the absence of any real connection between the picture and the prose which follows seems, however, to justify its exclusion. Other borderline examples are Peyton's *The Glass of Time in the two first Ages divinely handled* 1620, Thomas Stirry's *A Rot amongst the Bishops, set forth in lively Emblems*, 1641, Robert Farlie's *Kalendarium humanae Vitae* 1638, T. Jenner's *A Work for None but Angels and Men* 1658, none of which are emblem books by the criterion established above. Books on heraldry have been excluded for the same reason. It appears from titles such as these quoted that the word 'emblem' was sometimes used indiscriminately to signify the illustrations of any type of book. It was also used in the sense of a short prose essay in the following:

[1] Published after Donne's Sermon of the same name. Colman ends his book with a short poem entitled 'The Author's Apologie for the title of his book injuriously conferd by Roger Muchill, upon a Sermon of Doctor Donnes', in which he maintains that his title was stolen to grace Donne's book.

APPENDIX 1

John Maxwell. *Emblema Animae* or Morall Discourses reflecting upon Humanitie. Written by John du Plessis now Cardinal of Richelieu. Translated by I. M. 1635.

Donald Lupton. *Emblems of Rarities*: or Choyce Observations out of worthy Histories of many remarkable passages, and renowned actions of divers Princes and severall Nations. Collected by D. L. 1636.

There are no pictures in either book: the first contains moral essays on topics of general interest such as Providence and Foresight, the Choice of Friends, Poverty, and also descriptions of the Seven wonders of the World, the Four Monarchies, the Thirteen cantons, etc. The second is made up entirely of strange pieces of information, some of which are copied verbatim from Maxwell and the rest derived from Pliny, classical history and myth; it is a hotchpotch of miscellaneous scraps of knowledge, A Description of a Phoenix, A Description of Seneca, A Description of Whales, a strange History of a King devoured by Mice, etc. These two books are plainly not emblem books, despite their misleading titles.

Emblem books continued to be written in the eighteenth and nineteenth centuries but they had then ceased to be a serious literary form and I have not therefore thought it necessary to continue the Bibliography after 1700.

Appendix 2

LORD SHAFTESBURY'S *SECOND CHARACTERS*
OR THE LANGUAGE OF FORMS

Although there was much contemporary discussion of the exact
nature of the emblem as a form of expression, interest was chiefly
directed towards distinguishing the genre from others akin to it, and
little or no effort was made to discuss it as a whole. Thus Henri
Estienne, the author of *L'Art de faire les Devises*, in common with other
critics and with the emblem writers themselves, devotes most of his
book to an account of the differences between the various offspring of
the Hieroglyphic—'Aenigmas, Symbols, Fables, Parables, Emblems,
Sentences, Reverses of Medals, Arms, Blazons, Cimiers, Cyphres, and
Rebuses.' Abraham Fraunce, the first English critic to publish a book
on the subject, makes some attempt at a general classification when he
divides the ways in which mental concepts are expressed into two
groups, by speech and gesture for those present, and by writing and
pictures for those removed from one another by time and space.[1] In
Shaftesbury's *Second Characters*, however, an elaborate scheme is
worked out, and the whole of what formed the second group for
Abraham Fraunce is subdivided into three types of Character. Among
the material collected for the intended book is a chart accompanied by
explanatory notes in which the three types are defined. The part of the
chart concerned with emblems is quoted in the text on page 17.
What follow here are Shaftesbury's notes in full.

Characters.

(1) FIRST. *Notes.* Marks of sounds, syllables, words, speech, and
of sentiments, senses, meanings by that medium, viz. of
sounds and speech. Thus ciphers, shorthand, Cicero's invention.

(2) SECOND. *Signs. Signa. Sigilla.* Imitation of real forms and
natural beings, plastically (convex or concave), or lineally
and graphically by lines and colours, from the superficies and
extremities of the bodies, according to optics.

(3) A THIRD and middle sort, emblematic. As when the latter
signa are used as mediums (speech being passed over) to
convey sentiments, senses, meanings, etc. (but not sentences,

[1] Abraham Fraunce, *Insignium, Armorum . . . Explicatio.* 1588.

241

diction, etc.). For when the figure of an animal stands as a mark, arbitrarily and without relation to his form, nature, passion, history, then is this no more than an ordinary first character (as α,β,γ). But if natural history, passion, habit, form, be taken in, then ought this to be fine and beautiful and just: else it is lame and imperfect in its kind.

Of this latter sort, the *true*, therefore, is emblematic and graceful without mixture; the *false* enigmatic merely, mixt and barbarous: as the Egyptian hieroglyphics. Nor can the mixture of middle characters with first, as in the Egyptian way of obelisks, be any other than monstrous upon examination, as it appears *prima facie* to the slightest examiner or novice: however this hieroglyphic may have been extolled by travelling philosophers and admirers of the wonders of Egypt.

That our particular science therefore, of design or signature may emerge from this chaos of barbarity, we distinguish first characters from barbarous forms conjoined with those first (as in Egyptian hieroglyphics) leaving only the beautiful anaglyphics (relief-works and inwrought of the polite ancients) as a true species of art and workmanship: in the emblematic way. But this also being slightly touched and explained, we pass over to the unmixed, the simple and pure, viz. 'design, plastic art; second, poetry, imagery, iconography, typography (improperly applied to printing characters), by type, prototype and ectype; and the just imitation of nature according to natural history and the ideas or species of the several forms, animal or vegetative, to some end and with some intent'.[1]

[1] *Second Characters.* Ed. cit. pp. 90–3. 'Plastics. An Epistolary Excursion in the Original Progress and Power of Designatory Art.'

Appendix 3

BIBLIOGRAPHICAL NOTE ON
PARTHENEIA SACRA

The works ascribed to Henry Hawkins are as follows:

1. A Translation of Fr. John Floyd's *Synopsis Apostasiae Marci Antonii de Dominis*. St. Omer. 1617.

2. *Certaine Selected Epistles of S. Hierome* as also the Lives of Saint Paul the first Hermite, Of Saint Hilarion the first Monke of Syria, and of Saint Malchus; Written by the same Saint. Translated into English. n.p. (Paris) 1630.

3. *Fuga Saeculi* or the Holy Hatred of the World. Conteyning the Lives of 17 Holy Confessors of Christ, Selected out of Sundry Authors. Written in Italian by the R. Fa. Iohn-Peter Maffaeus of the Society of Jesus. And translated into English by H. H. Paris. 1632.

4. *The History of S. Elizabeth,* Daughter of the King of Hungary. According to sundry Autours who have authentically written her Life, distributed into III books. By H. A. n.p. (St Omer) 1632.

5. *Partheneia Sacra* or the Mysterious and Delicious Garden of the Sacred Parthenes; symbolically set forth and enriched with pious devises and emblemes for the entertainment of devout soules; contrived all to the honour of the Incomparable Virgin Marie Mother of God; For the pleasure and devotion especially of the Parthenian Sodalitie of her Immaculate Conception. By H. A. Iohn Cousturier. (Rouen) 1633.

6. *The Devout Hart* or Royal Throne of the Pacifical Salomon. Composed by F. St Luzvic S.J. Translated out of Latin into English. Enlarged with Incentives by F. St Binet of the same S. and now enriched with Hymns by a new hand. Iohn Cousturier. 1634. (By H. A.)

7. *The Life of St Aldegunda* translated by H.H. from the French of Fr. Binet. Paris. 1636.

This list with the exception of the *Devout Hart*, which has been ignored by all bibliographers, is given in G. Oliver's *Collections towards illustrating the biography of the Scotch, English and Irish members of the*

Society of Jesus, 1845, in A. de Backer's *Bibliothèque de la Compagnie de Jésus* ed. C. Sommervogel 1890–1909, and in the *Dictionary of National Biography*; in accordance with it, therefore, most authorities have ascribed *Partheneia Sacra* to Hawkins. A problem, however, is raised by the fact that some of the works are initialled H. A., some H. H., one is anonymous, and in none does the name Hawkins actually appear. The ascription was lately queried by Professor Praz, who proposed instead 'the Catholic poet Henry Aston'.[1] This suggestion was made originally by Fr. Gervase Mathew and the poet referred to is Herbert Aston, second son of Lord Aston of Tixall, Staffordshire, the friend of Michael Drayton. The Astons were a Catholic family in which, according to a Jesuit record, 'almost always some member is distinguished for his sanctity'. Herbert's sister and two of his daughters entered the convent of St. Monica's Louvain: and his son, another Herbert, entered the Society of Jesus where he was 'called and regarded by one and all as a saint'.[2] Herbert the elder was himself something of a poet. A little of his work is printed from manuscript in A. Clifford's *Tixall Poetry*, 1813. and some biographical details can be found in the same editor's *Tixall Letters*. More of it is in a manuscript Commonplace Book, now in the Huntington Library, which was made by Constance Fowler, Herbert's youngest sister, and contains a number of poems by Habington, Ben Jonson, Henry King, etc.[3] Constance was deeply attached to her brother and besides engineering a marriage for him with a lady of considerable charm who seems, from her letters before their marriage, to have shared his taste for literature—'How infinit a time will it seem till I se you: for lovers hours are full eternity. Doctor Dun sayd this, but I think it,'[4] she was an eager reader of his poetry and her letters are full of complaints at the delay in the arrival of promised verses. The Commonplace Book is not dated but seems to be of about 1640. Among the poems are a number above the cipher H. A. which are probably by Herbert Aston. They are all of a secular nature—amorous or moral—and are considerably inferior to those in *Partheneia Sacra*. Neither do they bear any resemblance to them in technique. It would, therefore, have to be supposed that Constance's collection represents work written by Herbert between 1633 and 1640 and that Herbert's style changed radically, and for the worse, after the

[1] Mario Praz, *Studies in Seventeenth Century Imagery*. 1939. p. 72.
[2] Annual Letter of St. Omer's College 1684 printed in Henry Foley, *Records of the English Province of the Society of Jesus*. 1877. Vol. V. pp. 448–9.
[3] H.M. 904.
[4] Katherine Thimelby to Herbert Aston. n.d. *Tixall Letters* ed. A. Clifford. 1815. p. 147.

publication of *Partheneia Sacra*: but even on those assumptions it is odd that Constance should not have included any of the published poems in her collection. Another difficulty is that Herbert was born in 1614 and would therefore have been only nineteen when *Partheneia Sacra*, which does not appear to be the work of a very young man, was published. Herbert Aston might well have been the author of a devotional book of this kind for he had poetic ability and Catholic interests, but without strong external support, which is lacking, no convincing case can be made on the evidence of the Commonplace Book alone.[1]

Among other possible contemporary H. A.s there is no one else to whom works so distinctively Catholic can be ascribed: Henry Austin, author of *The Scourge of Venus or the Wanton Lady* by H. A. 1613. and Henry Ainsworth, author of various anti-Catholic works such as *Counter-Poyson—Considerations touching points of difference between the godly ministers and people of the Church of England and the seduced brethren of the separation.* by H. A. London. 1642. may be dismissed without further investigation. Henry Annesley, who is mentioned by W. C. Hazlitt in a note on *Partheneia Sacra*, I have not been able to trace.[2]

It seems difficult therefore to establish any strong case against Hawkins's authorship, and on the positive side we have the witness of contemporary bibliographers.

The most important authority is Philip Alegambe, whose *Bibliotheca Scriptorum Societatis Jesu* of books published before 1642 appeared in 1643. This gives a brief biography of Hawkins and attributes to him the translation of Floyd and *Partheneia Sacra*. Hawkins was still alive and working in England at the time. A new edition of the *Bibliotheca* was printed in 1675 and in this the biography was brought up to date and all the works since attributed to Hawkins, except the *Devout Hart*, are listed. This edition has probably been the source of all information about Hawkins's writings. A bibliography of books on

[1] I am greatly indebted to Fr. Gervase Mathew for much helpful discussion of English Catholic books and to the late Mr. Bernard Newdigate for his great kindness in lending me his photostat copy of the Commonplace Book and for the information about the Aston family which he gave me. I should here like to record my thanks for so much generous assistance. Mr. Newdigate had not identified all the poems in the Commonplace Book—many other contemporary poets are probably represented. The exact extent of H. A.'s work is not even certain; I have traced one of the poems—'When by sad Fate from hence I summoned am'—given by Constance above his initials to Owen Felltham's *Lusoria*, printed in the 8th edition of *Resolves* 1661, which seems to cast doubts on her reliability.

[2] Hazlitt, *Bibliographical Collections and Notes.* 1st Series. 1876. p. 205.

the Virgin which was published two years after Hawkins's death also ascribes *Partheneia Sacra* to him, following Alegambe.[1] There seems, therefore, to be no contemporary doubt as to the Hawkins canon. Further support is given by W. C. Hazlitt who quotes an inscription inside the vellum cover of the copy of *Partheneia Sacra* before him: 'For Dame Benedicta Hawkines w(r)itten By her Borther Henery Hawkines of the Societie of Jesus'.[2] This is corroborated by Hasted who gives Benedicta as the name of one of Hawkins's six sisters.[3] It may, I think, be said with reasonable certainty that the book was written by Henry Hawkins though why he chose to sign some of his works with the initials H. A. and some H. H. must remain a mystery. Alegambe calls attention to the difficulty by noting that *Fuga Saeculi* was translated 'praescriptis nominis sui elementis H. H.' Hawkins's *alias* was Brooke (perhaps chosen in memory of the friendship between the Hawkins family and Sir Basil Brook who was one of Sir Thomas Hawkins's collaborators in the translation of *The Holy Court* and to whom *Fuga Saeculi* was dedicated) so no enlightenment comes from that source. There seems no doubt that the works of H. H. and H. A. are from the same hand. *Fuga Saeculi* itself, for instance, though mainly a translation, contains a number of original poems which closely resemble those of *Partheneia Sacra* in technique and theme. Nor is there any difference in kind between the two groups of writings: Hawkins did not, like William Hale White, strive for anonymity in his original work only; H. A. wrote *Partheneia Sacra* but he also translated the *Devout Hart*. H. H. translated Saints' Lives but he also wrote poetry.

The *Devout Hart*, overlooked by Alegambe and consequently by all other bibliographers, is unquestionably by the same author as *Partheneia Sacra*. The epistle dedicatory 'To the Worthy and Vertuous Couple W Standford Esq. and Elizabeth his wife' is signed H. A. and the prose is too much like Hawkins's best style to allow of any other conclusion.

Two other bibliographical questions remain to be discussed in connection with *Partheneia Sacra*. Several of the bibliographers mention an edition printed in Rouen in 1632 as well as that by John Cousturier in the following year. I have not seen any copies of this nor are there any detailed references to it: in fact it seems doubtful whether it ever existed. The edition is first mentioned in Alegambe as follows:

Parthenia [sic] Sacra, de Symbolis Beatissimae Virginis, cum Versibus et Imaginibus. Rhotomagi. MDCXXXII. in 8.

---

[1] Ippolyto Marracci. *Bibliotheca Mariana*. Rome. 1648.
[2] W. C. Hazlitt. Loc. cit.
[3] E. Hasted, *The History of Kent*. Vol. III. p. 4.

Other bibliographers who mention this edition—I. Marracci, C. Dodd, G. Oliver, A. de Backer, S. Halkett and J. Laing, all follow Alegambe's spelling and phrasing, though the later ones mention also the 1633 edition. It seems reasonable to conclude that the only edition ever printed was that by John Cousturier in 1633 and it was to this that Alegambe was inaccurately referring.

Secondly it has been suggested by some bibliographers that *Partheneia Sacra* is a translation. The foreign appearance of the woodcuts (see for example the house in the reproduction of the frontispiece on page 184), the choice of the olive and the palm for emblems of trees, and the fact that no other work of Hawkins's is entirely original have combined to suggest that *Partheneia Sacra* could not be so either. Both Dodd and Gillow call it 'A Translation' but neither gives any indication what it is a translation of.[1] The source of the idea is probably again Alegambe whose bibliography is ambiguously phrased and I think on the whole that it is mistaken.[2] There is no book among those written by Jesuits upon the Virgin—Alegambe gives a list in which *Partheneia Sacra* is included—which bears a title identical with Hawkins's: I have examined several which sounded like sources—e.g. *Ortulus florum beate marie virginis* 1508, Francis de la Croix's *Hortulus Marianus* n.d., Francis Coster's *Libellus Sodalitatis* 1588. Jan David's *Pancarpium Marianum* 1607—all without result. The investigation, however, was confined to Jesuit books and was by no means exhaustive in that one field so that the possibility of a foreign source remains. But there is little in *Partheneia Sacra* itself to encourage the belief: the book was printed abroad

[1] Charles Dodd. *The Church History of England.* 1742. Vol. III. pp. 118–19. J. Gillow. *A Bibliographical Dictionary of English Catholics.* Vol. III. p. 192.

[2] The first part of Alegambe's list is as follows:

Transtulit e latino Anglice
> Synopsim de Apostasia Marci Antonii de Dominis a Fideli Annoso con-scriptam. Andomari. 1617.
Edidit etiam polito sermone Anglicano.
> Parthenia Sacra de Symbolis Beatissimae Virginis cum versibus et imaginibus. Rhotomagi. 1632. in 8.
Reddidit praeterea ex Italico Anglice praescriptis nominis sui elementis H.H.
> Vitas 17 Confessorum scriptas a Nostro Ioanne Petro Maffeio. Parisiis. 1636. in 4.
> Vitam S Aldegundae scriptam a nostro Stephano Binetto Gallice. Parisiis. 1632. in 12.
> etc.

Probably ' Transtulit e latino Anglice' applies only to the first book mentioned just as the 'reddidit ex Italico' applies only to the *Lives of the 17 Confessors*.

and the plates made by a Dutch engraver which would account for their foreign appearance; the palm tree and the olive were familiar and frequently recurring symbols in English literature by 1633. There is also far too much contemporary allusion scattered through the book for even the best of translators to have introduced into a foreign text. A reference to Dowland in the section on 'The Nightingale', a quotation of the Epitaph on Argalus and Parthenia from *Arcadia* 'which a certain Poet of ours had framed' in 'The Palm', a reference to 'our *England*' which 'is knowne also by the name and title of our *Ladies Dowrie*' [1] and elsewhere to '*the Covent-Garden*, the Garden of the *Temple*, nor that of the Charter-house, or of *Grayes Inne Walke*, to be had and enjoyed at home';[2] and many casual phrases such as 'a mounsier of Paris' occur so naturally and are so deeply imbedded in their contexts that they make translation improbable. It is noticeable, too, that Hawkins's prose is much richer and more idiomatic in *Partheneia Sacra* than in any of his other works; it gives the impression of complete freedom in the treatment of the material.

[1] *Partheneia Sacra.* p. 180.　　　　　　[2] Ibid. p. 111.

Appendix 4

THE AUTHORSHIP OF *ASHREA*

The authorship of *Ashrea* is obscure. The epistle dedicatory 'To the Lady M. B.' is signed E. M. and the initials have been accepted as those of a certain Edward Manning who had the previous year published a pamphlet called *The Mask'd Devil*,[1] but there is little evidence to support the ascription. The pamphlet is an attack on seven Quakers who were alleged by Manning to have evaded justice by failing to appear when the ship in which they were to be transported was ready finally to sail after many false starts. The Quakers replied in another pamphlet [2] in which they offered 'an utter refutation of a Lying Paper published under the hand of one Edward Maning' by defending themselves on all counts. The details of the dispute are not important— the Quakers' main argument was that the shipmaster, Thomas May, had refused to transport them since in his view, and their own, they were 'innocent persons'—but it throws some light upon the character of their accuser. He was officious and disreputable, and his object simply that of gratuitous persecution. According to the Quakers he had no interest in the ship and no connection with them: they had, in fact, been ordered finally to ignore any commands from him and to wait for a dispatch from the shipmaster himself. Manning had apparently no means of subsistence of his own and far from providing the prisoners with beds, as he claims in the pamphlet, he had 'not so much as a bed for himself to lie upon'; they had been obliged to pay their own expenses while negotiations with the shipmaster were proceeding and 'indeed oft-times, like one of them called a shirk, he thrust himself upon us, and eat of our Victuals, and drank of our wine, which we had provided to have served us at sea'. It seems unlikely, if not impossible, that this same 'shirk' should the following year have produced a devotional work of the type of *Ashrea*. Although, as the Quakers observed in their last Parthian shot, he could quote Latin and Scripture to serve his argument, these are not the quotations of a particularly

[1] In the British Museum Catalogue. I have found no references to *Ashrea* elsewhere. The pamphlet is *The Mask'd Devil, or Quaker, neither fearing God nor reverencing man*. By Edward Maning. London. 1664.

[2] *A True and Impartial Narration of the remarkable providences of the Living God of Heaven and Earth, appearing for Us his oppressed servants called Quakers.* 1664.

249

learned or a particularly religious man. Altogether there seems little
in the pamphlet to discredit his victims' estimate of Manning's character: the attack is entirely personal and made in the cause of detraction
rather than of religion.

If *Ashrea* were merely hack work the ascription might be convincing
but its merits both as devotion and as literature lift it above that level.
The cuts and the verses are certainly crude enough, but the prose has
an individuality of phrasing and a fervour of tone that makes it comparable at times with that in *Partheneia Sacra*. It may well have been
the work of a Jesuit, slightly camouflaged to delude the censor. In
1669 there was published '*A Journal of Meditations for every day in the
year. Gathered out of divers Authors*. Written first in Latine by N. B.
and newly translated in English by E. M.'[1] This E. M. was Edward
Mico *alias* Harvey or Baines, an English Jesuit who came to England
some time before 1666. The *Journal* is a collection of meditations for
the whole Christian year including meditations on each of the Beatitudes based on the method of Fr. Luis Puente, and Fr. Mico made
considerable additions to the original. He was also the author of some
Meditations and Prayers which were never published. There is no
positive evidence to prove that Mico was the E. M. of *Ashrea*, but there
is enough likeness between their interests to suggest that it might be so.

[1] A second edition appeared in 1674. This is the only work ascribed to Mico
by Alegambe and de Backer, but their bibliographies were not complete: *The
Devout Hart*, for instance, is ignored by both in their lists of Hawkins's works.
Mico was born in 1630 and died in 1678 in prison where he had been confined
as a result of the Oates plot. For an account of his life see J. Gillow. op. cit.
Vol. V. p. 7.

INDEX OF EMBLEMS

(List of Emblems and Personifications mentioned in the Text)

251

INDEX OF EMBLEMS

GENERAL INDEX

(The most important reference to each Emblem writer is in heavy type)

GENERAL INDEX

254

GENERAL INDEX